Google
Your Family *Tree*

UNLOCK THE HIDDEN POWER OF GOOGLE

DANIEL M. LYNCH

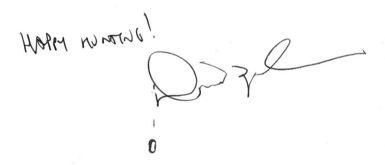

HAPPY HUNTING!

FamilyLink.com, Inc.

www.GoogleYourFamilyTree.com

Publisher's Cataloging-in-Publication Data

Lynch, Daniel M.
Google your family tree : unlock the hidden power of Google /
Daniel M. Lynch.—1st ed.—Provo, UT : FamilyLink.com, c2008.

    p. ; cm.

    ISBN: 978- 0- 9820737- 1- 1
    Includes bibliographical references and index.

    1. Genealogy—Computer network resources—Handbooks,
manuals, etc. 2. Google. 3. Web search engines—Handbooks,
manuals, etc. 4. Internet research—Handbooks, manuals, etc. I. Title.

CS21.5 .L96 2008   2008934913
025.06/9291   0810

Published by FamilyLink.com, Inc.
1234 N. 900 East
Provo, UT 84604
www.familylink.com

Published 2008.
13 12 11 10 09   3 4 5

ISBN: 978-0-9820737-1-1

Managing Editor and Interior Design: Matthew Wright
Cover Design: Barry Hansen

Printed in Canada

This book is dedicated to all my ancestors—Irish, Italian, and American—but especially to my maternal grandmother, Louise Ditoto Lombardo (1911–1991). I often think about how much she would have enjoyed the Internet and the many places she could have visited and things she could have learned, all without leaving the comfort of her favorite chair.

Also to my daughters, Hannah and Eliza, who have never known a world without the Internet. It's difficult to imagine the technology that will be commonplace when they are my age, but I can only hope that they will continue to use it to research, record, and share our family history with their children.

Louise Ditoto Lombardo
(photo by Bernard M. Lynch, Jr.)

CONTENTS

List of Illustrations

Google is the world's leading search engine. And it is most likely the world's leading genealogy search engine. With hundreds of millions of users in more than 160 countries searching more than 20 billion documents, countless individuals have searched for their own name, or for their family names, or for individuals in their family tree.

But until now, there has not been a book written with the sole purpose of helping family historians use Google to discover their family tree. *Google Your Family Tree* is the right book, describing the right search engine, written by the right author, and released at the right time. I think it has the potential to help millions of family history researchers become more successful online.

I first met Dan Lynch in March 1998 while I was CEO of a (then) small startup company called Ancestry.com. Our website was quickly becoming the most popular genealogy website in the world. Dan expressed interest in what we were doing, and with his tremendous background in direct marketing and his clear passion for genealogy he was a great fit. After several meetings, during which Dan demonstrated the depth and breadth of his understanding of the genealogy community and the technology sector, he accepted a position with Ancestry.com as vice president of business development. I had the privilege of working closely with Dan for the next few years.

Since leaving Ancestry in 2001, Dan has worked as a consultant with such organizations as The Statue of Liberty-Ellis Island Foundation and FindMyPast.com (UK), has appeared on national and local television several times, and has been published in many leading genealogy publications. He has become a top online affiliate for major genealogy companies, and his website, 1930census.com, ranks No. 1 on Google, Yahoo!, and MSN (Live.com) for the phrase "1930 census." When he told me he was writing this book, my instincts told me this had the potential to be the best-selling genealogy book of all time. I thought it might outsell the very popular *Netting Your Ancestors* by the well-known Cyndi Howells, and perhaps in a few years, even catch up to *Genealogical Helper* by Everton Publishers, which has sold 1.2 million copies in 11 editions, over a 50-year period.

As an Internet entrepreneur since 1995, and knowing what I do about search engines and genealogy, I didn't expect to learn anything new when I read the manuscript cover to cover. But Dan delivered. I found myself several times shaking my head in disbelief that I've used Google since 1999 and didn't know several of the keys to successful research, from date range searches to historic newspaper archives to advanced wildcard searches. This book will help you understand some of the most powerful and sometimes hidden features of the world's best search engine by teaching you the simple commands and approaches that unlock this power.

And, that is the magic of this book. It takes one of the most common Internet experiences—a Google search—and puts it in a new light, making it seem brand new. I vouch for its usefulness for both the serious Web searcher as well as someone that is new to the world of Google.

—Paul Allen, FUGA, chief executive officer of FamilyLink.com, Inc.;
co-founder of Ancestry.com

ACKNOWLEDGMENTS

When I started this project, it seemed impossible to think of all the expert advice and feedback that would be needed for successful completion. As it turned out, knowledgeable and helpful people surrounded me all along—all I had to do was ask. I now have a much deeper appreciation for the specialized skills of those responsible for content development, design, editing, layout, and production. My most sincere thanks to Paul Allen, Sharon DeBartolo Carmack, Don Coddington, Dick Eastman, Ben Edwards, Jim Garrity, Jake Gehring, Giuseppe Gianfagna, Chandler "Bud" Henley, Kathleen Hinckley, Louise E. Lynch, Rita Ditoto Mongillo, Halvor Moorshead, Stephen Morse, Elizabeth Oravetz, Mark Pearson, Joy Rich, Loretto Dennis Szucs, Maureen Taylor, Richard Tomlinson, Matthew Wright, Ed Zapletal, Peg Zitko, and John Zmijewski. Their contributions and support have been critical to the successful completion of this project.

I also extend a special note of thanks to William J. Pape II, publisher of the *Waterbury Republican-American* newspaper, for access to his collection of historical images by photographer Frederick Stone. Many of the wonderfully detailed images within this book are courtesy of his collection.

Although I have never met or spoken with them, I also extend my thanks to Google founders Larry Page and Sergey Brin for having the vision and determination to create a service that has redefined innovation. They are proof that entrepreneurs can hold firm to their vision and still achieve success in a commercial, public marketplace.

This book's dedication notwithstanding, I also thank my parents for their contributions to this and many other projects. Thanks, Mom and Dad.

Google is an amazing company with extraordinary products. And, no, I'm not an employee or stockholder, I say this simply because I use Google products every day and have developed a deep appreciation for how well they serve my needs. It's not that other Internet search engines aren't helpful in their ability to quickly find needles in the worldwide haystack, it's just that it seems there is no end to the innovation that has come from Google in its relatively short corporate life. But why an entire book focused on Google and genealogy? After all, it's not as if Google engineers had genealogists in mind when they built their service—or did they? Before we step forward to answer that question, we have to step back to look at a brief history. Probably just what you'd expect from a genealogist, right?

Not long ago, family historians could be found dutifully writing letters and visiting archives, libraries, and cemeteries in search of clues detailing the lives of their ancestors. The tools of the trade were pencil and paper, microfilm and microfiche, and one-of-a-kind ledger books tucked away in thousands of vaults throughout the world—unless fire or flood had destroyed them first. With limited discretionary time and 9-to-5 hours at most research venues, many would-be genealogists were forced to wait until retirement to pursue their ancestral roots. By that time, most of their family elders had passed on, making it more difficult for them to preserve their unique family heritage for children and grandchildren of their own.

Back in those days, only the most dedicated family historians traveled to Salt Lake City, headquarters of The Church of Jesus Christ of Latter-day Saints (LDS Church) and the undisputed mecca for genealogists worldwide. Similarly, millions of visitors each year would make another pilgrimage of sorts to Ellis Island and the Statue of Liberty. These landmarks situated in New York Harbor are recognized throughout the world as symbols of the largest human migration ever recorded. For many family historians, the thought of finding their ancestors' names among the millions recorded on centuries-old passenger lists represented a lifetime of genealogical achievement.

But that was all genealogy B.C. (Before Computers). Today, thanks to personal computers and the Internet, even first-time researchers can point their browser to <www. familysearch.org>, the LDS Church's online genealogy homepage, providing free access to millions of records for anyone interested in researching their heritage. The future looks even brighter for genealogists with a promise from the LDS Church that it will continue to digitize much of its prized collection of family records from around the world. And many can still recall the April 2001 launch of the Ellis Island website at <www.ellisisland. org>. With the prospects of finding valuable clues about their immigrant ancestors, tens of millions of visitors flooded the website on opening day causing officials from The Statue of Liberty-Ellis Island Foundation to place limits on inbound site traffic just to keep the servers working for those lucky enough to establish a connection. Those were the days of dial-up connections, and very few websites were offering researchers a view of the actual digitized record—let alone offering it for free. In an instant, it seemed, microfilm was no longer good enough. The bar had been raised for an entire generation of genealogists.

It's nearly impossible to pinpoint a single event or date, but family historians during the last decade have certainly witnessed the most significant changes to ever occur in genealogical research. With an abundance of content now available online to anyone at any time, the Internet has become a critical resource and Google an important tool for every family historian—beginner, intermediate, or professional. Luckily, mastery of this powerful tool can be achieved in a relatively short period of time and can also pay dividends in other areas of life as well. Having lectured on the use of technology for more than a decade, I have paid close attention to the emergence, growth, and changing landscape of the Web. As a fellow genealogist with little time to devote to my own research, I have paid even closer attention to any tool or research technique that could save me time or prevent wasted effort.

The topics covered within these pages are those that I believe to be the most useful for anyone conducting genealogy research online—regardless of the country you call home. Google has a tremendous range of products and services available to a worldwide audience—well beyond those covered in the pages of this book. Throughout this project, one of my biggest challenges has been to stay focused on the elements within Google that have an undisputed role in helping family historians research and record their family history. Over time, I've certainly found a way to squeeze some genealogical benefits from almost every Google feature or application, but I've decided to include only those with the most broad-based application and likelihood of yielding the greatest return with a minimum of time invested by each researcher.

As a frequent lecturer, one of the most common questions about Google asked by attendees is "How did you become such an expert at Google?"—and the answer is easy. I use Google every day and I'm always visiting its "About Google" pages to learn what they're working on next. Google often launches new services in a Beta version and you just have to be willing to try new products in a sometimes rough, unfinished state. In many cases, if you try something new or make a mistake, Google will let you know. I encourage every reader to spend a few minutes every day trying a new command or search technique. Keep a notebook or index cards and try searching for one of your most elusive ancestors. Write down the number of results achieved and how the query was structured to obtain those results. Continue to refine your query until you have success. Once you have mastered a new technique, try using it in combination with another command (a Syntax Summary is found in Appendix E). You may sometimes find it helpful to search for people and places you have found previously. This will allow you to sharpen your search skills without getting immediately distracted by links to another website. And since the Web is growing and changing every day, submit the same query on a regular basis and use other search engines so you can compare results. You might even try searching for yourself to see what information is available online about you for others who may be trying to contact you about their family research.

I put this book together in a specific way to make it easier, I believe, to learn and practice the concepts that will make you a great searcher of Google. Following are some notes to guide you on the way:

Icons & Layout

This book is specifically designed to be an active workbook that you can refer to on a regular basis to grow your knowledge of Google as you research your family history online. We have left some room around the edges for notes, and there are suggestions throughout for how to test the instructions with your real-world examples.

Screen Shots

Sample screen shots are shown throughout this book, either in whole or in part, to visually support the text describing the feature being discussed. With the majority of personal computers using Microsoft *Internet Explorer* (~55%), I use this as my browser as well. Depending upon which version of *Internet Explorer* you use, your screen may look different. If you are using *Firefox, Chrome, Mozilla, Safari,* or *Opera,* your screen may have slight differences in appearance, as well.

Google It!

The *Google It!* boxes call your attention to exercises you can do to test the technique being described. Since many of the concepts discussed in this book are cumulative, I recommend pausing when you see this box so you can try a few Google searches for yourself using the technique described.

Partially Obscured Text

To show results for certain commands, some screen images may contain personal information (email, phone, etc.) of the author or others. To ensure privacy, some text may appear distorted.

Web Addresses

Throughout this book, I list Web addresses (also called URLs—Uniform Resource Locators) for your convenience in visiting the page or site being discussed. I enclose URLs in brackets < >, but you do not need to type the brackets when providing the address. For example <www.google.com> is accessed by typing **www.google.com**

One last thing before we begin our journey together down the road to all things Google. Technology, the Internet, and Google are great, but they aren't a replacement for libraries, archives, or participation in local genealogy clubs and societies. Every time I visit a library or archive, I learn something new. Not just from the books or microfilm, but from the knowledgeable staff that serve as custodians of these sources. They are perhaps more eager to help now than at any time in the past because the flow of patrons has slowed to a trickle. In a similar way, clubs and societies have experienced a lack of participation in local events, yet one of the best places to learn new tips and techniques is by talking with a fellow attendee at one of these local functions. So after you've learned how to find anything using Google, be sure to search for the name of a society or research center near you. Turn off your computer and pay them a visit, not just online, but in person. Yes, genealogists still do that!

If you have a favorite Google tip or technique not covered in this book, but one that may be of interest to fellow family historians, please visit the companion website for this book at <www.GoogleYourFamilyTree.com>. Updates will be shared online along with other tools of interest to family historians.

Happy hunting!

CHAPTER 1

Search Engine Basics

Chili, Clam Chowder, and Web Search

It might seem odd to start a book about Google with a comparison to chili or clam chowder, but I'm certain you will nod your head in agreement as you read further. When you think of chili or clam chowder, chances are good in both cases that you know what to expect—regardless of which recipe is being used or how long it's been since you last enjoyed a bowl of either. Hot and spicy? Thick and creamy? We each have our own distinct favorite, but we also have a general understanding that variations exist from one chef to another depending upon the exact mix and weighting of special ingredients. The same holds true for Internet search engines and their formulas for presenting search results.

In most cases, even novice computer users are familiar with the basic function expected of all Internet search engines. Look for an empty white box, type in a word or two, and press enter with an expectation that somehow the results will satisfy a need for specific information. Like the secret recipes of world-famous chefs, each search engine provider has its own ingredients and weighting factors that are used to determine how and which results are displayed. (They call this their algorithm.) During the last few years, Google has grown to dominate the world of online search, but Yahoo!, MSN (Windows

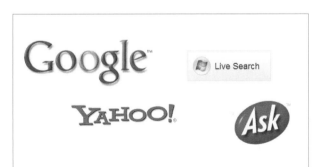

Live Search), Ask.com and others certainly still have a loyal following. Each continues to refine their "recipe" based on intelligence gleaned from millions of daily searches.

What does a Search Engine do?

At its most basic level, the function of a search engine (Google or any other) is to simply compare a string of characters provided by the user with those stored on one or more computers to determine if a match exists. This seems simple enough, but when the results can be scattered across billions of computers located anywhere in the world, you can begin to appreciate the magnitude of the task. As researchers, we type in names, locations, or other phrases with special meaning to us. The search engine doesn't understand that meaning at all. It simply takes that string of characters ordered in a certain way and returns a list of pages where the same characters are found in the same order specified. It is our job, therefore, to help the search engine better understand the meaning of our search.

Why Google?

This book is focused on the specialized use of Google for family history research for two simple reasons—market share and functionality. The chart below contains overview

Provider	Searches (000)	Share of Searches
Google Search	4,331,153	60.0%
Yahoo! Search	1,304,889	18.1%
MSN/Windows Live Search	770,592	10.7%
AOL Search	376,331	5.2%
Ask.com Search	143,231	2.0%
Comcast Search	45,438	0.6%
My Web Search	38,550	0.5%
AT&T Worldnet Search	30,272	0.4%
NexTag Search	17,901	0.2%
Dogpile.com Search	15,418	0.2%

statistics for the U.S. online search market according to Nielsen Online (a division of A.C. Nielsen). Google has earned a strong lead position at 60.0%, more than triple its closest competitor. Having followed Google and other online search providers for more than a decade, I believe Google provides the strongest overall offering for conducting genealogy research. Certain unique and useful features of other search engines are discussed as part of Appendix C.

How does Google work?

No need to worry—you don't have to become an expert on *how* Google works, just on how to use it to your best advantage to retrieve the best possible results in the shortest period of time. It will be to your advantage, however, to have a basic understanding of how a search engine works, Google or any other.

Before Google can provide results, it must have a database to search. Using a program called a Web crawler (or *spider*), Google visits websites page by page, link by link, while analyzing and recording information about the content of each page for its ever-growing worldwide index. As part of this process, it also takes a snapshot of each page as a temporary record of the material in its index (called a *cache*). The more popular a website, the greater the frequency of visits by Google's crawler in its never-ending effort to deliver the most comprehensive and up-to-date content to Web users worldwide.

"I THINK YOU SHOULD BE MORE EXPLICIT HERE IN STEP TWO."

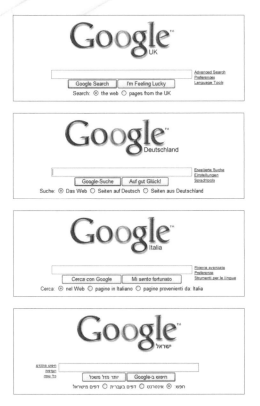

Does Google Work the Same Everywhere?

Google the company and its flagship site <www.google. com> are based in the United States, but the company offers more than 160 international versions of its online service. While some Google applications and services may differ from one geographic location to another, the overall process of information search and retrieval is remarkably consistent across sites.

I apologize in advance to readers and family historians living outside the United States. Most screen shots used in this book are based on the U.S. version of Google, and many examples involve U.S. place names. Where possible, special notes have been included to point out differences between Google's U.S. and International versions. Special foreign language capabilities are discussed in detail as part of Chapter Four—Language Tools.

What is Google's Interest in Genealogy and Family History?

As a company, Google does not have any specific interest or focus on genealogy or family history. It does, however, have an overall corporate goal that is quite beneficial from the standpoint of the millions of family history enthusiasts throughout the world.

In what is perhaps one of the best corporate mission statements you will ever read, in just fifteen words, Google shares on a very broad scale what it is trying to accomplish as a company. Interestingly, the term *search* is not among the fifteen words. Ask anyone on the street what one word they would use to describe Google and most will say *search*. I tried this while writing this section and scored seven out of ten for *search*. The eighth response was "*the Internet,*" the ninth was "*information,*" and the tenth was "*What's a Google?*" (We'll just have to assume this one person has been living under a virtual rock for the last five or

"GOOGLE'S MISSION IS TO ORGANIZE THE WORLD'S INFORMATION AND MAKE IT UNIVERSALLY ACCESSIBLE AND USEFUL."

ten years.) The words *genealogy*, *family history*, *heritage*, *vital records*, *census,* or *grandparents* are nowhere to be found in the Google mission statement. Or are they?

It is said that beauty is in the eye of the beholder. The words *organize, information, universally accessible and useful* are all terms that genealogists love to behold. So, selfishly, I read the Google mission statement and appreciate its dedicated focus in addressing our need for someone to organize all those vital records, census schedules, and old family photographs, and make them universally accessible and useful.

Google Corporate Overview—You can read more about Google (the company) on its website at <www.google.com/intl/en/corporate/index.html>.

The Google Home Page—Your 'Mission Control'

Since its inception, Google has been recognized for its sparse white home page and colorful, but simple logo. Despite all its innovation and powerful features, it has remained true to its initial design. As of this writing, there are just eighteen individual items that can be directly accessed with a single click from Google's default home page.

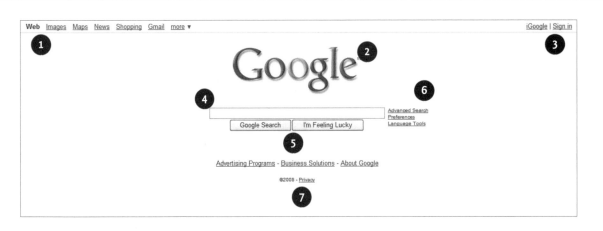

① Located in the upper left corner of the Google home page are a series of text links. The default is **Web** and instructs Google to search general Web results when you enter a query. This is the most typical search type for Internet users. Alternate links are for **Images**, **Maps**, **News**, **Shopping**, **Gmail** and **more, which** provide access to additional Google content types and features. Over time, Google has changed the links in this list and their location on the page.

② The Google logo (shown in grayscale on our pages) is adapted from the Catull typeface in blue, red, yellow, blue, green, red. Clicking on this logo throughout the site will generally return you to the Google home page or the top-level of the content type or feature you are using. To commemorate special events, holidays, or other historically significant dates, Google often entertains users with special adaptations of the logo with artwork by employee Dennis Hwang.

③ Two text links in the upper right provide access to a range of customization features available through Google. One is **iGoogle,** which enables you to customize your home page, but is a departure from the classic look. The other enables you to sign in to your Google account to access your personalized settings, free **Gmail** account, and other optional user accounts.

④ The input box is the central component of the Google interface and is where users enter their search terms. This box limits each query to no more than thirty-two words or a maximum of 2,048 characters (including spaces). Although queries this long are rare, Google will simply ignore words or characters that exceed the established limits.

⑤ Below the input box are two buttons: the Google Search button and the I'm Feeling Lucky button. Clicking on the Google Search button has the same effect as pressing the Enter or Return key on your keyboard. If, after entering your search terms, you click on the Google Search button, Google will present your results, but will also display a tip letting you know you can save time by pressing the Return key on your keyboard instead. The I'm Feeling Lucky button is simply a time-saving option. Clicking here will take you directly to the website listed as the top most relevant site based on your query.

⑥ To the right of the Google input box you will see three small text links. Links for *Advanced Search* and *Preferences* first appeared in this location in November 2000 with a *Language Tools* link being added in October 2001. These three small text links provide access to powerful features that will be described later in this book.

⑦ Centered along the bottom of the Google home page is a simple copyright insignia, along with three text links. While the number of links may change in the future, they currently include links to *Advertising Programs* (Google's primary source of revenue), *Business Solutions*, and an *About Google* link. If you are curious and patient enough you can learn a lot about the inner workings of Google products and services by following any number of link trails accessible from the About Google page. A *Privacy* link takes you to a Privacy Center and details for all Google privacy policies, as well as some helpful videos

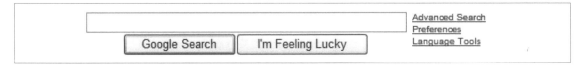

Search Input Box—Close-up view of the Input Box (#4), the two search buttons (#5), and the text links (#6) to access advanced search and customization features.

Keywords—The Main Ingredient of Web Search

The most basic search ingredient used by Google and other Web search engines is called a *keyword*—a word representing the topic you're trying to research. While single-keyword queries will generate many results, you will typically find a more manageable number of highly relevant results by using a carefully crafted query comprised of multiple keywords (called a *keyword phrase*) and perhaps one or more special commands or operators. Most operators and commands can be used in combination with one another to more precisely define your query.

In the example below, I conducted a series of Google Web searches seeking pages that may contain information about my great-grandfather Eugene Lynch. Each search grows in level of complexity as I include additional keywords to instruct the search engine to filter out unwanted results. The commands and syntax used in the queries below are discussed in detail on the following pages.

Google Web Search Query	Results
lynch	42,800,000
lynch family	363,000
lynch family connecticut	141,000
eugene lynch family connecticut	45,500
"eugene lynch" family connecticut	51
"eugene * lynch" family connecticut	815
"eugene * lynch" family connecticut ~genealogy	117
"eugene * lynch" family connecticut ~genealogy waterbury OR bridgeport	8

Keyword Phrases for Genealogy

For genealogists, *people*, *places*, *dates*, *events*, and *data types* will be among the most useful elements when structuring a query. Different surnames may require careful consideration depending upon how common or unique they are, especially if the name has one or more common alternate uses (e.g., Brown, Ford, White, Smith). In the table above, consider how even the most basic commands can be used alone or in combination to filter billions of results and deliver just a few meaningful pages for the diligent researcher.

Remember, before you begin any Google search session, the most important thing you can do to increase your chance for success is to select a combination of keywords that answer the basic genealogical questions—who, where, and when. With more than 20 billion pages indexed by Google, your goal is to carefully filter out unwanted pages and leave a manageable enough group so that you can individually inspect each result and determine if the content is relevant to your family.

Case Insensitive

As you carefully craft your queries for Google, note there are only two instances where case sensitivity matters—when using the Boolean commands **AND** and **OR,** as discussed later in this chapter. In all other instances, Google is case insensitive and will deliver the same results regardless of the combination of upper and lowercase letters you use in your query.

	Google Web Search Query	Results
1	genealogy	127,000,000
2	Genealogy	127,000,000
3	GENEALOGY	127,000,000
4	gEnEaLoGy	127,000,000
5	GeNeAlOgY	127,000,000

In the previous example, all five variations of a query for the single keyword term *genealogy* result in the same 127 million results and are presented in the same order of relevancy. Most examples throughout this book are shown using lowercase characters.

Automatic AND

Google uses a technique called an *automatic AND* (sometimes called an *implied AND*). For any query containing multiple keywords, Google will process the search as though each additional keyword is preceded by the command **AND**. This requires each word in the query to appear on the resulting pages unless other commands or syntax instruct Google to perform otherwise.

An example of the automatic AND can be seen below. Note that both queries generate nearly identical results. Although I have not been able to determine why, there are sometimes very slight differences in the reported volume of search results.

Google Web Search Query	Results
lynch genealogy Connecticut	84,500
lynch **AND** genealogy **AND** Connecticut	84,600

Ordering Keywords

Google returns different results to similar queries based on the ordering of keywords. The first keyword or phrase listed is generally considered more important that words or phrases that may follow. Genealogists are encouraged to use surname first, followed by place name as qualifying keywords. If your search yields few or no results, try reversing the keyword order. The proximity of one word to another can also impact your search results, but only when you use specific commands to instruct Google that the words need to be next to or near each other.

Did You Mean Genealogy?

It's no secret that *genealogy* is often misspelled, even among genealogists. We've already established that Google doesn't even know what genealogy is. To Google, it's simply an ordering of nine characters that results in 127 million pages when searched alone. Google does, however, recognize patterns based on billions of individual queries and can sometimes try to save us from our own mistakes.

A very common misspelling for genealogy is geneology, with the letter 'o' instead of an 'a' in the fifth letter position. Google is smart enough to realize that the user probably spelled the word wrong, but it performs the search as requested. A single keyword search for **geneology** results in 4.9 million pages, but Google will also prompt us with "Did you mean: **genealogy**", enabling us to submit a correctly spelled search with a single click.

Google does not publish a list of terms for which it recognizes a possible error. You can test this feature by using the example described above or submit a search term of your own. In all cases, the suggestion will appear at the top left, beneath any sponsored results that may exist, but above the natural results which appear. To view a list of commonly misspelled words, you can visit the Internet Accuracy Project at <www.accuracyproject.org/confusedwords.html>.

Word Variations—Stemming

When evaluating a search query, Google uses a technique called *stemming* in which it searches for the word and variations of that word depending upon the nature of the query. Other variations may include the plural form of the original word, as well as past, present or future tenses. An example of this technique is a query for the keyword *jumping*. Search results would include *jumping*, but might also include *jump*, *jumped*, and *jumps*. Since genealogists commonly search for information about deceased ancestors, this is an important and helpful concept. Your search using the keyword *died* would also yield results including *die* and *dies*.

Commonly Occurring Words—Stop Words

In the past, Google's search algorithm ignored commonly occurring words and certain single characters entered as part of a query, unless you used special operators to instruct them otherwise. These *Stop Words* included *a*, *of*, *the*, *and*, *to*, *where*, *how*, and many others. Google's reasoning was sound—including frequently occurring words slowed their response time without providing any meaningful benefit to users among the listings provided.

While Google reports it no longer ignores stop words, it has refined its handling of these terms depending upon the overall structure of the query. In the example above, a query for *the land of the free* is processed similar to, but not exactly the same as, a two-word query for *land free*. The table that follows shows differences in the volume of results found with and without stop words. This issue should not impact your search, especially once you become familiar with basic operators and syntax used to perform simple filtering as discussed later in this chapter.

	Google Web Search Query	Results
1	the land of the free and the home of the brave	688,000
2	"the land of the free and the home of the brave"	136,000
3	land free home brave	2,010,000
4	"land of the free" "home of the brave"	385,000
5	"land of the free" -"home of the brave"	1,380,000
6	"land of the free" **OR** "home of the brave"	228,000

Query Structure

In the examples below, similar queries are submitted with only slight differences in the ordering of keywords and/or the use of basic syntax. You can see that even slight changes in your query can yield a tremendous difference in the number of results returned. The remaining pages of this chapter, as well as Chapter Three, will describe in detail the use of basic and advanced commands and operators, some of which are shown in bold below.

	Google Web Search Query	Results
1	the statue of liberty	9,530,000
2	"the statue of liberty"	2,100,000
3	statue liberty	5,790,000
4	statue **AND** liberty	957,000
5	statue-liberty	5,450,000
6	statue -liberty	4,960,000
7	statueofliberty	5,840,000
8	statue +liberty	5,800,000
9	+statue +liberty	5,800,000
10	statue **OR** liberty	160,000,000
11	liberty statue	446,000
12	"statue * liberty"	911,000
13	"statue ** liberty"	617,000
14	"statue *** liberty"	610,000

Basic Search Operators

There are dozens of simple yet powerful commands that will direct Google to filter through billions of records to retrieve just those with the highest degree of relevance for your search. Mastery of the following operators is critical to establishing an overall foundation for success with using Google as your most powerful tool for researching your family history. Most of the following operators are also recognized by other leading search engines.

Google It!	As you read this section, you may find it useful to pause after each command and try a few similar searches. First use the examples given, then substitute the name of your ancestor and their town. Be sure not to get too side-tracked if your results yield an unexpected find. Remember, the better you get at using Google, the more expected each of these finds will become.

Unlocking the Mystery of Query Syntax

The table below describes in detail the results generated by the similar, but vastly different queries in the table on the previous page.

1	Find pages that contain all four words. Since no other instructions are given, results will include pages with words in any order and with no specific proximity to one another. A very broad search like this one is likely to yield a large number of results.
2	Adding quotations around the phrase requires resulting pages to include all keywords in the exact order specified in the query. This narrows results.
3	Find pages with both **statue** and **liberty** in any order and any proximity. Google inserts an *automatic AND* between keywords unless instructed otherwise.
4	Requesting pages with both **statue** and **liberty** in any order and any proximity. Essentially this is the same query as 3, but for reasons not clear to the author, Google responds with fewer than one-fifth the results despite its friendly reminder on query 3 that "The 'AND' operator is unnecessary— we include all search terms by default."

5	Find pages with both **statue** and **liberty** where any character or string separates the two keywords (see also query 12 for use of proximity wildcards).
6	Find pages with the term **statue,** but excludes results if the page also contains the word **liberty.** (Note the difference from query 5 is a single space before the minus).
7	Find pages that include the matching 15-character string of **statueofliberty,** appearing anywhere in the page content, web address, or page structure.
8	Find pages with the keyword **statue** and also with exactly the word **liberty,** excluding other common variations for liberty (e.g., liberties).
9	Find pages with exactly the word **statue** and exactly the word **liberty** appearing anywhere on the page in any proximity, but excluding common variants for each keyword (e.g., statues and liberties).
10	Find pages containing either **statue** or **liberty** including common variants. Note how these two very broad terms generate a substantial number of results.
11	Similar to query 3, but with the order of terms reversed, Google seeks pages with the term **liberty** and also **statue** in any proximity to one another. You can see from the significantly lower number of results that keyword order does matter.
12	Similar to query 2, but the asterisk **(*)** allows one word to separate **statue** from **liberty**.
13	Building on query 2 and 12, two asterisk (**) symbols increase the proximity between keywords to allow two keywords to appear between **statue** and **liberty**.
14	Extending query 13 with one additional asterisk further extends proximity.

Command: AND

Use the word **AND** (all uppercase letters) between keywords to direct Google to find results containing *all* the keywords in your query. Note that while all keywords will be present on the resulting Web pages, they will not necessarily have any connection or relevance to one another.

AND	▶ eugene **AND** lynch
	▶ eugene **AND** lynch **AND** connecticut
	▶ eugene **AND** lynch **AND** connecticut **AND** waterbury

Even though Google will insert an 'Automatic AND' between the terms shown in the above examples, try typing them in so you can become more familiar with the syntax as we begin to combine operators for more powerful filtering. Once you've mastered these commands, you can then save yourself some typing!

Google will often try to help you improve your search skills by calling your attention to simple things it does automatically on your behalf. In the graphic below, you can see the message Google displays beneath the search box to let you know the AND is not required.

Thinking Beyond AND

For most genealogists, it is quite easy to demonstrate why the AND command alone is rarely sufficient when searching for an ancestor online. In the examples above, we asked Google to return results that included keywords *Eugene* AND *Lynch*. The nearly 700,000 pages that result from such a query include many with characteristics similar to the example

Google | statue AND liberty | | Search | Advanced Search   Preferences

The "AND" operator is unnecessary -- we include all search terms by default. [details]

Google It!   Use the boxes below to write a few different queries dealing with your own family history. Start with a simple query using first and last name, then increase your level of complexity to watch how the volume of search results changes. In general, the more filters you apply, the fewer the results.

shown below. One highly ranked result includes an article on <www.slate.com> written by **Eugene** Volokh about Private Jessica **Lynch**. Unless you happen to also be related to this soldier, this is not a relevant result despite the fact that both your keywords appeared prominently on the page and within close proximity to one another.

Command: " "

Placing quotation marks directly around two or more words directs Google to seek results containing exactly the same string of characters specified inside the quotations and in precisely the same order and proximity to one another as they appear in your original query.

Does Pfc. Jessica Lynch Own the Movie Rights to Her Life?

By Eugene Volokh
Posted Monday, April 14, 2003, at 4:17 PM ET

A star, whether she likes it or not

NBC is planning to make a movie about Pfc. Jessica Lynch, the rescued American POW, even if it doesn't get her permission. Can the network do that? Doesn't NBC need to buy the movie rights to her life?

Yes, it can, and, no, it doesn't—so long as NBC sticks to the facts.

People don't own "movie rights" to their lives. Facts, even facts about particular people, are not exclusively owned by anyone. That's why newspapers may write about people without their permission, and why

" "	▶ "eugene lynch"
	▶ "lynch, eugene"
	▶ "eugene lynch" **AND** connecticut
	▶ "eugene lynch" connecticut
	▶ "eugene lynch" **AND** "elizabeth o'rourke"

I recommend placing quotations around an ancestor's name as shown in the examples above. Since some transcriptions posted online by others may display the surname before a given name, be sure to try both options. Combine quotations for a name with the AND before a place name to narrow results more precisely. Since the AND is optional, it is shown with and without, so you can develop a familiarity in reading queries both ways.

One of the most important benefits of using quotations is a concept called *proximity*. This simply means that words appear next to or near one another. By submitting a simple AND query for **eugene AND lynch** (or **eugene lynch**), you can have millions of Web pages including Eugene and Lynch, but with no relevance to one another. An entry early in the page might deal with an individual named **Eugene** Smith with another entry further down the page for Patrick **Lynch**. Because Google found both terms on the page, it was included in your results. Quotations tell Google that both keywords must appear next to one another!

One Name—Many Possible Listings

Genealogists know better than most Internet users the challenges involved in searching for someone or some place with a name that is often prone to being misspelled. Google even recognizes that *genealogy* is frequently misspelled with an 'o' instead of an 'a' as the

Google It!

Build on the queries you tried on the previous page or try others dealing with other family lines or related research. Using quotations can be very helpful for genealogists so be sure you try several examples so you can be comfortable with this concept before moving forward.

fifth letter and can suggest the proper spelling for us. Even relatively simple names, such as Eugene Lynch, require some careful thought to the structure of your query.

On the previous page, you learned how quotations can help remove unwanted results by requiring that *eugene* and *lynch* appear next to one another. When you conduct an exact phrase match search however, you need to keep in mind that Google will return results exactly in the order you requested. Therefore, a query for "*eugene lynch*" *will not* return pages with results where the name may appear in reverse. In the example shown below, a transcribed passenger list appearing on <www.immigrantships.net> includes a listing on line 18 for "Lynch, Eugene." This could be exactly the person you're looking for, but unless you give some careful thought to your query you may never find your ancestor.

Immigrant Ships
Transcribers Guild

SS Bolivia

Glasgow, Scotland via Moville, Ireland to New York
1 December 1880

DISTRICT OF NEW YORK - PORT OF NEW YORK

I, John J. Small, Master of the Steam-Ship Bolivia do solemnly, sincerely, and truly swear that the following List or Manifest, subscribed by me, and now delivered by me to the Collector of the Customs of the Collection District of New York, is a full and perfect list of all the passengers taken on board of the said S. S. Bolivia at (nothing is filled in this blank) for which port said (nothing filled in) has now arrived, and that on said list is truly designated the age, the sex, and the occupation of each of said passengers, the part of the vessel occupied by each during the passage, the country to which each belongs, and also the country of which it is intended by each to become an inhabitant; and that said List or Manifest truly sets forth the number of said passengers who have died on said voyage, and the names and ages of those who died. So help me God. (signed) John J. Small
Sworn to this 1st of Dec 1880 before me (signed) E. A. Merritt

---

> **Structuring Name Queries**—Genealogists should always be sure to search for at least three variations of an ancestor's name as shown below:
> ▶ "eugene lynch" **OR** "lynch, eugene" **OR** "eugene * lynch"
> (The **OR** and * commands are described on the following pages.)

Command: * (wildcard)

Use of one or more asterisk (*) symbols has a special meaning in Google when it is used within quotations. While you might consider this an advanced command, it is being included in this section immediately following the description of quotation marks because of the special usage of these two commands in conjunction with one another.

The placement of a single asterisk serves as a wildcard that instructs Google to accept any character or consecutive string of characters in place of the asterisk. Genealogists will find this especially valuable since many ancestors' names may be listed with a middle name or middle initial between the first and last name. If you conducted a simple query for *"eugene lynch"* Google would perform the task as requested, but would ignore pages that might list **Eugene P. Lynch** or **Eugene Patrick Lynch** in its results. This is also helpful in cases where transcriptions may include maiden names for female ancestors. A search for "*elizabeth lynch*" would find just that, nothing more and nothing less. A similar query for "*elizabeth * lynch*" would find results that might help you find a previously unknown maiden name (e.g., **Elizabeth O'Rourke Lynch**).

*	▶ "eugene * lynch"
**	▶ "eugene ** lynch" **AND** connecticut
	▶ "eugene * lynch" connecticut
	▶ "eugene * lynch" **AND** "elizabeth * lynch"

To work as described, the use of an asterisk must occur inside quotations and will take the place of any string of non-space characters. For this reason, a query like the first one shown in the box above will not include results for pages with an occurrence of "**eugene lynch**" because there are no characters appearing between eugene and lynch. Use of multiple asterisks is permitted, with each asterisk representing a unique string of characters. Results for a wildcard search of "**eugene ** lynch**" could include Eugene Patrick Joseph Lynch or Eugene P. J. Lynch.

Command: OR

Use the word **OR** (all uppercase letters) between keywords to direct Google to find results containing *any* of the keywords specified in your query. Note that while either or both of the keywords adjacent to the OR command may be present on the resulting Web pages, their presence together will not necessarily have any connection or relevance to each another. A piping symbol (|) can be used in place of the word OR.

OR	
OR |	▶ phalen **OR** phelan ▶ patrick **OR** eugene **AND** lynch ▶ "lynch, eugene" **OR** "eugene lynch" **OR** "eugene * lynch" ▶ lynch **AND** waterbury **OR** bridgeport ▶ patrick **OR** eugene **AND** lynch **AND** waterbury | bridgeport

If you have frequent variant spellings for a surname, the OR operator can be helpful in capturing all possible results. Combine the use of OR with AND or quotations to add more precise filters to your searches. In the third example, one search can be conducted to obtain results for pages about any main variation of Eugene Lynch. The last example directs Google to conduct a query based on either of two given names and either of two place names, but in all instances, the keyword lynch must be present. Note that Google recognizes the \| symbol and interprets it the same as the OR operator. These queries take some practice to get the desired results. Another way of submitting the same query using different syntax is **"patrick lynch" OR "eugene lynch" AND (waterbury \| bridgeport)**

Queries that combine AND, OR, and quotation marks can yield some of the most useful filtered results for family historians. While these queries can also be submitted using an Advanced Search Form (discussed in Chapter Three), they are well worth practicing for use with other more advanced filters.

Command: - (NOT)

The word **NOT** is *not* recognized as a command by Google, but the negative function can be performed by using a minus sign directly in front of a word, phrase, or command. Note that there should not be a space following the minus sign when it is used in this fashion. Queries submitted with the minus sign will instruct Google to remove all results pages containing the word or phrase specified.

-	▶ waterbury -vermont ▶ "eugene lynch" **AND** waterbury -vermont ▶ hilton -paris -hotel -celebrity -conrad -hilton.com ▶ ferris -wheel -amusement -bueller -university

This operator is especially helpful when family historians are researching a surname with other common meanings (e.g., Ford, but excluding auto-related results) or when a place name is known to occur in many locations (e.g., Canton, but not China, not Ohio, etc.).

In one example, I was asked by a seminar attendee for recommendations on researching the surname Ferris. The minus sign could help remove ferris wheel, Ferris Bueller, Ferris State University and other unwanted listings that dominate search results, but other more advanced query techniques can readily solve this challenge. Also, given the current

Google It!	Since the minus symbol can be interpreted differently by Google depending upon its use, be sure to place your keywords immediately following the sign to achieve the desired results.

popularity of teen singing sensation Miley Cyrus as Hannah Montana, just imagine how many unwanted Web pages now exist including the words Hannah and Montana, but having nothing to do with Pacific Northwest genealogy. Using -"Hannah Montana" -"miley cyrus" would certainly be in order here!

Tips on Using a "Negative Search"

Excluding one or more search terms as part of your query definition can be an effective technique for filtering out unwanted results that you know from prior experience are likely to otherwise appear in matching results. For genealogists, this can be especially helpful given the reoccurrence of certain place names. In the example that follows, a search for *roxbury* yields first-page results for Massachusetts, New Jersey, New York, and Connecticut. You could easily narrow your selection by changing your query to *roxbury massachusetts*. But what if you're not certain? Perhaps a family Bible includes an entry as

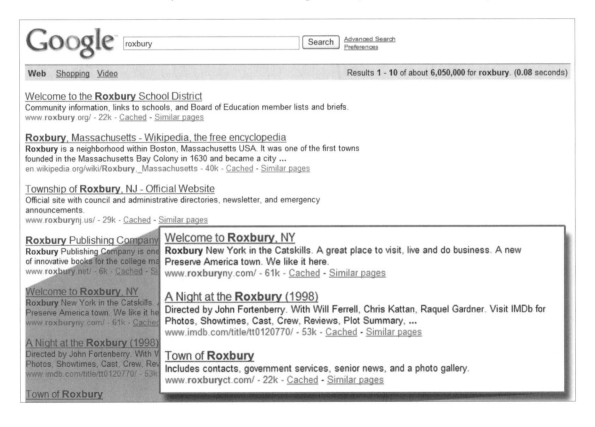

born March 15, 1762 in Roxbury. If you know from other sources that the family lived in Massachusetts, then Connecticut, then New York, you may choose to exclude New Jersey from possible results by using a negative search operator.

Command: + (plus sign)

The plus symbol is used to instruct Google to find results with pages containing exactly the word specified, not any variants of the word (see *Stemming* described on page 16). Many users confuse the use of **AND** and the **plus sign** as interchangeable because they yield similar results, but there are slight differences. Preceding a word with **+** has the same effect as placing that single word in quotations (e.g., ***+married*** is the same as ***"married"***). When used in this manner there is no space following the plus sign.

+	▶ "eugene lynch" +brother ▶ "eugene lynch" +sibling ▶ "eugene lynch" +phelan +waterbury -vermont

I often find it helpful to use the plus symbol liberally, especially in combination with other operators and special keywords commonly used in genealogy.

A somewhat rare occurrence when using Google is to submit a query yielding exactly one matching result. In the example shown below, that is exactly what happened for this query: **"eugene lynch" +grandfather waterbury OR bridgeport -vermont**

Web   Images   Maps   News   Shopping   Gmail   more ▼   Sign in

Google ["eugene lynch" +grandfather waterbury OR bridgeport -vermont] [Search]   Advanced Search
                                                                                      Preferences

Web   Results **1 - 1** of **1** for **"eugene lynch" +grandfather waterbury** OR **bridgeport -vermont**. (0.13 seconds)

Marriage Annacoument's Times Picayune Submitted by: see each ...
A Reception Followed At The New Orleans Sheraton Hotel In The **Waterbury** ...... Mr. Curry,
Whose Mother Was The Former Miss Nancy Curtis Of **Bridgeport**, ...
ftp.rootsweb.com/pub/usgenweb/la/orleans/vitals/marriages/paper/tp-c.txt - 433k -
Cached - Similar pages

Command: ~ (tilde)

The **tilde** (~) symbol is used to find similar words for a specific keyword. (This symbol can be found on your keyboard located as the uppercase character to the left of the number one.) Similar words are also called synonyms; although the tilde has a broader meaning extending beyond the true definition of synonyms. Note there is no space separating the tilde and the desired keyword for which you seek similar words.

~	▶ lynch ~genealogy
	▶ "eugene lynch" ~genealogy
	▶ "eugene lynch" ~birth
	▶ brown **AND** family **AND** "new york" ~genealogy

This operator is especially useful for genealogy research because it can direct Google to find pages with a surname and/or place name, but only those that have something to do with genealogy. As a result, Google will filter out pages not meeting this criteria and leave only pages directly related to your research interests.

Although Google does not publish any list of synonyms, you can determine which words are treated as such by executing successive queries as follows:

▶ ~genealogy –genealogy

▶ ~genealogy –genealogy –family

▶ ~genealogy –genealogy –family –tree

▶ ~genealogy –genealogy –family –tree –surname

Using this technique, the following synonyms were found for the keyword **genealogy** in a search using the ~ command: ancestry, family, family history, family tree, genealogical, genealogical records, genealogists, genealogical, geneologists, geneology, records, roots, surname, tree, vital records.

<table>
<tr><td>Google It!</td><td>Using ~genealogy can be one of the most useful filters for family history enthusiasts conducting research online. I strongly recommend making this part of your initial search efforts for a new ancestor or family line.</td></tr>
</table>

Google Web Search—Building a Genealogy Query

On page 13, I shared a variety of simple techniques to demonstrate how commands can be used to filter Google Web search results. The table is repeated below for your reference. The first query is the most general, using only surname and generating the highest number of results—far too many to evaluate for relevance to your family history. As each search is refined, note the item in bold that was added to the query appearing immediately above. This was done in an attempt to filter results until a manageable number could be found.

Google Web Search Query	Results
lynch	42,800,000
lynch **family**	363,000
lynch family **connecticut**	141,000
eugene lynch family connecticut	45,500
"eugene lynch" family connecticut	51
"eugene * lynch" family connecticut	815
"eugene * lynch" family connecticut ~**genealogy**	117
"eugene * lynch" family connecticut ~genealogy **waterbury OR bridgeport**	8

Using a surname from your family and eventually a place name corresponding to that individual, build a similar set of queries and make a note of the results for each one. You may also find it helpful to note the date in the margin so you can compare the number of results at some future time for the same queries. You may even wish to compare the results found on Google with those found on other leading search engines. (See Appendix C for a listing of search engines.)

Google It!

Google Web Search Query	Results

Building a Genealogy Query—Exercises

The following tables are provided so you can repeat the exercise from the previous page, either for different ancestors and family lines or for the same queries repeated over time to compare the volume of search results. You may even wish to compare the results found on Google with those found on other leading search engines. (See Appendix C for a listing of other Internet search engines.)

Google Web Search Query	Results

Google Web Search Query	Results

Google Web Search Query	Results

Interpreting Web Search Results

Sifting Through the Haystack

In the previous chapter we discussed the basics of how a Web search engine works and why it can be an invaluable tool for genealogy research. As you become more proficient with structuring your queries, you will accomplish an important task without even realizing it. By submitting more thoughtful queries, you will quickly reduce the size of the virtual haystack of results that will require individual inspection before you walk away with your "needle"—details for your elusive ancestors.

The average Google query had long been reported to consist of three words, but a Google presentation in February 2008 noted that the average query is now comprised of four words. Prior examples have already demonstrated how adding each incremental keyword and operators can reduce the number of results. If your Google Web query generates 150,000 results, the default settings will display them ten per page, but Google will only display the first 1,000 before suggesting that you may need to refine your query.

In this chapter, you will learn how to quickly evaluate the *Google Web Search Results* page. Each results page follows the same basic template and is packed with information. If you sometimes find yourself overwhelmed with all the results, you're in good company. A simple query for **the statue of liberty** yields a page introducing nearly 9.5 million results, more than 575 words on the page, and a total of 84 different links waiting for your decision—and that's just on the first page! It's easy to understand why a novice user might be intimidated by all these options, but after carefully reviewing this chapter, anyone should feel right at home on this important destination page.

Note that different templates exist for searching different content types within Google. The Google Image Search displays results using one template while Google News displays results using a template better suited for that content type. The Google Web Search is the most common type, so understanding this template will build a solid foundation for all other content types.

Primary Elements of Google Web Search Results Page

The following is an overview summary. Numbers correspond to the graphic at right.

1	The Google logo, primary text links, and the search input box are carried over from the Home page and are always visible in the upper left corner of your screen. Your search query is also carried forward to this page, enabling you to refine your original query or submit a new one as desired.
2	A summary line showing the number of results found, the time it took Google to perform the search, and links to the primary keywords used in your query.
3	Sponsored links may appear either above the natural search results, along the right side of the page, or in both locations. These advertisements are based on keywords in your query and represent a primary source of Google's revenue.
4	In some instances a Google Web Search will return images, maps, or video as the leading result, based on your query.
5	The core of Google's Web Search Results Page, each result is summarized by up to four lines of text in a specific format. Google's default settings will display 10 results per page using various colors so you can quickly scan the results. Understanding the layout of these results is critical to your success.
6	For some queries, Google will follow basic text results with one or more links to Google Books with titles that match your search criteria. This can be a valuable addition for family historians as more 19th- and 20th-century books are scanned and made available online.
7	In some cases, Google will follow the 10 results with one or more text links labeled "Searches related to:". These links represent similar topics that Google has determined through prior search history may be of interest to you.
8	An expanding Google logo is located above numbered text links enabling direct navigation to more results pages for your query.
9	As a user convenience, Google repeats the search box located in the upper left corner of the screen so you can refine your original query.
10	Google copyright notice and links to Google Home and business information.

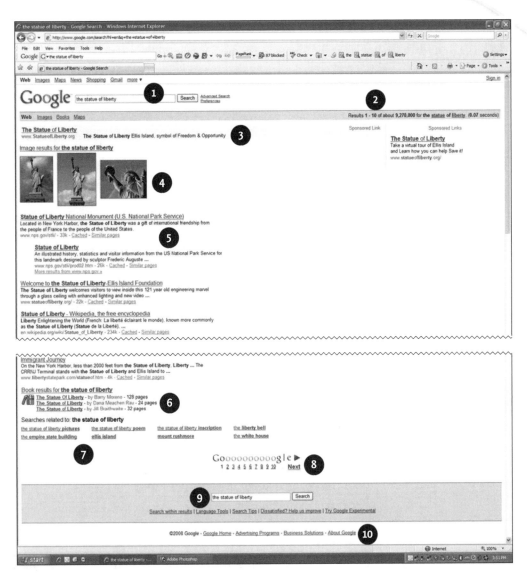

Google Web Search—Results Page

Your mastery of Google will be closely tied to the queries you submit, but also to how well you can understand the results as they are displayed on Google's various results pages. The following pages will dissect the Web Search Results Page, explaining how you can quickly determine if your search has led to meaningful results.

Results Page Part 1—Results Header

As a convenience to the user, the top of each results page is essentially a miniaturized version of the Google homepage. The most important navigational links appear within close proximity to the Google logo. In fact, the logo itself is also a link and will take you directly back to the home page where you can start fresh if you prefer.

One of the most useful items found within the results header is your original query in the search box. This enables you to quickly refine your query as needed. If your query generated 12 million results, you may decide to add quotations or another operator to filter out unwanted listings.

Web   Images   Maps   News   Shopping   Gmail   more ▾
Google™ [the statue of liberty] [Search] Advanced Search Preferences

The dynamic links above the Google logo will switch you to another content type while retaining the subject of your search as the active query. The *Advanced Search* and *Preferences* links to the right of the Search button are described in more detail in Chapter Three.

Images	Click the *Images* link to go directly to the Images results page for the query shown in the input box.
Maps	Click the *Maps* link to go directly to the Maps results page for the query shown in the input box.
News	Click the *News* link to go directly to the News results page for the query shown in the input box.
Shopping	Click the *Shopping* link to go directly to the Products results page for the query shown in the input box.
Gmail	One-click access to your free account on Google Gmail. (You can sign in here or register for an account.)
more	Links to Google Video, Groups, Books, Scholar, Finance, Blogs, YouTube, Calendar, Photos, Documents, Reader, and more.

Results Page Part 2—Result Statistics

Immediately below the results header is a blue bar running horizontally across the page. Along the upper right corner of your screen you will find statistics for the search you just executed from either the Google Home page or from within another content page.

> Results **1 - 10** of about **9,270,000** for the <u>statue</u> of <u>liberty</u>. (0.07 seconds)

In the example above, we see that our query for ***the statue of liberty*** generated 9.27 million results and that it took Google less than 1/10th of a second to respond to the query. The keywords ***statue*** and ***liberty*** also appear as bold text links. Clicking on either keyword will direct you to <www.answers.com> and a variety of definitions for your keyword term. Note that *the* and *of* were included in our search but their status as Stop Words (see Chapter One) prevents them from being treated with the same importance as *statue* and *liberty*.

Results Page Part 3—Sponsored Results

Sponsored results are exactly what the name implies— small text advertisements placed on the results page by advertisers interested in capturing your attention. These advertisements are based on the keywords of your query. Sponsored results—also called *paid listings*, *paid results* or *pay-per-click ads*—are the lifeblood of the multi-billion-dollar revenue engine that drives Google innovation.

How do Sponsored Links work?

Advertisers create an account with Google called *Google AdWords*. They specify the keywords they are interested in, how much they are willing to pay, and how often they want their

The Statue of Liberty   Sponsored Link
www.StatueofLiberty.org   The Statue of Liberty Ellis Island, symbol of Freedom & Opportunity

ads to appear. Each time a search is submitted containing one of the desired keywords, Google displays one or more ads in pre-determined locations on its results pages; the ads are also labeled *Sponsored Links*. Some other search engines use the controversial practice of mixing sponsored links with natural, or free, results (see page 44), making it difficult or impossible for the user to determine which results are based on true relevance. Advertisers are typically charged only when you click to view their message (therefore the term *pay-per-click* advertising).

Sponsored Links

The Statue of Liberty
The Statue of Liberty Ellis Island,
symbol of Freedom & Opportunity
www.StatueofLiberty.org

Where do the Sponsored Ads appear?

Google's Web Results page has two locations reserved for sponsored ads. One is a horizontal band running about three-quarters the width of the page. This is the most valuable real estate for advertisers because Google will list no more than three text ads in this space. The second area reserved for sponsored links is a column filling the remaining righthand quarter of the results page. These narrow text ads can be stacked as many as eight high, often with a link at the bottom to More Sponsored Links.

While some sponsored links may not be of interest to you, the keyword-based system is at least one mechanism used to match advertisers with consumers that are predisposed to their products or services. You may find some useful genealogy products or services by following a sponsored link on your results page, but look before you leap and keep in mind the Latin phrase Caveat Emptor—'let the buyer beware.' Google may be good, but it can't possibly be responsible for every product or service promoted by its advertising sponsors.

Results Page Part 4—Alternate Content in Web Results

As Google continues to refine its service, it uses data gathered from billions of individual searches in an effort to determine what you *might be* searching for, even though you may not have asked for it yet. In the case of our search for pages about ***the statue of liberty***, Google executes our Web search as requested, but, recognizing that many similar queries are seeking images, it displays a sampling of related images as well. These related images are included as a convenience and will appear below the sponsored results, just above the ten natural listings.

In other instances, Google may recognize that a particular query has a high likelihood of being satisfied by displaying a miniature map with phone and address information. In this case, a result similar to the one shown below may appear within your natural results. From time to time, you will also see a range of other content types appearing within your Web Search Results, including video, news archives, blog postings, music, and more.

Image results for **the statue of liberty**

If your carefully crafted genealogy query presents a results page with a non-traditional format, you should explore the results. Google does a very good job and you may be pleasantly surprised with what you find.

In the examples below, you can see both a screen shot and a close-up view of local business results that may appear in response to a Google Web Search. For genealogists, this can be very useful in obtaining a list of churches, cemeteries, libraries, and town halls in a particular place.

Ritz-Carlton-Ny **Battery Park** ⊘
www.ritzcarlton.com

2 West St
New York, NY 10004
(212) 344-0800
Get directions

☆☆☆☆☆ 183 reviews and more »
"Overall, great rooms, great location, looks good, but let down by the details."

In the two examples shown below, the Google Web Search was:

cemeteries waterbury ct

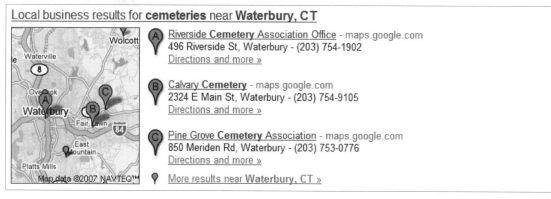

In certain instances, Google may determine that one specific site is extremely relevant given the terms used in your original Web search. In an effort to save you time, Google may present you with a modified summary of the site, including multiple links that will enable you to navigate directly to the most relevant portion of the target website.

In the example shown at the top of the opposite page, a general Web search was conducted for ***ellis island***. Google has determined that the website located at <www.ellisisland.org>

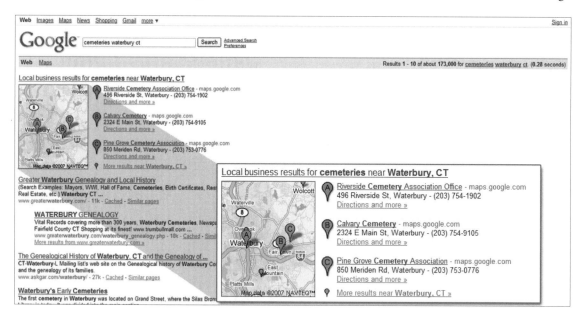

Ellis Island - FREE Port of New York Passenger Records Search
Ellis Island is the symbol of American immigration and the immigrant experience. Use our Free Search to find your immigrant ancestors arriving through the ...
www.**ellisisland**.org/ - 27k - Cached - Similar pages

New Search	Ellis Island
Visiting Ellis Island	Photo Albums
Ellis Island History	Advanced Search
Immigrant Experience	Ellis Island Timeline

More results from ellisisland.org »

is highly relevant, therefore it is placed as the leading natural result. In addition to the standard layout (described more fully on the following two pages), there are eight text links that will take you directly to the corresponding portions of the Ellis Island website.

Video Content

Depending upon the nature of your Google Web Search, your results may occasionally include a summary similar to the one shown below. These video summaries may appear intermingled with your general text results and can be identified by the thumbnail image, as well as the running time of the video (3 min 51 sec, in this example) and the 1–5 star rating as voted by users who have viewed this video.

Video content is described more fully in Chapter Eight—Images & Video.

 YouTube - **Statue of Liberty** Disappears
David Copperfield makes **Statue of Liberty** disappears...
⊞ Watch video - 3 min 51 sec - ☆☆☆☆☆
www.youtube.com/watch?v=9S6tJpUxvOU

Results Page Part 5—Natural Results

One of the most important aspects of using Google is to have a clear understanding of the format used to summarize search results. By understanding how to quickly interpret Google's summary results, you can save a great deal of time and will also become more proficient at structuring future queries.

There are two basic types of listings that can appear on a Google Web Search Results page—*sponsored results* and *natural listings* (also called *organic* or *free listings*). Google typically displays natural results ten per page, ordered from most relevant to least relevant according to its proprietary algorithm. The better job you do selecting meaningful keywords and using basic or advanced operators as filters, the more relevant your natural results will be.

Statue of Liberty National Monument (U.S. National Park Service)
Located in New York Harbor, **the Statue of Liberty** was a gift of international friendship from the people of France to the people of the United States.
www.nps.gov/stli/ - 33k - Cached - Similar pages

Statue of Liberty
An illustrated history, statistics and visitor information from the US National Park Service for this landmark designed by sculptor Frederic Auguste ...
www.nps.gov/stli/prod02.htm - 26k - Cached - Similar pages
More results from www.nps.gov »

Keywords in Bold

In the partial screen shot shown above, you can quickly determine the original query because Google highlights keywords from each Web search in bold type. In the example above, a Google Web query for **the statue of liberty** results in two summary listings from among the top ten results, which are pages on the U.S. National Park Service website <www.nps.gov>.

The second listing is indented slightly because the page is part of the same website. Google highlights up to two relevant pages from a given site, followed by a link to access other relevant pages from that same site. It is limited to two pages to safeguard any one site from monopolizing the natural search results for a given topic.

The table at right provides a detailed description of each element used in Web search results. Slight differences may exist depending upon your query, but the general layout will be the same. As you review this section, you may find it helpful to be near a computer and to submit a basic Google Web search for the term **the statue of liberty** as used in these examples. The colors used on screen will help you more quickly identify the various sub-components of each search result.

Natural Results Layout Summary

These listings represent the most information-packed portion of the search results screen. Taking the time to understand this standard layout will help you quickly master Google.

[Page Title]	The link on line 1 is featured in blue text and contains text from the title of the target page. This is the text that would appear in your browser title if you visited this Web page.
[Summary Text]	Typically one or two lines of black descriptive text with content from the target Web page (either visible content or words hidden in the code called meta-tags).
[URL]	Light green text typically appearing on the fourth line of each summary result, this is the URL or Web address for the target page. A small number (e.g., 33k) often follows to indicate the file size of the corresponding target page.
Cached	A link to the most recent snapshot of this page as stored in the Google index. This feature can be very useful when a link to the live page cannot be established.
Similar pages	A link whereby Google executes a search based on keywords found on the original target Web page.
More results from...	When Google finds multiple relevant results from a single website, it displays the second result below the first and indents it slightly. Additional pages from this same site can be accessed by using the *More results from...* link.
View as HTML	For certain content pages stored in alternate file formats, Google offers an automatic translation into the standard HTML format for your convenience. Automatic translations are typically available for .doc, .pdf, .xls, .ppt, .csv, and other popular formats.
Translate this page	Google will display this conditional link for pages that are in a language other than the native language where your search originated. If, for example, your query results in Italian content, you can view an automatic translation of that page in English by using this link.

Natural Results—Optional Links

You can see from the examples provided on the last few pages that Web search result summaries will enable you to quickly determine if a link is likely to be of interest to you. Before proceeding, there are two additional items that are worth noting briefly, but will not be discussed in detail until later in this book. These two features are sometimes visible within Web Search results as *Translate this page* and *Note this* text links.

Translate this page

If you submit a Google Web Search from an English-based version of the site and it detects relevant results from a page written in another language, Google will place a conditional link offering to translate the page into your native language. Keep in mind that the translation will be a machine-based one and, while not perfect, will be a great help for those who may not speak the other language at all. In the example below, a page with Italian content is included in results for our search for the ***statue of liberty***. This feature is part of Google's Language Tools covered in more detail in Chapter Four.

Statue of Liberty - New York - Recensioni su **Statue of Liberty** ...- [Translate this page]
Statue of Liberty: Vai su TripAdvisor, la tua fonte di quanto di meglio offre il web su recensioni imparziali e articoli su **Statue of Liberty** a New York, ...
www.tripadvisor.it/Attraction_Review-g60763-d103887-Reviews-**Statue_of_Liberty**-New_York_City_New_York.html - 97k - Cached - Similar pages - Note this

Note this

Another optional link that may appear in search results is typically found on the last line to the far right and reads ***Note this*** as seen in the example above. This is a special feature of Google Notebook, which will be discussed in greater detail in Chapter Twelve. By clicking on this link, a user of the Google Notebook application would quickly save a clipping of this search result for future inspection without having to leave the results page or interrupt his or her current thought process.

Since Google is continually refining its service and adding new applications, it is possible—and in many ways likely—that additional links may appear in some future iteration of these Web Results summary. If you see a link not discussed here, follow it to see where it may lead you!

Results Page Part 6—Google Books

One of the many extraordinary projects Google has undertaken in recent years is its digitization and search effort called simply *Google Books* (originally Google Print). Google's ambitious goal is to digitize the world's collection of books and make them accessible through its advanced keyword search algorithm. This feature of Google is discussed more thoroughly in Chapter Five, but of special interest to genealogists is the fact that older books no longer covered under copyright and now in the public domain—including many family and local histories from the 1800s and early 1900s—are available for online viewing and free download in PDF format.

Book results for **the statue of liberty**
The Statue Of Liberty - by Barry Moreno - 128 pages
The Statue of Liberty - by Dana Meachen Rau - 24 pages
The Statue of Liberty - by Jill Braithwaite - 32 pages

As in the example shown above, Google displays up to three titles beside one of several distinct icons. The exact location on the Web Results page has changed over time, but most often it will appear at the bottom of the page, following the ten natural listings for this same topic. By following one of the featured links, the user is taken to the Google Books view (shown on the following page).

Results Page Part 7—Related Searches

Occasionally, Google will list one or more related search links at the bottom of the page, following the natural listings for your query. Based on keyword intelligence gathered from millions of previous queries, Google suggests common similar queries that may be of interest. In the example below, our query for ***the statue of liberty*** has resulted in eight alternate suggestions—three of which incorporate similar keywords, but the remaining suggestions are an interesting collection of local and national landmarks.

Searches related to: **the statue of liberty**			
the statue of liberty **pictures**	the statue of liberty **poem**	the statue of liberty **inscription**	the **liberty bell**
the **empire state building**	**ellis island**	**mount rushmore**	the **white house**

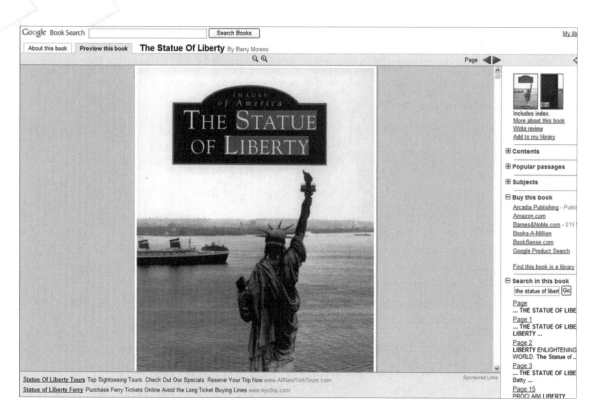

Genealogy

A single word query for ***genealogy*** generates more than 78 million natural results and another dozen sponsored links. At the bottom of the results page, you can see from the image (opposite) that Google also suggests the following terms—*genealogy mormon*, *genealogy charts*, *rootsweb*, *surnames*, *coat of arms*, *us census*, *birth records*, and *lds*. It can sometimes be interesting to intentionally submit a single-word query just to see the related topics that Google suggests.

Results Page Part 8—Navigation

As part of the footer for each results page, Google uses an ever-expanding logo which will act as an accordion depending upon the number of search results found for your query. Many queries generate millions of results—at ten per page, that's quite a few pages. You can navigate through relevant results by clicking the previous/next buttons, the arrows to the left and right of the logo, or simply by clicking on an individual page number to jump directly to those results.

As noted earlier, Google may find millions of results matching your query, but will only display the first 1,000 results. If I've done my job in helping you understand the use of keywords and commands, you should never see this warning notice.

Although Google has not published any specific statistics on search results by page or position on the page, it is estimated that 85 to 90 percent of users select a result from those presented on page one. Relatively few searchers advance to page two, three, or beyond, although some studies have shown a small percentage visiting through page five. In most cases, if a user cannot find results from the first page of listings, he or she refines the query and tries again. This is why most companies spend a great deal of time, effort, and money to ensure that their product or service is listed on page one. If they can't achieve that in the natural listings, they will generally feature their offering as one of the Sponsored Links using the process described earlier in this chapter.

Results Page Part 9—Search Box

For your convenience, Google repeats the search box (described in part 1) at the bottom of each results page. The box contains the query as you submitted it, and you can refine it and re-submit it or you can submit an entirely new query.

Results Page Part 10—Company Links

The last line of each results page is Google's copyright notification, which is followed by text links to return to the Google home page as well as links to additional information about the company. For those readers interested in learning more about any aspect of Google, this is the place to visit.

©2008 Google - Google Home - Advertising Programs - Business Solutions - About Google

About Google

In my opinion, one of the most important links on the entire Google website is included at the footer of every page—*About Google*. By following any number of paths originating from this single text link, you can learn a tremendous amount about Google products and services. Much of the learning that enabled me to become expert in the use of Google originated through curiosity and inspection of these pages. So take time to visit this page!

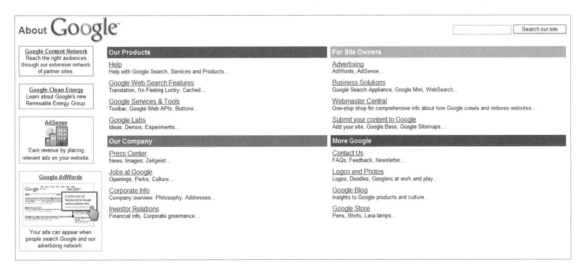

For those readers who enjoy technology as much as I do, be sure to visit the *Google Labs* link located under the blue *Our Products* section of the About Google page. Google Labs is the place where you can learn about what's on the Google drawing board.

CHAPTER 3

Advanced Search Techniques

Building on a Foundation of Basics

Before you can build a house you need a strong foundation to serve as a base. The same is true with using Google. While many of the advanced commands and operators that will follow here are easy to understand, I highly recommend that you spend time at your computer with the sole purpose of playing with Google. Build your foundation of basics so you can squeeze more value from the advanced techniques that will follow. There is no better way to become fluent in search engine basics than to spend an extra ten or fifteen minutes each day searching for something—anything at all— simply for the sake of building your search skills.

In the first chapter, you learned the following important concepts:

- Careful selection of keywords
- Google's automatic AND
- Automatic searching on word variations (e.g., Stemming)
- Google's treatment of common words *(e.g., Stop Words)*
- Use of "quotation marks" and the * as a wildcard
- Synonyms and similar terms
- Use of the OR command
- Removing undesired results with a minus sign

Using Advanced Search

There are at least two ways of leveraging the power offered by Google's many advanced search commands and special operators. One way is to use the Google Advanced Search form, which guides you through the process of building a query by using input boxes and drop-down menus and essentially writes the syntax for you. Other users, especially those with a technical background, prefer to have more direct control and would rather type the commands themselves.

In this chapter, both techniques will be discussed in detail. No matter which method you prefer, be sure to review each command since the results of the Advanced Search form are simply achieved by executing one or more commands on your behalf behind the scenes.

Accessing Advanced Search

The Advanced Search form can be accessed from the Google home page by clicking on the small text link located to the right of the input box. The link is also displayed as part of the common header on most results pages, regardless of content type. The main portions of the Advanced Search form are described below. You may find it helpful to point your Web browser to this page on your screen so you can review this discussion in full size and color.

Google Advanced Search

In mid-March 2008, Google launched the new Advanced Search form, which is a dramatic improvement over the prior version. Essentially, five main components of the page are used as needed to harness the power of more than a dozen power filtering commands.

1	The top box in light blue is reserved by Google to display the syntax of your query as you build it using the advanced search components available. You cannot edit contents in this box.
2	A combination of input boxes and drop-down menus to construct an advanced query based on common nested operators and commands.
3	Additional advanced options to refine your query even further using some lesser-known commands, operators, and filters.
4	Accepts a full URL as input and then directs Google to perform one of two advanced operations on your behalf.
5	Topic-specific search can direct Google to search a specific content type or base of information for more specialized results.

Use the form below and your advanced search will appear here ❶

Find web pages that have...

all these words:

this exact wording or phrase: _tip_

one or more of these words: OR OR _tip_

But don't show pages that have... ❷

any of these unwanted words: _tip_

Need more tools?

Results per page: 10 results

Language: any language

File type: any format

Search within a site or domain:

(e.g. youtube.com, .edu)

⊟ Date, usage rights, numeric range, and more

Date: (how recent the page is) anytime

Usage rights: not filtered by license

Where your keywords show up: anywhere in the page ❸

Region: any region

Numeric range: ..

(e.g. $1500..$3000)

SafeSearch: ⦿ Off ◯ On

[Advanced Search]

Page-specific tools:

Find pages similar to the page: ❹ [Search]

Find pages that link to the page: [Search]

Topic-specific search engines from Google:

Google Book Search
Google Code Search New!
Google Scholar
Google News archive search

Apple Macintosh
BSD Unix
Linux
Microsoft

U.S. Government
Universities

❺

Advanced Search Part 1—Query Builder

A welcome addition to the new Advanced Search form is an automatic query builder. In previous versions of Advanced Search, Google simply accepted user input and processed the query. With the introduction of this one line—and lots of intelligence behind the scenes—Google displays the syntax of your query as you fill out the other parts of the form. Although you cannot currently edit this syntax view, I expect this will be allowed at some point in the future. By reading the syntax as you build your query, you can become more familiar with the command structure of a query and thus will become a more effective online researcher.

In the example below, the syntax for a query was automatically created using only the basic components of the Advanced Search form. If you build an advanced query that needs slight modification, you can highlight and copy the full text of the query, paste it directly into the Google search input box on the home page, and directly edit it as needed there.

Google™ Advanced Search   Advanced Search Tips | About Google

lynch family ~genealogy "eugene lynch" connecticut OR bridgeport OR waterbury

Find web pages that have...

all these words:	lynch family ~genealogy		
this exact wording or phrase:	eugene lynch		tip
one or more of these words:	connecticut	OR bridgeport	OR waterbury	tip

But don't show pages that have...

any of these unwanted words:		tip

Need more tools?

Results per page:	10 results
Language:	any language
File type:	any format
Search within a site or domain:	

(e.g. youtube.com, .edu)

⊞ Date, usage rights, numeric range, and more

Advanced Search

Topic-specific search engines from Google:

Google Book Search	Apple Macintosh	U.S. Government
Google Code Search New!	BSD Unix	Universities
Google Scholar	Linux	
Google News archive search	Microsoft	

Advanced Search Part 2—The Basics

The main section of the Advanced Search form enables users to answer one or more questions about what they are researching. Google will dynamically begin building a query based on the user's input. (This is the syntax as described on the previous page.) There are currently a total of seven input boxes and three drop-down menus. To obtain meaningful results for a genealogy query, I recommend using either the first or second input box at minimum, then using other options to refine the query definition.

Find web pages that have...			
all these words:	lynch family ~genealogy		
this exact wording or phrase:	eugene lynch		tip
one or more of these words:	connecticut	OR bridgeport	OR waterbury	tip
But don't show pages that have...			
any of these unwanted words:			tip
Need more tools?			
Results per page:	10 results		
Language:	any language		
File type:	any format		
Search within a site or domain:			
	(e.g. youtube.com, .edu)		

The three main components of this Advanced Search section help structure a basic query and then introduce the user to some popular advanced tools.

Find Web pages that have...	Five input boxes guide you through the process of building a basic query that will use **AND**, **OR**, and " ". Either the first or second boxes should be considered required; the other three are optional.
But don't show pages that have...	Employs **NOT** logic (the minus sign) to remove unwanted results by excluding certain keywords. This requires that other query parameters have been specified in the section described above.
Need more tools?	Enables you to specify the number of results per page, the language of results pages, and certain file types, or to direct the search to a specific domain or domain type (*e.g., .edu, .gov, or .lib*).

Advanced Search Part 3–Expanded Capabilities

After providing basic keyword definitions as described on the previous page, you may wish to expand your use of filtering based on the expanded capabilities of Advanced Search. A text link with a plus symbol is labeled "*Date, usage rights, numeric range, and more.*" Click on this link (note that the plus symbol now becomes a minus) to reveal expanded capabilities of the Advanced Search form as shown below and described in detail on the following page.

⊟ Date, usage rights, numeric range, and more	
Date: (how recent the page is)	anytime
Usage rights:	not filtered by license
Where your keywords show up:	anywhere in the page
Region:	any region
Numeric range:	..
	(e.g. $1500..$3000)
SafeSearch	⊙ Off ○ On

Google Advanced Search   Advanced Search Tips | About Google

lynch family ~genealogy "eugene lynch" connecticut OR bridgeport OR waterbury

Find web pages that have...

all these words:	lynch family ~genealogy	
this exact wording or phrase:	eugene lynch	tip
one or more of these words:	connecticut OR bridgeport OR waterbury	tip

But don't show pages that have...

any of these unwanted words:		tip

Need more tools?

Results per page:	10 results
Language:	any language
File type:	any format
Search within a site or domain:	
	(e.g. youtube.com, .edu)

⊞ Date, usage rights, numeric range, and more

Advanced Search

Topic-specific search engines from Google:

Google Book Search	Apple Macintosh	U.S. Government
Google Code Search New!	BSD Unix	Universities
Google Scholar	Linux	
Google News archive search	Microsoft	

©2008 Google

Expanded Capabilities Defined

To access the expanded capabilities of Advanced Search, click the link shown below. It will reveal the screen as shown at left.

⊞ Date, usage rights, numeric range, and more

Expanded Capabilities of Advanced Search

Date of Page	A drop-down selection allows the user to seek results from pages that have been posted during a specified time frame. Choose from any time, the past 24 hours, past week, past month, past two months, past three months, past six months, or past year.
Usage Rights	Limits results to pages with content that may or may not have usage restrictions based on copyright or other claims. Choose from one of five options: 1) not filtered, 2) free to use or share, 3) free to use or share (even commercially), 4) free to use, share, or modify, and 5) free to use share or modify (even commercially).
Keyword Location	Enables you to specify where on the page certain keywords or phrases appear. Select from one of five options: 1) anywhere on the page (default), 2) in the title of the page, 3) in the text of the page, 4) in the URL of the page, or 5) in links to the page.
Region of the World	Limits a query to results coming from a specific region of the world as defined by an extensive list of countries. Defaults to any region.
Numeric Range	Expands the definition of a query to include pages where numbers in a certain range are specified by beginning and ending parameters.
SafeSearch Filtering Preferences	An On/Off option based on your individual preference settings. This enables you to filter out certain results that may be objectionable based on the keywords being researched. (e.g., A query for information or images dealing with breast cancer or human anatomy may trigger inappropriate content without the use of SafeSearch filtering.)

Advanced Search Part 4—Page-Specific Tools

In addition to the expanded capabilities discussed on the two previous pages, two additional search filters appear when the Advanced Search screen is expanded. In both of these cases, Google will execute a query based on a Web address (URL) provided by the user and will ignore any keywords or filters specified elsewhere on the form. Each option is followed by an individual Search button, which will cause the query to be performed.

Find pages similar to the page:	Using the **related**: command described in greater detail later in this chapter, Google uses information from its index for the Web page specified and then presents other results that have similar characteristics—most notably keywords or phrases used in the content of the page and/or in the structure of the Web page itself. See the **related**: command for more details.
Find pages that link to the page:	Similar to the option above, this input box requires a Web address as user input. Clicking on the corresponding Search button will perform the query. Any keywords or other information appearing elsewhere on the Advanced Search form will be ignored. Results will include other websites that link to the specified target site. This is achieved through the Google **link**: command described later in this chapter.

Advanced Search Part 5—Topic-Specific Search Engines

To cater to researchers who may have specialized needs, Google offers a variety of topic-specific versions of its search service. These can be found at the bottom of the advanced search page. When used, each version will provide users with the same capabilities of the more familiar interface, commands, and syntax, but results will be limited to a more narrowly defined content area.

Topic-specific search engines from Google:

Google Book Search	Apple Macintosh	U.S. Government
Google Code Search	BSD Unix	Universities
Google Scholar	Linux	
Google News archive search	Microsoft	

The list currently includes: **Book Search**, Code Search, Scholar, **News archive search**, Apple Macintosh, BSD Unix, Linux, Microsoft, **U.S. Government**, and **Universities**. From the standpoint of family history research, those listed in bold type will be of special interest. For more details on similar functionality, see the description of the **site:** command on page 67.

Advanced Search—U.S. Government Search

Among the topic-specific features provided by Advanced Search, genealogists should take special note of the Google U.S. Government Search. Results for queries through this search will restrict results to only those pages or files appearing on a U.S. Government website—those ending in a .gov domain name extension.

This can be especially helpful when searching for government forms and other information required to make a formal request for copies of documentation for one or more of your ancestors. This service can be accessed by visiting Google's Advanced Search page or by pointing your browser directly to <www.google.com/ig/usgov>.

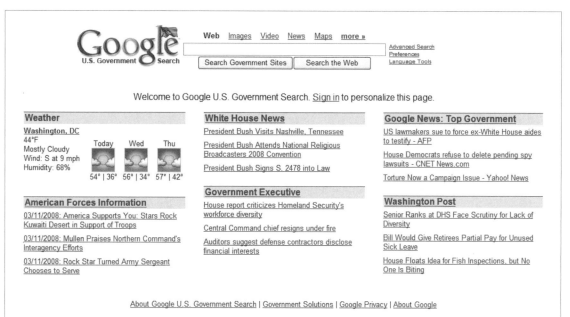

Advanced Search–University Search

Similar to the U.S. Government Search, Google's University Search provides a quick and easy interface to limit your query to a specific college or university. Genealogists may find it useful to query a college or university attended by an ancestor to see if any old alumni postings are among the pages of its website. If the name of the university you want to search is not yet on Google's list, you can still execute a similar search from the command line using the **site:** command (see page 67 for details). This service can be accessed by visiting Google's Advanced Search page or by pointing your browser directly to <www.google.com/options/universities.html>.

Advanced Search Form vs. Command Line Syntax

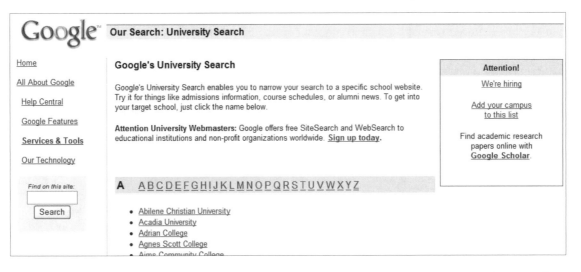

As the information on the previous few pages demonstrates, the Advanced Search form offered by Google is an especially powerful tool for those with little technical background or experience in conducting research online. For genealogists, this form can be easily adapted to perform useful searches based on surname and place name, as well as more advanced searches involving date ranges and other filters. Despite the usefulness of this form however, I strongly encourage all researchers to become familiar with the commands and syntax that Google is using in the background to perform queries on your behalf. Even though Google will surely make continual improvements to the Advanced Search, there are many more quick refinements you can make by understanding the commands used to execute your query.

Remember that this book is focused on the use of Google for genealogy research. There are many additional commands and techniques that you may find helpful in other aspects of your life (a few favorites are included in Chapter Fourteen), but many more won't be included in these pages because they don't directly connect to helping you improve your family sleuthing skills. Use of the following commands is discussed in detail, including their use and limitations through the Advanced Search form. For your quick reference to these advanced commands, the pages in this section will use a special format. The four-part formatting used to detail each command includes:

1. Command Description
2. Syntax
3. Appearance on the Google Advanced Search Form
4. Special Relevance to Genealogists

Commands & Syntax of Advanced Search

wildcards (*)	Specifying proximity of keywords in an exact-phrase match
numrange (..)	Using dates and other numeric ranges in your query
related:	Viewing pages that have similar content to a target page
site:	Restricting search efforts to a specific site or site type
cache:	Viewing previous versions of a Web page
intext:	Restricting search efforts to the visible text of a page
intitle: / allintitle:	Restricting search efforts to the words in a page title
inurl: / allinurl:	Restricting search efforts to the words in a Web address/URL
filetype:	Searching for or excluding specific file types
phonebook:	Searching residential and business phone listings
calculator functions	Performing mathematical calculations using Google
conversions	Performing various conversions from the Google search box

Command: AND, OR, " ", - , + , ~

In Chapter One, I discussed how to structure a basic query with carefully selected keywords and the use of basic operators **AND, OR,** " ", the minus sign, plus sign, tilde, and others. Each of these commands can be used individually or in combination with one another to structure detailed queries. The syntax may look complex, but the Advanced Search form will help remove the mystery and you will quickly be typing them on your own.

Syntax

lynch family ~genealogy "eugene lynch" connecticut **OR** bridgeport **OR** waterbury

Appearance on Advanced Search Form

Find web pages that have...			
all these words:	lynch family ~genealogy		
this exact wording or phrase:	eugene lynch		tip
one or more of these words:	connecticut	OR bridgeport	OR waterbury	tip
But don't show pages that have...			
any of these unwanted words:			tip

Special Relevance to Genealogists

As you carefully craft your queries for Google, note that there are only two instances where case sensitivity matters—the use of the Boolean commands **AND** and **OR** as discussed previously in this chapter. In all other instances, Google is case insensitive and will deliver the same results regardless of the combination of upper and lowercase letters used in your query.

Command: .. (numrange)

Google will recognize the use of two periods placed immediately between two numbers and will seek results including your keyword terms, in addition to any numbers on the page that are in the specified range. Note that there are no spaces before, after, or between the two periods. Examples of numbers in a range can include dates, weights or other units of measure, and amounts. This command is most helpful when used in combination with one or more basic commands.

Syntax

"eugene lynch" born 1840..1890

Appearance on Advanced Search Form

Special Relevance to Genealogists

In addition to surnames and place names, dates serve as a key element for all family historians. When an exact date isn't available, an approximate range in years is often helpful to filter out unwanted results from tens of thousands of entries that may exist for similar names. Consider the example below where I am searching for census information for an individual named exactly Eugene Lynch. The range of years 1860 to 1910 will instruct Google to include any pages that may mention the exact name as given, but will limit results to pages also noting years between or including 1860 and 1910.

> ▶ "eugene lynch" census 1860..1910
> ▶ "eugene lynch" "elizabeth o'rourke" **OR** "elizabeth rourke" married 1865..1885

In the example above, I included the names of two ancestors known to have married sometime between 1865 and 1885. Since the bride's name was often written incorrectly, the **OR** command captures the surname as both **O'Rourke** or **Rourke**.

Command: related:

This command instructs Google to find other Web pages related to the same topic as that covered by the page being specified. By analyzing keywords on the page, Google can determine which other pages in the Google index are likely to be of interest. This has the same result as clicking on the *Similar pages* link found in the natural listings for most Google Web searches.

Syntax

related:www.ditota.com/domenico_ditota.php

Appearance on Advanced Search Form

To access this feature from the Advanced Search page, you must click the link to expand additional capabilities for Date, usage rights, numeric range, and more (see below).

⊕ Date, usage rights, numeric range, and more

Page-specific tools:

Find pages similar to the page:		Search
Find pages that link to the page:		Search

Special Relevance to Genealogists

When you find a useful Web page dealing with some aspect of your family, especially one dealing with a particular ancestor, surname, or place name, you should try a **related:** query. You can do this easily by highlighting the full Web page address from your browser's address bar, then pasting it into a Google search box. Before pressing Enter, place your cursor at the very beginning of the line, remove the http:// if it is present, and type the word **related:** Note that there should be no space between the colon and the Web address.

▶ **related:**www.ditota.com/campobasso.php

Command: site:

The **site:** command directs Google to either exclude a particular site or to search only a specified site using the keywords and other operators provided. When used from the command line, this feature will direct a query to a designated site unless you precede the command with a minus sign, which will instruct Google to perform the query excluding the site in question.

Syntax

site:lynchonline.com patrick lynch 1850**..**1900

Appearance on Advanced Search Form

Search within a site or domain:	
	(e.g. youtube.com, .edu)

Special Relevance to Genealogists

In the sample syntax noted above, the query returned just three results. By removing the numrange series, the query generated 17 results. In my opinion, the **site:** command is one of the most useful advanced commands supported by Google. You are strongly encouraged to test this from the command line, especially for large websites that contain hundreds of pages dealing with your ethnic or geographic areas of interest.

Specifying just an extension (e.g., gov, net, edu, lib, co.uk, etc.) is also a useful filter to limit results to a range of sites, rather than just a single site. Using the minus sign will similarly remove one or more sites from a query. (Use of the minus sign to exclude sites is a capability not currently available through the Advanced Search form.)

> ▶ **site:**www.immigrantships.net "eugene lynch" 1850..1890
> ▶ **site:**gov "patrick lynch" 1850..1900
> ▶ patrick lynch 1850..1900 **-site:**lynchonline.com

In this example, the command is directing Google to query the website of the Immigrant Ships Transcribers Guild, a very large and popular site with thousands of pages of transcribed passenger lists. Using a simple version of this query with just the surname specified, results yield 833 occurrences of the surname Lynch. Adding the given name Eugene narrows the field to just 89. Adding the date range continues to filter unwanted results leaving just 35 pages. While this number is small enough to inspect one-by-one, adding quotations around the exact name results in a single matching result. Ah, if only this were our man.

Using the site: Command for Google Images

To this point, our examples have emphasized using advanced search techniques to flush results from a Google Web Search. These same commands are equally useful—sometimes even more useful—when searching other content types. The **site:** command can be an especially effective tool for searching Google Images for pictures relating to your family story. The syntax is identical, but you must direct the search by clicking on the *Images* link found on both the Google homepage and the header of most results screens.

The image above is an enlarged view of the page header, taken from the full-page screen shot shown opposite. By using the **site:** command, Google has been instructed to find image files that appear on the official Statue of Liberty website at <www.statueofliberty. org>. This same technique can be employed to find images or other files on any target website. For more detail on searching and using Google Images, see Chapter Four.

Command: cache:

The **cache:** command, which is accessible via a standard link included with most Web Search results, provides users with the ability to see a prior version of the target Web page as last indexed by Google. This snapshot is stored in Google's index and serves as a useful backup for instances where a page has been renamed, modified, or retired.

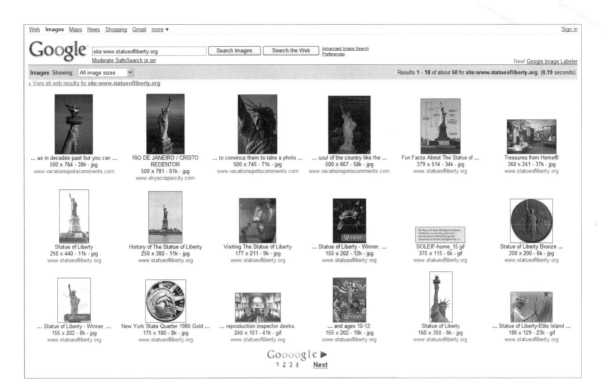

Syntax

cache:www.ditota.com/campobasso.php

Appearance on Advanced Search Form

Although the **cache:** command does not have an exact counterpart on the Advanced Search form, the form does include a Date feature that enables users to query pages based on their age. The resulting lists will include a Cached link that can then be used to access the page file.

⊟ Date, usage rights, numeric range, and more	
Date: (how recent the page is)	anytime
Usage rights:	not filtered by license
Where your keywords show up:	anywhere in the page
Region:	any region
Numeric range:	--

Special Relevance to Genealogists

Millions of pages have been published to the Web dealing with some aspect of genealogy. With the proliferation of Web publishing tools, it has become quite easy to publish portions of our research online for the benefit of others. The **cache:** command is a useful safety net to obtain information that is otherwise in jeopardy of being lost. If you find something relevant to your family via a cached copy of a page, be sure you print a copy of the page so you can retain it for future reference.

Example of a Cached Search Result

Cached page files can be very useful for genealogists. The Internet is always in a state of change as pages are being published, modified, renamed, and retired on a regular basis. If your search yields a result summary that looks promising, but your attempt to access that result fails, be sure to click the *Cached* link to capture whatever you can before that page disappears forever.

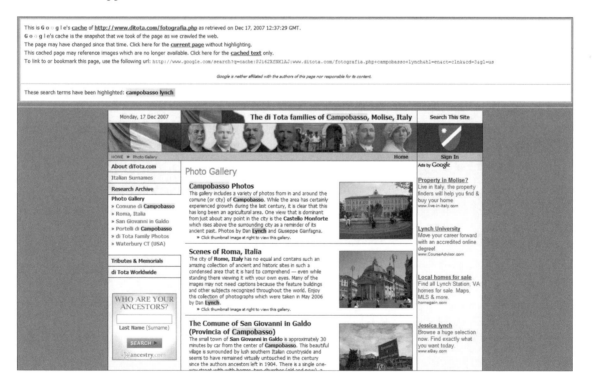

The screen shot on the opposite page shows a Google Web Search result accessed using the cache: command. The page header (shown enlarged below) includes special information about the page, the date it was last indexed by Google, and links to view the most recent version of the page. If keywords were also specified as part of your query, they would be highlighted as shown in this example.

> This is G o o g l e's cache of **http://www.ditota.com/fotografia.php** as retrieved on Dec 17, 2007 12:37:29 GMT.
> G o o g l e's cache is the snapshot that we took of the page as we crawled the web.
> The page may have changed since that time. Click here for the **current page** without highlighting.
> This cached page may reference images which are no longer available. Click here for the **cached text** only.
> To link to or bookmark this page, use the following url: http://www.google.com/search?q=cache:PJi62XfNK1AJ:www.ditota.com/fotografia.php+camp
>
> *Google is neither affiliated with the authors of this page nor responsible for its content.*
>
> These search terms have been highlighted: **campobasso lynch**

Command: intext:

This command instructs Google to execute the query as specified, but requires that the word or phrase following the command be found in the text of the Web page as opposed to other parts of the page indexed by Google (e.g., page title, URL, anchor text, etc.). This can be especially helpful when used in conjunction with other similar commands.

Syntax

~genealogy **intext:**"eugene lynch"

Appearance on Advanced Search Form

This feature is included as part of the extended capabilities of the Advanced Search form and uses the drop-down menu to specify the location of the terms being searched.

> ⊟ Date, usage rights, numeric range, and more
>
> Where your keywords show up: anywhere in the page ▼
> anywhere in the page
> in the title of the page
> in the text of the page
> in the URL of the page
> in links to the page

Special Relevance to Genealogists

Search results can sometimes frustrate genealogists who arrive at a page only to realize their keywords were not visible within the page content, but instead were part of the code used to create the page or some element other than the page text itself. This command will be used sparingly, but may help more advanced users working on common surnames or place names.

> ▶ **intext:**"lynch genealogy" 1850..1890
> ▶ "eugene lynch" ~genealogy connecticut **intext:**waterbury
> ▶ "eugene lynch" ~genealogy 1880..1900 waterbury **-intext:**vermont

Command: intitle: / allintitle:

These two related commands direct Google to search the title of potential result pages for the occurrence of one or more keywords as specified immediately after the command. When placed at the beginning of a query, the **allintitle:** command requires the presence of all keywords in the title of the resulting pages. The **intitle:** command can be used anywhere in the query. Keywords placed after the command will be required in the title, but others will not. Placing the **intitle:** command before each keyword will generate the same results as using the **allintitle:** command. There is no space between the colon and the keyword.

Syntax

lynch **intitle:**family
lynch **allintitle:**"family history"
allintitle:lynch family history
census records connecticut **intitle:**lynch

Appearance on Advanced Search Form

> ⊟ Date, usage rights, numeric range, and more
>
> Where your keywords show up: | anywhere in the page ⌄
> anywhere in the page
> in the title of the page
> in the text of the page
> in the URL of the page
> in links to the page

Special Relevance to Genealogists

This is a tricky but useful command, especially in scenarios where you are researching a very common surname or place name. By structuring a query with certain keywords occurring anywhere in your results, but others being required in the title, you will likely narrow your results to a smaller, more qualified group of pages. Unless you use this command regularly, it is one of several commands that's easier to use through the Advanced Search form.

You may find it helpful to use these commands in combination with the **intext:** command discussed previously, which will then require certain keywords to appear in the title and others to be included as part of the page text.

Command: inurl: / allinurl:

This pair of commands directs Google to search the entire URL string (Web address) for one or more keywords as specified immediately after the command. When placed at the beginning of a query, the **allinurl:** command requires the presence of all keywords in the title of the resulting pages. The **intitle:** command can be used anywhere in the query. The keyword placed immediately after the command will be required in the URL, but others will not. Placing the **inurl:** command before each keyword will generate the same results as using the **allinurl:** command. There is no space between the colon and the keyword.

Syntax

lynch **inurl:**genealogy

lynch **inurl:**"family history"

allinurl:lynch family history

census records connecticut **inurl:**lynch

Appearance on Advanced Search Form

⊟ Date, usage rights, numeric range, and more

Where your keywords show up: | anywhere in the page ⌄

anywhere in the page
in the title of the page
in the text of the page
in the URL of the page
in links to the page

Special Relevance to Genealogists

As with the **intitle:** / **allintitle:** command pair, this can be a difficult command to master, but it will generally help you find very qualified pages if you structure your query correctly. By structuring a query with certain keywords occurring anywhere in your results, and others being required in the URL, you will increase the likelihood of relevant results. Unless you use it regularly, this command is also easier to use through the Advanced Search form.

Command: filetype:

This command directs Google to search its index for your query as defined, but to limit results to those of a particular filetype. The **ext:** command performs the same function. To exclude a particular file type from your results, use a minus sign immediately before the command as shown in the third syntax example on the opposite page. As of this writing, only the command line execution of this command allows the removal of filetypes, not the Advanced Search form.

Syntax

lynch ~genealogy **filetype**:pdf

Appearance on Advanced Search Form

Need more tools?

Results per page:	10 results ⌄
Language:	any language ⌄
File type:	any format ⌄

any format
Adobe Acrobat PDF (.pdf)
Adobe Postscript (.ps)
Autodesk DWF (.dwf)
Google Earth KML (.kml)
Google Earth KMZ (.kmz)
Microsoft Excel (xls)

Special Relevance to Genealogists

As most family historians know, the worldwide community of genealogists is a large, diverse, and sharing group. Our collective efforts are frequently published online as Microsoft *Word* documents, transcriptions in Microsoft *Excel* spreadsheet format, files converted for universal sharing using the popular Adobe *Acrobat* PDF file format, and many others. By using the **filetype:** or **ext:** commands in careful combination with other commands and operators, you can search for items with almost pinpoint accuracy. Use the first example below to find copies of genealogy presentations covering certain topics of interest (by replacing *census* with other keywords). The Advanced Search form doesn't support GEDCOM, but you can manually instruct Google to search the Web for such files using syntax similar to the last example shown below.

filetype:	▶ ~genealogy census workshop **filetype:**ppt 2005..2008
ext:	▶ irish passenger arrivals 1840..1860 ext:xls
	▶ irish passenger arrivals 1840..1860 -**filetype:**xls
	▶ lynch waterbury **OR** bridgeport **filetype:**ged

Command: phonebook:

This command will search for anyone with a specified name and within a geographic area of interest (U.S. cities, zip codes, and states only) resulting in an alphabetized list including name, phone, mailing address, and a text link to the corresponding Google Map for the corresponding street address.

Syntax

As shown in the image below, the syntax requires either zip code, city, or state. For major cities (e.g., Boston, New York, and Philadelphia) you can omit the state, but it will be required for frequently occurring city or town names (e.g., Canton, Mansfield, and Springfield). You can search using **firstname lastname state** or **firstname lastname city** or **lastname city** or **lastname zip**, but Google appears to place limits on the most general search using **lastname state**, showing no more than 600 results for any such query.

The phonebook command is not currently available from the Advanced Search page and should be typed from the Google Web Search command line.

Special Note—*The results contained in the image above and at right have been partially distorted as a courtesy to those whose names may appear in this sample search.*

Special Relevance to Genealogists

Similar to any number of online phone directories, this command can be useful in your efforts to connect with distant relatives who may still be living in the city or town of your ancestors. It may be a long-shot for those with common surnames, but it can be extremely useful for those with unique surnames or Americanized spellings of European names.

Google Phonebook Results

In the example below, Google is directed to search phonebook listings for the surname Barnes that may exist in the town of Mansfield, Ohio. The abbreviation for Ohio could have been typed as oh, Oh, or oH but was typed as OH to emphasize a point. If this query had specified Portland, Oregon, the user could have typed **phonebook:barnes portland OR**. In this one instance, Google would recognize the uppercase OR was being used as a qualifier for Oregon and not as the OR command. The OR command is not supported within a Google Phonebook search.

On the sample results page below, you can see the familiar screen layout that includes the common header in the upper left, results statistics in the upper right, and the specified keywords appearing in bold type throughout the page.

Reverse Phone Number Lookup

You can often obtain a name and address for a particular phone number (land line, not cell phone) simply by entering the number into the Google command line. For best results, enter the number in quotes as "(555) 555-5555."

Google Residential vs. Business Listings

For family historians with an in-depth familiarity with Google, you may recall more specialized commands for residential (**rphonebook:**) and business (**bphonebook:**) phonebook listings. While certain aspects of these commands can still yield results, advancements in other Google features have reduced the usefulness of these commands and rendered them nearly obsolete. Business listings can be obtained through general Google Web or Google Maps searches as shown below.

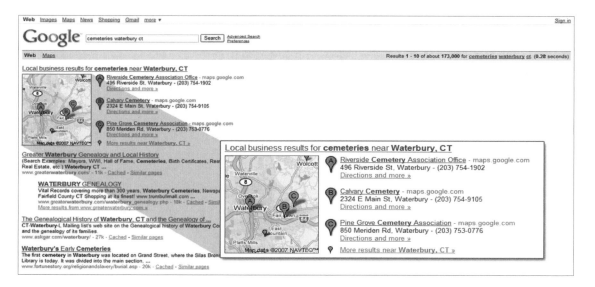

Simple Phone Lookup

If you are simply trying to look up the phone number and address for an individual or business, you can try finding it directly from the Google command line. Type the name and location, separated by a comma. Although the state is not required, you will get better results if you use it.

Web   Images   Maps   News   Shopping   Gmail   more ▾

Google™ | john mongillo, ocala fl | [Search]   Advanced Search
Preferences

Web

Phonebook results for **john mongillo, ocala fl**
☎ **John Mongillo** (352) 347-0955 ███ ███ ███ ██. Ocala, FL 34473 Map

Google Phonebook Name Removal

At the bottom of each Google Phonebook results page, a text link is included that reads
"Request to have your name removed from this list."

If your preference is to remove your residential and/or business contact information
from the Google Phonebook service, Google provides simple instructions for making such
a request. In both cases, Google warns that such a removal from its service is permanent
and that it is not possible to add your number in the future.

IMPORTANT NOTE: Removing your phonebook listing will not remove your personal information from other
pages on the web or from other reverse phone listing lookup services, such as:

- Anywho
- Switchboard.com
- Whitepages.com
- Reverse Phone Directory
- Phonenumber.com
- Smartpages.com

For a comprehensive list of reverse phone lookup services, try a Google search.

Please enter all information exactly as it appears in your phonebook entry:

Enter your name
[   ]

Enter your city and state (e.g. Mountain View, California)
[   ]

Enter the phone number to be removed
([   ]) [   ] - [   ]

Reason for removal
○ My phone number is incorrect
○ Privacy concerns

Command: Calculator Operations—Addition & Subtraction

Google can interpret a number of mathematical signs, perform the desired operation, and provide a quick answer. The numbers should be placed directly in the search input box. Pressing Enter will generate an answer page that repeats the original query. Google will perform these calculations with or without a space around the plus or minus sign.

Syntax

1892+78   (addition)
2008-1911   (subtraction)

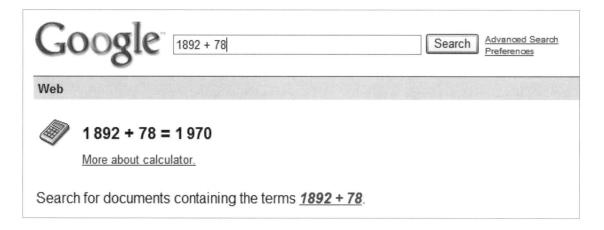

Special Relevance to Genealogists

This feature can be used to double-check your calculations of age, approximate year of birth or death, and many other calculations when you don't have a calculator on hand and don't trust your own math skills. Answer quick questions like the following:

- How old would my great grandfather be in the 1930 census if he was born in 1856?
- A headstone lists year of death as 1839, aged 83. When was this person born?
- If Grandma arrived at Ellis Island when she was 17 and she was born in 1898, what year did she arrive?

While working on this book, I wrote to Google requesting the addition of a more advanced query that would convert a death date and exact age at death into a precise date of birth. These calculators are common online, and I think it would be nice functionality as part of Google.

Calculator Operations—Multiplication & Division

Working from left to right, Google will perform simple or nested multiplication and division, as well as addition and subtraction. The order of operations is consistent with the rules of math—anything inside parenthesis is solved first, then multiplication and division working from left to right, then addition and subtraction working from left to right.

Syntax

12 * 4	(multiplication)
696 / 12	(division)
12 * 2 / 3	(nested operations)

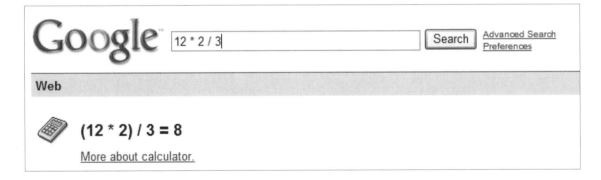

Special Relevance to Genealogists

These calculations may not be nearly as relevant for genealogists, but it's always good to know that Google can execute these basic commands in case you find yourself needing to check a more complex calculation. For instance, how much will it cost to order t-shirts for your next family reunion if they are $12.50 per shirt and seventy-eight people have already responded that they want to buy one?

Calculator Operations—Unit Conversion

In addition to the mathematical operations already discussed, Google can perform a number of freeform conversions using *in* as an operator. From the Google command line, you can convert distance, temperature, time, currency, weights, and a variety of other values.

Syntax

27 kilometers **in** miles

500 usd **in** south african money   *(see sample result below)*

27 miles **in** kilometers

789 months **in** years

550 dollars **in** euros

68 degrees fahrenheit **in** celsius

1 US dollar **in** russian currency

120 dollars **in** japanese money

500 U.S. dollars = 3 970.45978 South African rands

Special Relevance to Genealogists

Whether you're planning a trip to an ancestral village or trying to interpret an old handwritten recipe from your great-grandmother, the conversions available through Google may come in handy. Some examples are shown above, but Google can also help answer more basic questions like:

- How many pecks in a bushel?
- How many days in a fortnight?
- How many stones are in a pound?
- How many teaspoons in a cup?

1 US bushel = 4 US pecks

Command: define:

The **define:** command can be used to obtain the definition for any word or phrase. Typing this command followed immediately by a word or phrase will yield a results page containing brief definitions and a link to the corresponding source for further inspection.

Syntax

define:cooper

define:jack of all trades

Using This Command

This functionality is not available through the Advanced Search form so it should be typed directly from the command line. Also, it operates differently from the Definition link that appears as part of search results in the result statistics portion of the screen. Similar functionality can also be accessed by simply typing the question (e.g., what is a cooper), but the results are typically limited to one.

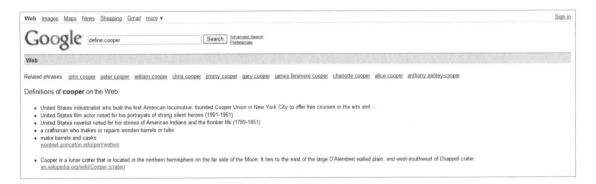

Special Relevance to Genealogists

Many surnames have one or more special meanings that can provide clues about an ancestor's occupation or place of origin. Or, as you review an old document, you may encounter a term that is no longer in common use. The **define:** command can be used to help expand your understanding of your research.

Specialized Keyword Queries for Genealogy

In addition to the special syntax and commands that can be adapted for genealogical use, there are also some simple keyword queries that are likely to produce good results. As most seasoned family historians know, even the smallest clue can lead to an important find. While many facts about the lives of our ancestors are found in official sources, there are many others that can be equally as important that originate from one-of-a-kind sources shared online by another researcher.

With more than 20 billion pages already indexed by Google, with new pages published daily, chances are good that someone somewhere may be working on a similar aspect of your family history—albeit from a different point of view. The queries below are designed to help you quickly locate pages dealing with the key genealogical events in your ancestors' lives. Note that commands can be combined with one another to narrow results as needed.

was born was born in	*Designed to find pages detailing birth information for an individual. By adding* was born *or* was born in, *you are further refining results* ▶ eugene lynch was born or "eugene lynch was born" ▶ "eugene lynch was born" waterbury **OR** bridgeport ▶ "patrick * lynch was born" ***(see sample result below)***
married	*Designed to find pages detailing marriage information for an individual* ▶ eugene lynch married or "eugene lynch married" ▶ "eugene lynch married" waterbury **OR** bridgeport ▶ "eugene * lynch married"
died died on	*Designed to find pages detailing death information for an individual* ▶ eugene lynch died or "eugene lynch died on" ▶ "eugene lynch died" waterbury **OR** bridgeport ▶ "eugene * lynch died"
was buried	*Designed to find pages detailing burial information for an individual* ▶ eugene lynch was buried or "eugene lynch was buried" ▶ "eugene lynch was buried" waterbury **OR** bridgeport ▶ "eugene * lynch was buried"

Claire's Ancestry - Lynch
1870, brother of Bernard Lynch, had migrated to USA and **Patrick Neeson Lynch was born** there. Patrick's mother was Eleanor Neison b. approx. 1804. ...
www.claires-rosleaancestry.co.uk/Lynch_family_register.htm - 29k - Cached - Similar pages

Automatic Vital Records

This is a genealogist's dream come true, but there's a catch. These commands only work for notable individuals with a great deal of content coverage on the Internet. So you know you've really made it if Google can automatically provide your vital records.

birthday	Returns the date of birth for the person specified, as well as a link to the source of the information. ▶ birthday thomas jefferson ▶ birthday tiger woods
married	Returns the date of marriage for the person specified, as well as information about children and a link to the source of the information. ▶ married tiger woods ▶ married sting
spouse	Returns the spouse and marriage date for the person specified, details for children, and a link to the source of the information. ▶ spouse gwen stefani ▶ spouse britney spears
died	Returns the date of death for the person specified, as well as a link to the source of the information. ▶ ronald reagan died ▶ william mckinley died

Tiger Woods — Date of Birth: 30 December 1975
According to http://www.brainyquote.com/quotes/authors/t/**tiger_woods**.html - More sources »

Gwen Stefani — **Spouse**: Gavin Rossdale (14 September 2002 - present) 1 child
According to http://www.imdb.com/name/nm0005461/bio

William McKinley — **Died**: September 14, 1901 (aged 58) Buffalo, New York
According to http://en.wikipedia.org/wiki/**William_McKinley**

CHAPTER 4

Language Tools

For many family historians worldwide, at least one piece of the genealogical puzzle involves passenger records. At different times and for different reasons, family members left their homes to establish roots in a different part of the world. In some cases an ancestor can be found traveling alone, in other instances entire villages re-established their communities elsewhere. Family historians in North America, South America, and Australia share ancestral ties to Europe, Asia, and elsewhere. For those living in the United States, Ellis Island is a powerful and lasting symbol of the "Golden Era" of American immigration. From 1892 to 1924, more than twenty million passengers arrived through the Port of New York and Ellis Island. Some were travelers, but many were immigrants seeking a new life in America.

Foreign Ancestry	U.S. Population (millions)	Percent of Total
German	46.4	16.5%
Irish	33.0	11.7%
English	28.2	10.0%
Italian	15.9	5.7%
French	9.7	3.4%
Polish	9.0	3.2%

Source: U.S. Federal Census, 2000 (ranked by foreign ancestry).

Today's American families represent a diverse ethnic mix and for most family historians, connecting to their ancestral village is an important chapter in their family story. This task is easier for recent immigrants, but for those with three or four generations separating them from their immigrant ancestors, the challenge can be a daunting one. The 2000 U.S. Federal Census recorded a total population of 281.4 million. German, Irish, English, and Italian were among the most common ethnicities claimed—representing just four of the 160 countries served by Google.

What are the Google Language Tools?

Currently, six individual components of Google deal with some aspect of foreign language. All share a similar goal in helping extend the overall user experience by making features and content available in a variety of languages. Genealogists will appreciate the ease with which these features can extend their foreign language skills and thus make new types of research possible.

The components discussed in this section include:

1. Search across foreign languages
2. Translate text input by users
3. Translate content found on Web pages
4. Use the Google interface in one of nearly 120 languages
5. Access a localized version of Google
6. Translate words via the Google Toolbar

Accessing Google Language Tools

From the Google homepage, you will see a small text link labeled *Language Tools* just to the right of the search input box. This link provides access to five of the six tools noted above. (The one exception is discussed in Chapter Eleven.)

1	Search Across Languages—Allows users to input a query in their native language, obtain results from pages originally published in another language, and receive text back that is automatically translated into the native language.
2	Text Translator—Enables users to type or cut/paste text into a box, select a target language, and obtain a translation.
3	Web Page Translator—Directs Google to a target Web page to translate results using one of nearly 30 built-in translators.
4	Foreign Language Interface—Allows users to set their Google preferences to display the homepage, messages, and buttons in one of more than 120 languages.
5	International Google Sites—Provides quick access to the Google site for any one of 160 countries of the world.

Google Language Tools

Search across languages

Type a search phrase in your own language to easily find pages in another language. We'll translate the results for you to read.

Search for: [   ]

My language: [English ▾]   Search pages written in: [Spanish ▾]   **(1)**

[Translate and Search]

Tip: Use <u>advanced search</u> to restrict your search by language and country without translating your search phrase.

Translate text

(2)

[Spanish ▾] » [English ▾] [Translate]

Translate a web page

http:// **(3)**

[Spanish ▾] » [English ▾] [Translate]

Use the Google Interface in Your Language

Set the Google homepage, messages, and buttons to display in your selected language via our <u>Preferences</u> page.
Google currently offers the following interface languages:

(4)

- Afrikaans
- Albanian
- Amharic
- Arabic
- Armenian
- Azerbaijani
- Basque
- Belarusian
- Bengali
- Bihari
- Bork, bork, bork!
- Bosnian
- Breton
- Bulgarian
- Cambodian
- Catalan
- Chinese (Simplified)
- Chinese (Traditional)
- Corsican
- Croatian
- Czech
- Danish
- Dutch
- Elmer Fudd

- English
- Esperanto
- Estonian
- Faroese
- Filipino
- Finnish
- French
- Frisian
- Galician
- Georgian
- German
- Greek
- Guarani
- Gujarati
- Hacker
- Hebrew
- Hindi
- Hungarian
- Icelandic
- Indonesian
- Interlingua
- Irish
- Italian
- Japanese

- Javanese
- Kannada
- Kazakh
- Klingon
- Korean
- Kurdish
- Kyrgyz
- Laothian
- Latin
- Latvian
- Lingala
- Lithuanian
- Macedonian
- Malay
- Malayalam
- Maltese
- Maori
- Marathi
- Moldavian
- Mongolian
- Nepali
- Norwegian
- Norwegian (Nynorsk)
- Occitan

- Oriya
- Pashto
- Persian
- Pig Latin
- Polish
- Portuguese (Brazil)
- Portuguese (Portugal)
- Punjabi
- Quechua
- Romanian
- Romansh
- Russian
- Scots Gaelic
- Serbian
- Serbo-Croatian
- Sesotho
- Shona
- Sindhi
- Sinhalese
- Slovak
- Slovenian
- Somali
- Spanish
- Sundanese

- Swahili
- Swedish
- Tajik
- Tamil
- Tatar
- Telugu
- Thai
- Tigrinya
- Tonga
- Turkish
- Turkmen
- Twi
- Uighur
- Ukrainian
- Urdu
- Uzbek
- Vietnamese
- Welsh
- Xhosa
- Yiddish
- Yoruba
- Zulu

If you don't see your native language here, you can help Google create it by becoming a volunteer translator. Check out our <u>Google in Your Language</u> program.

Visit Google's Site in Your Local Domain **(5)**

www.google.ad   www.google.ae   www.google.com.af   www.google.com.ag   www.google.com.ai

Part 1—Search Across Languages

This tool accepts input of a Google search query using the same syntax and commands that are described earlier in this book. Users select their native language from one of twenty-three options, and then instruct Google to search for Web pages in another language. In the example below, a user selects his or her language as English and directs Google to search for pages published in Italian.

Search across languages

Type a search phrase in your own language to easily find pages in another language. We'll translate the results for you to read.

Search for: campobasso family history

My language: English   Search pages written in: Italian

Translate and Search

Tip: Use advanced search to restrict your search by language and country without tr...ase.

Arabic
Bulgarian
Chinese (Simplified)
Chinese (Traditional)
Croatian
Czech
Danish
Dutch
Finnish
French
German
Greek
Hindi
Italian
Japanese
Korean
Norwegian
Polish
Portuguese
Romanian
Russian
Spanish
Swedish

Translated Search Results

Using the query example above, Google returns 34,300 results for pages published in Italian that match the query definition as translated into Italian—*campobasso storia familiare*. A results screen is shown at right. The left side of the results screen contains listings that have been translated into English; the right side retains the original Italian results. A simple text link allows the user to *Hide Italian results*, if desired.

Not Quite Right?

Google uses advanced technology for translating large volumes of text, but also recognizes that there is no replacement for human translation. Several text links enable users to receive a more meaningful translation of the content based on their familiarity with both the original language and the target translation.

Translated Search Results & Dictionary

At right, a close-up view of built-in language dictionaries, which enable the user to perform a quick look-up for a particular word in a dozen dictionaries.

Special Relevance for Genealogists

I have had success in searching localized pages for content, especially about the history of towns and villages. It is logical to believe that like-minded individuals and small organizations throughout Europe and elsewhere are digitizing and publishing content in their native tongues. These pages, once translated, can provide interesting clues about the lives of our ancestors and the history of our ancestral homelands.

Part 2—Text Translator

For genealogists who need help translating an old letter, postcard, or notation on the back of an old family photo, this free text translator is a great addition to the family history toolbox. Simply type or cut/paste into the text box, select a translation option, and click the Translate button.

Translate text

```
Hello. My name is Dan and my great grandmother came from
the village of Campobasso, born 1884.  I just found your
Web site and hope you can help me.  I am planning a trip
to Campobasso later this year and want to visit the
church, cemetery, and local archives.

Can you offer any suggestions?
```

Spanish to English ▾   Translate

English to Dutch
English to French
English to German
English to Greek
English to Italian
English to Japanese
English to Korean
English to Portuguese
English to Russian
English to Spanish
French to English

Translation Complete

The text below may not be perfect, but pasting the translated text into the body of an email to the address found on an Italian website may reach a willing recipient with better English skills. I have used this method successfully on many occasions. In one instance I even reserved a room at an Italian hotel following multiple email exchanges, all of which were translated back and forth using the English/Italian and Italian/English translator options.

Automatically translated text:

Ciao. Questo è il mio nome e la mia bisnonna provenivano dal villaggio di Campobasso, nato 1884. Ho appena trovato il vostro sito Web e di speranza mi puoi aiutare. Sono in programma un viaggio a Campobasso nel corso di quest'anno e vuole visitare la chiesa del cimitero, e gli archivi locali.

Potete offrire qualche suggerimento?

⊞ Suggest a better translation

Special Relevance for Genealogists

The translator tool is one of the most powerful tools for genealogists working on connections to their ancestral towns and villages in Europe and elsewhere without a familiarity of the local language. This tool is also helpful in translating foreign documents that you may have obtained online or via microfilm from an LDS Family History Center. By carefully typing in the text as it appears, you may have a close approximation for the contents of the original document. I'm still hoping for a Latin to English translator!

Genealogy Example—Italian to English Translation

In May 2006, I traveled to southern Italy as part of a genealogy case study about researching Italian heritage. While visiting the Archivio di Stato di Campobasso (Molise), the Google language tools were very handy for several reasons. Since I couldn't read or speak Italian and the staff in this rural region three hours from Rome didn't read or speak English, even the simplest requests were a challenge. Hand gestures, pedigree charts, and Google Language Tools were my primary means of communication when my distant cousin Giuseppe wasn't there to translate. Requests were made, official forms were signed and submitted, and various ledgers began to appear. It didn't take long before I had several birth, marriage, and death records that matched the preliminary research I had conducted via microfilm in the United States.

The image at right is a page photographed from the 1862 birth records for the small village of San Giovanni in Galdo, Campobasso, located in the Molise region of southern Italy. In this case, the birth record belongs to my great-great-grandmother Teresa di Cesare. By typing the text into the Google translator, a machine translation is provided. Though it isn't perfect, it provides a basic outline of what the document contains. Luckily, I visit my Italian translator monthly—a barber born in southern Italy who enjoys translating these old Italian documents for his Irish-American customer!

Clues Obtained Through Translation

By reading, transcribing, and then translating the source document shown at right, I added the following clues to my profile for my second great-grandmother:

- Born 1862
- Father was John (Giovanni) di Cesare, the son of Francis
- Father was 46 years old at the time of his daughter Teresa's birth
- Father's occupation was that of farmer and he resided in the village of San Giovanni in Galdo
- Mother was Maria Vincenza Pesce

Often times, the bigger challenge is deciphering the old handwritten text, so don't rush to judgment based on facts you gather using this method of discovery.

Atto di Nascita

Foglio 4

N. d'ordine 41

L'anno milleottocentosessantadue il dì *ventuno* di *Agosto* alle ore *tredici* avanti di noi *Gaetano Passarelli Agg.* *son Delegato Uff. del Sindaco in congedo*, ed uffiziale dello Stato Civile di *San Giovanni in Galdo* Provincia di Molise, è comparso *Giovanni di Cesare* figlio del fu *Francesco* di anni *quarantasei* di professione *contadino* domiciliato in *questo Comune*, il quale ci à presentato una *femmina* secondo che abbiam ocularmente riconosciuto, ed à dichiarato che la stessa è nata da *Maria Vincenza Perce*, sua legittima moglie di anni *trentasei* domiciliata con *esso* e da lui dichiarante di anni *come sopra* di professione *come sopra* domiciliato *come sopra* nel giorno *venti* del suddetto mese alle ore *cinquette* nella casa di propria abitazione *strada Porta del Piano*.

Lo stesso inoltre à dichiarato di dare alla *medesima* il nome di *Teresa*.

La presentazione e dichiarazione anzidetta si è fatta alla presenza di *Tommaso Mioggi* di professione *contadino* regnicolo domiciliato in *questo Comune* e di *Vincenzo Dino* di professione *contadino* regnicolo domiciliato *quivi* testimoni intervenuti al presente atto e da esso Signor *Giovanni di Cesare* prodotti.

Il presente atto è stato letto al dichiarante ed a' testimonii, ed indi si è firmato da noi, *avendo detto il dichiarante e testimoni di non saper scrivere*

Gaetano Passarelli

G. D. Passarelli Segretario Comunale

Il Parroco di *questo Comune* ci à restituito nel dì *trentiquattro* di *Agosto* anno corrente —

Il notamento che gli abbiamo rimesso nel dì *ventuno di Agosto* —

anno suddetto in piè del quale à indicato che il Sacramento del battesimo è stato amministrato a *Teresa di Cesare*

nel giorno *ventitre dell'istesso mese* del quale si è accusato la ricezione.

L'Uffiziale dello Stato Civile

G. Passarelli

Part 3—Web Page Translator

Translate a Web Page

| http://www.comuni-italiani.it/070/066/ | Italian to English ▼ | Translate |

This tool is used to translate the contents of a target Web page from one language to another, using one of more than two dozen pre-defined translation filters provided by Google. This is the same functionality discussed in Chapter Two whereby Google places a *Translate this page* link next to Web Search results that may appear but are not published in your native language.

Type or paste a Web address into the box (as shown above), select a language filter, then click the Translate button to view the page in the language selected (see example below).

Part 4—Foreign Language Interface

The Foreign Language Interface sets your Google preferences to display the Google homepage, messages, and buttons in one of more than 120 languages currently supported by Google. Both the *Preferences* and *Language Tools* text links are accessible from Google's homepage, located just to the right of the search input box.

For those very observant readers, you'll notice that Google even supports a few special languages not likely to be used by family historians, but entertaining nonetheless. See the list below, and note especially Bork, bork, bork!, Elmer Fudd, and Pig Latin.

Use the Google Interface in Your Language

Set the Google homepage, messages, and buttons to display in your selected language via our Preferences page. Google currently offers the following interface languages:

Afrikaans	English	Javanese	Oriya	Swahili
Albanian	Esperanto	Kannada	Pashto	Swedish
Amharic	Estonian	Kazakh	Persian	Tajik
Arabic	Faroese	Klingon	Pig Latin	Tamil
Armenian	Filipino	Korean	Polish	Tatar
Azerbaijani	Finnish	Kurdish	Portuguese (Brazil)	Telugu
Basque	French	Kyrgyz	Portuguese (Portugal)	Thai
Belarusian	Frisian	Laothian	Punjabi	Tigrinya
Bengali	Galician	Latin	Quechua	Tonga
Bihari	Georgian	Latvian	Romanian	Turkish
Bork, bork, bork!	German	Lingala	Romansh	Turkmen
Bosnian	Greek	Lithuanian	Russian	Twi
Breton	Guarani	Macedonian	Scots Gaelic	Uighur
Bulgarian	Gujarati	Malay	Serbian	Ukrainian
Cambodian	Hacker	Malayalam	Serbo-Croatian	Urdu
Catalan	Hebrew	Maltese	Sesotho	Uzbek
Chinese (Simplified)	Hindi	Maori	Shona	Vietnamese
Chinese (Traditional)	Hungarian	Marathi	Sindhi	Welsh
Corsican	Icelandic	Moldavian	Sinhalese	Xhosa
Croatian	Indonesian	Mongolian	Slovak	Yiddish
Czech	Interlingua	Nepali	Slovenian	Yoruba
Danish	Irish	Norwegian	Somali	Zulu
Dutch	Italian	Norwegian (Nynorsk)	Spanish	
Elmer Fudd	Japanese	Occitan	Sundanese	

Part 5—International Google Sites

Google currently offers 160 international versions of its online search and related services. While it is unlikely that any researcher will ever need them all, it's comforting to know that Google is working toward its mission of "organizing the world's information."

To access Google as it is offered within a particular country, select from the alphabetized list found on the Language Tools page.

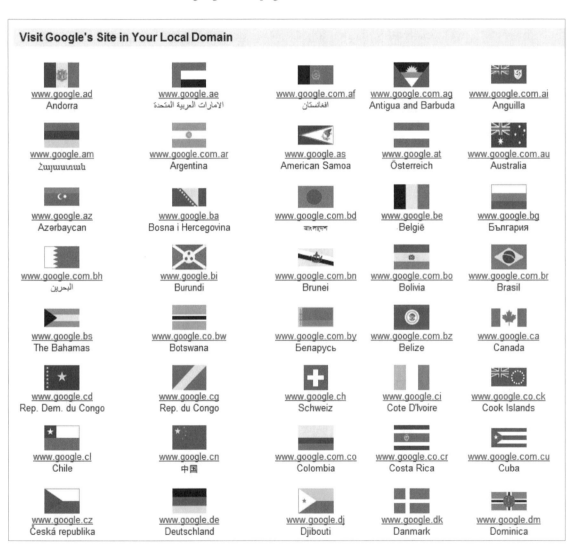

Google Worldwide

As of this writing, Google provides access to its services through 160 different websites worldwide. So whether your have ties to Romania, Zimbabwe, Liechtenstein, or elsewhere, chance are good that Google's got it covered.

Google Israel — www.google.co.il

The image above shows the Google Home page as it appears in Israel. The image below is a sample results page. Note that the screen layouts are right to left in keeping with the Hebrew style of reading and writing.

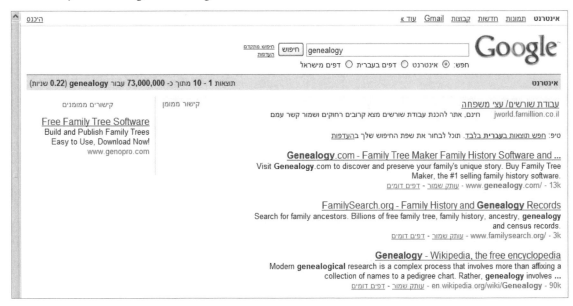

To view an international version of Google, simply visit the Language Tools page by clicking on the small text link to the right of the search box on the Google homepage. As you scroll down the page, you will see a collection of 160 flags corresponding to the countries listed in alphabetical order. Depending upon your foreign language skills and the depth of your research, you may find it helpful to view native Google search results for surnames and place names.

As you can see from the examples, the standardized layout of Google makes it possible to navigate sites in many languages, even if you can't read or easily translate the results.

 Google Italia – www.google.it

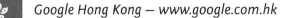

Google Hong Kong – www.google.com.hk

The Google Toolbar

The Google Toolbar, described in detail in Chapter Eleven, deserves special mention here because of one foreign-language feature that users will especially appreciate. For those readers interested in improving their understanding of foreign vocabulary, a simple on/off translator button is available through the Google Toolbar.

When the Translate button is set to the On position, the cursor becomes an on-demand translator. When you hover your mouse over almost any word on the page, you will see a small text box appear with a translation for that word. (The desired language can be set in the Toolbar options.)

In the example at right, the cursor is placed over the word *Southern* and the Italian translation appears in the text box as *del sud*. Below, the toolbar option is set to Italian, but it can also support Russian, Chinese (Simplified and Traditional), Japanese, Korean, French, German, and Spanish. I am confident this list of supported languages will grow over time.

Google Books: Your Own Genealogy Library

Imagine for a moment that your great-great-grandfather shared your passion for family history. Even better, imagine that he had compiled and published a detailed history of his ancestors dating back more than two hundred years. The original book was published in the 1850s and, while no copies are known to exist, you have several old family letters citing his book as their source. For years you've scoured local libraries, the LDS Family History Center and even online auctions hoping to find a copy for sale by some antiquarian bookseller, but no luck.

Google may eventually be able to make your genealogical dream come true through its Google Books service. First announced in the fall of 2004 as Google Print, this service is an aggressive initiative to partner with leading libraries throughout the world. Their goal is to digitize more than 15 million books within a decade and make the content available via the powerful keyword search algorithm that has driven Google's success to date.

Although a number of legal issues regarding volumes still protected by copyright were raised almost immediately after Google's announcement, I will focus on the genealogical benefits of the service. In this section, you will learn how to access many public-domain and out-of-copyright titles that can be useful in your family history research.

Family and Local Histories

Published family and local histories were quite popular in the 1800s and into the early part of the 1900s. Other so-called "mug books" were also published that contain brief biographical sketches and often photographs or etchings of prominent citizens from a town, county, or region. Family historians lucky enough to have one of these volumes in their personal collection will quickly attest to the value of this early research. Even though errors may have been included in these early family records, the depth and breadth of content can save an individual from years of digging for a particular family line. Your job instead is to use available resources to check the names, dates, places, and facts that were included in the work.

As of this writing, there are more than 62,000 titles in the Google Books collection that reference the term *genealogy*. While some are contemporary how-to books, many others are more than a century old and chronicle the lives of early American families and the cities and towns they helped to build. Exercise your keyword skills to find books for your family or town.

What is Google Books?

Google Books is just one of many search tools provided by Google and is centered on Google's effort to digitize millions of books in partnerships with libraries, universities, and publishers worldwide. The ever-growing database is an index to public domain, out-of-copyright, and copyrighted materials. Google's search algorithm helps connect users with titles that may be of interest given words or phrases specified in their query. A special feature enables public domain and some out-of-copyright material to be downloaded in the popular Adobe Acrobat PDF format.

Accessing Google Books

If Google finds relevant results matching your keyword query, the contents of Google Books may sometimes be displayed as summary results from a typical Google Web Search.

Book results for **the statue of liberty**
The Statue Of Liberty - by Barry Moreno - 128 pages
The Statue of Liberty - by Dana Meachen Rau - 24 pages
The Statue of Liberty - by Jill Braithwaite - 32 pages

If you wish to direct your search exclusively toward Google Books content, this service can be accessed from the Google Home page as follows:

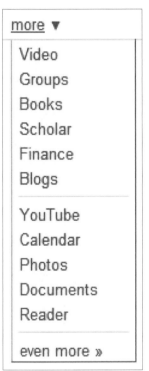

1. Point your browser to the Google homepage.
2. In the upper left corner, click the <u>more</u> ▼ text link.
3. Click the menu option for <u>Books</u>.

Current Limitations

The syntax for searching content within Google Books is nearly identical to other content areas within Google, although some advanced commands are not yet supported. If your first few attempts do not result in any matching entries, try fewer keywords for the surname or place name you are most interested in researching.

Two notable exceptions I am still disappointed to see are apparent lack of support for the tilde command to identify similar words (e.g., ~genealogy) and confirmed lack of support for the numrange syntax (e.g., specifying a date range using 1880..1900 as part of the command string query). Having used and studied Google since its Beta launch, I am confident these parameters will eventually be supported from the command line. In the meantime, we can use the Advanced Book Search.

Exploring Google Books

The main page (see below) features sixteen titles from the Google Books database—four from each of four sub-categories: Interesting, Classics, Highly cited, and Random subjects. Having read earlier chapters in this book, you will feel right at home with the familiar header navigation and search box featured prominently on each page. Special links for Advanced Book Search and Google Book Search Help are located to the right of the search input box.

Along the left side of the main page, Google includes text links for Fiction and Non-fiction, as well as a collection of randomized links for other subjects.

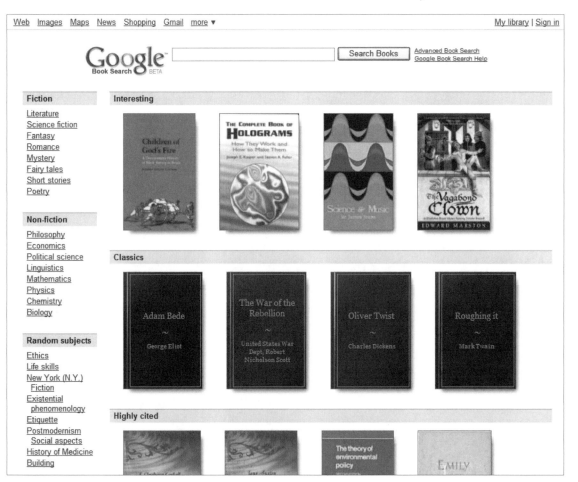

Search Results

As with most queries for family history, you will have the greatest success in using surnames and place names to locate content in the Google Books database. In the sample query below, I provide the city and state where my great-grandparents settled more than a century ago. Google Books responds in less than a second with more than 2,100 results.

Search terms: waterbury connecticut

Consistent with other Google services, the template for the results page incorporates a section along the right side for Sponsored Links. The overall screen layout is very similar to the Google Web Search. You may find it helpful to launch a similar query on your computer so you can view the screen more closely as we discuss individual elements of the page layout.

The Town and City of **Waterbury, Connecticut**
by Sarah Johnson Prichard - Waterbury (Conn.) - 1896
Vol. 1 by Sarah J. Prichard and others; v. 2 and 3 ed. by J. Anderson, with the assistance of Anna L. Ward.
Full view - About this book - Add to my library - More editions

---

Each individual result has an appearance similar to the Google Web Search results. A thumbnail image of the title page is displayed at left with the book title appearing as the first line; both are hyperlinks that take you to the online viewer (shown at right). The author's name and publishing date follow on the second line, along with a one- or two-line synopsis of the book. Books will be available in Full View (as in this case), Limited Preview, Snippet View, or No Preview Available. In general, I have found that many older titles appealing to my interest in genealogy and local history are available as Full View and in PDF format for download.

The view available to you through Google Books will depend upon the age of the book in question and whether or not it is part of the public domain or still protected under one or more copyright laws. In some ways, family historians are the ones who benefit most from this service because the older the book, the more interested we are in the content.

As noted, place name queries can be especially helpful in your research—even if the title didn't include information specific to your ancestors. By finding and reading through a local history for the town or city where your ancestors lived, you will learn about groups they may have joined, the places they may have frequented, and the industry that may have attracted them to the area to begin with. Many ethnic groups also settled in large numbers in various towns, so while your ancestor may not be mentioned in a local history, there may be a great deal of information of the settlement of your ethnic group in that region.

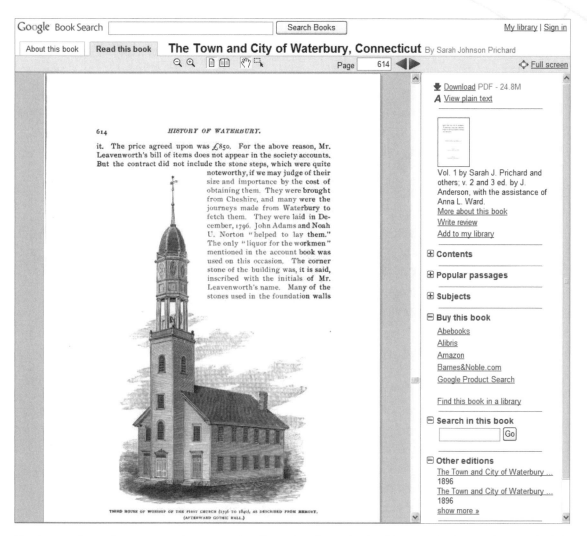

The image above shows a sample screen shot from Google Books, in this case the image viewer which is accessed by clicking on the 'Read this book' tab. Controls allow you to quickly magnify the image, click forward or backward, and even highlight a portion of the visible page for copying to another application. Note in the lower right corner of the screen how you can search for keywords within the book that is currently being displayed—an extremely useful too for family historians.

Anatomy of the 'About This Book' view

The numbered details below correspond to the About This Book image at right.

1	Title Page Thumbnail—A thumbnail view of the title page (if available) is shown. Beneath this are buttons to either switch to the Read This Book view or to download a PDF to your hard drive.
2	Publication Data—To the right of the thumbnail image, a brief summary of the book including author, title, date and place published, when the title was digitized and where the original copy was obtained for digitization, and links allowing you to add the title to your personal library or to write a review.
3	Buy this Book / Borrow this book—In the upper right corner of your screen, Google displays options for buying this title as well as a link to help you locate a copy of this book to borrow from a library or archive.
4	Contents—An indexed table of contents by subject and with corresponding page numbers. Click on an individual link to view that section directly.
5	Selected Pages—Thumbnail views of selected pages that often includes the title page, contents pages, as well as any pages with photos, drawings, or other images. The corresponding page number appears beneath each image. A More link reveals additional thumbnails of possible interest.
6	Search this book—A small search input box allows you to search for a specific word or phrase within the book. This is very helpful for large volumes that may only include your surname or place name in one small section.
7	Popular Passages—During the scanning and indexing process, Google compares the text to other books already indexed and can identify certain passages that appear in other publications. It flags each passage and adds a link so you can view other titles with this passage.
8	Related Books or Other Editions—Depending upon the title being viewed, you may see information on other editions or related books of possible interest.
9	Places Mentioned—A map view of places mentioned in this book. You can click on any place marker to view details for that place as well as the page number and reference to the location within the text of the book.

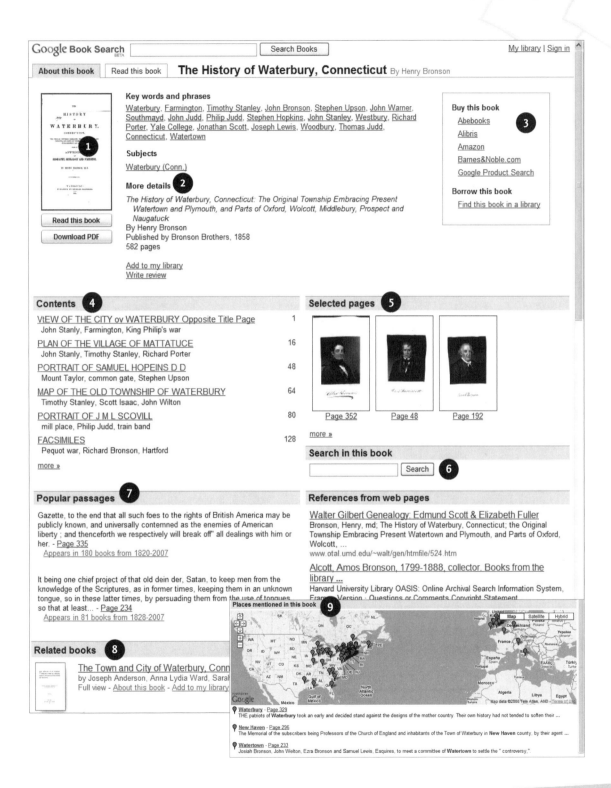

Add to my library

As an optional feature of Google Books, users can save items they have previously found in a *My Library* account, which is part of an overall Google Account that can be established free of charge. Here, users can write reviews that will then be visible to other members of the Google Books community. This can be useful to keep track of which titles you have already found during prior research sessions.

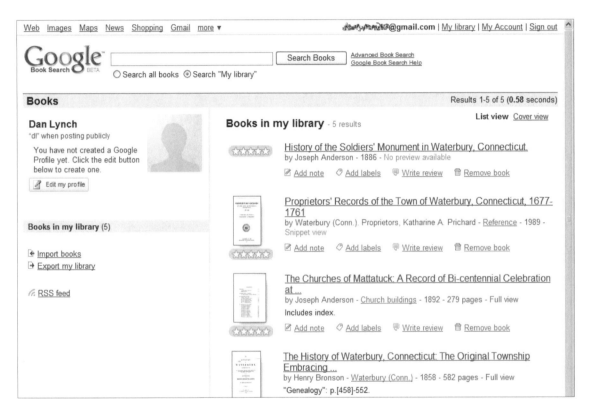

Download

The Google Books collection contains many books available for free download and viewing in the Adobe Acrobat PDF file format. The keyword search capabilities can help you discover even the smallest reference to your ancestors or their town, often in a source you may have never thought to look.

While in the *Read this book* view, you will see a small thumbnail image in the upper righthand corner of your screen. Click on the Download text link located above the image to initiate the download process. I strongly recommend creating a separate folder on your computer—either by surname, place name, or a general folder—for genealogy downloads from Google Books. This will help you find these files more quickly at any point in the future.

Download PDF - 24.8M

A **View plain text**

Vol. 1 by Sarah J. Prichard and others; v. 2 and 3 ed. by J. Anderson, with the assistance of Anna L. Ward.

More about this book

Write review

Add to my library

Search PDF Files

Once you have the PDF files on your computer's local hard drive, you can either browse the book with the free Adobe *Acrobat Reader* software or you can search the contents of these and other files using the Google Desktop application, which will be discussed in greater detail in Chapter Thirteen.

Free Adobe Acrobat Reader Software

If you have never used digitized documents in the PDF format, you can point your browser to Adobe at <www.adobe.com/products/acrobat/readstep2.html> or submit a Google query for ***free adobe acrobat reader***. The software to

File Download

Do you want to open or save this file?

Name: The_Town_and_City_of_Waterbury__Connecti.pdf

Type: Adobe Acrobat Document, 25.1MB

From: books.google.com

[Open] [Save] [Cancel]

While files from the Internet can be useful, some files can potentially harm your computer. If you do not trust the source, do not open or save this file. What's the risk?

read these book files is distributed freely. You can also download this software as part of the Google Pack discussed in Chapter Thirteen. You can access Google Pack software at <http://pack.google.com>.

Advanced Book Search

As noted earlier in this chapter, the current command line search for Google Books has some limitations, but they can be overcome by using the Advanced Book Search form shown below.

The Advanced Book Search looks and performs similarly to the capabilities described in Chapter Three for Advanced Web Search. You can conduct various keyword queries but also search based on author, title, publisher, subject, publication date, and ISBN number.

Special Note for Family History Research

I strongly recommend using the Advanced Book Search to search for books in your personal collection that may also be in Google's online collection. If you do find digitized versions that can be downloaded to your personal computer in PDF format, it is well worth your time. You will be surprised how quickly you can conduct a keyword query of a large volume to obtain the page number for one or more entries you want to read offline.

Special Relevance for Genealogists

It may not be immediately obvious, but once you start searching Google Books, you'll quickly appreciate the ability to conduct keyword queries on millions of books just as easily as you check your email inbox. And, you can often find important entries in unexpected places by using Google Books. I recently found a detailed entry in an 1882 Municipal Register about a cemetery I had been researching for more than a decade. Despite having access to a complete collection of these books in hardcopy format, I had never considered turning to them as a source for my cemetery research. The keyword query helped find this hidden entry.

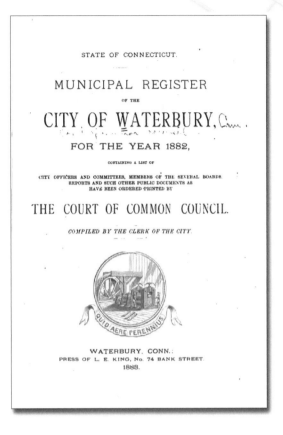

It is extraordinarily convenient to now have electronic copies of several decades worth of municipal registers, early city directories, gazetteers, and town histories sitting on the hard drive of my computer for quick reference anytime, anywhere. My current collection of titles is primarily U.S.-based, but Google's ongoing efforts to provide a worldwide offering should result in a more balanced collection over time. Copyright laws also differ from country to country, so it may be some time before users worldwide enjoy the same benefits as users in the United States currently have. In any case, as the number of titles in Google's collection grows, so too will the addiction of most family historians seeking free access to digitized, hard-to-find content from the comfort of home.

Google News Archive

News is a part of our everyday life, as it was for our ancestors. Although we certainly have more choices for how we receive our news compared to our ancestors, it's likely that we rely upon the content of these reports in much the same way they did in their day. We read, listen to, or watch weather forecasts to determine what to wear and when to travel. Financial reports help us decide whether to save or spend, as well as where and when to invest. Sports and entertainment news help us track our favorite team or plan an upcoming night on the town. And let's not forget more individual types of information such as birth notices, engagement and marriage notices, obituaries, probate, real estate transactions, and many others.

When looking at news from the standpoint of genealogy research, an interesting question comes to mind: When does a news item cross over from being contemporary news and become part of our collective history? My guess is that you can ask ten people this question and get ten different answers. I'm not sure I have a good answer for this question myself; it all depends upon the content we're looking for or looking at. After all, our family history is today, yesterday, last week, and last month—not just one hundred years ago. I recently received an obituary in the mail for a distant relative who had died less than a week earlier. Certainly this is still contemporary family news, but I found myself inspecting the details of the news clipping just as closely as if the notice had appeared in the newspaper a century ago.

Google appears to have set the contemporary versus historic threshold at thirty days, so we'll spend a little time looking at the differences between the Google News Search and the Google News Archive Search. You can decide for yourself the difference between new news and old news for your family history. Whatever you decide, I strongly encourage you to develop a close familiarity with the Google News Archive Search as part of your ongoing family research. Use the News text link, which appears in the upper left corner of the Google Home page and also above the Google logo on nearly all search results pages. From here, you can quickly access the historical archives through the New Archive Search link.

>Top Stories
World
U.S.
Business
Elections
Sci/Tech
Entertainment
Sports
Health
Most Popular

Make
Google News
Your Homepage

✉ News Alerts

Text Version

Standard Version

Image Version

RSS | Atom
About Feeds

Mobile News

What Is Google News?

Google describes its news service as a computer-generated news site that aggregates headlines from more than 4,500 English-language news sources worldwide. The company doesn't employ journalists or photographers to bring you the news, rather it leverages technology to find content published online by others and then presents that content in the most meaningful way based on your preferences and search requests.

In the same way that Google's sophisticated algorithm assigns relevancy to Web search results, it also evaluates published news content to determine what is timely and relevant. In all cases, when you click on a summary news result, you are taken to the original source to view the full context of that article. As of this writing, Google has more than 53 regional editions of the Google News service with a goal of expanding to full worldwide coverage over time.

Presentation of News Content

You can think of the main landing page for Google News as Google's equivalent of a newspaper's front page. There are nine primary categories to filter your view with a single click (as shown at left). If you're looking for the latest in sports news, simply click the Sports link and Google will present a range of sports content. In each case it lists the source for that content as well as how long it's been since the posting occurred. Age is typically stated in minutes (e.g., 35 minutes ago or seven hours ago) or by date. Content appearing within Google News is generally very timely, but no more than 30 days old. After 30 days, the content becomes accessible via the Google News Archive Search.

There are three main variations for viewing Google News content: Standard, Text and Image. The default Standard Version mixes text with small thumbnail images where appropriate. Use the small text links in the left navigation to quickly access the Text Version, which removes photos and looks very similar to standard Web Search results. Or choose Image Version to view stories represented by small photos with even smaller captions. It's always good to have a choice, but Google's Standard Version seems to be best suited for most users.

Google News Homepage

The image below shows the Google News homepage, as well as a close-up view of the menu to select from one of more than 53 different regional editions. Since our emphasis is focused on genealogy and historical research, I won't spend more time on the general news service. As you search for news items, keep in mind that many of the commands and operators discussed in earlier chapters are just as effective in filtering news

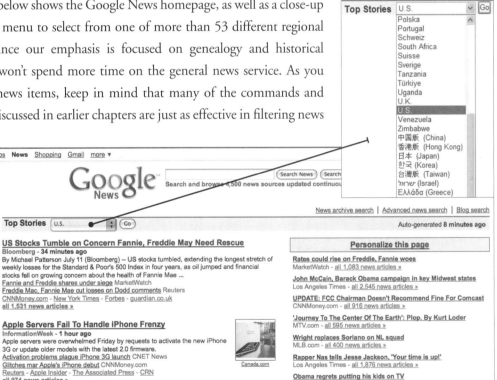

results as they are for general Web results. Categories appear in the upper left, lead news items appear in the main center column using a format similar to that described in Chapter Two for Web Search results, and secondary news items appear in a righthand column or further down the page.

What Is Google News Archive Search?

The Google News Archive Search is an extension of the Google News service, but one which is focused on historical archives, rather than contemporary news. In my opinion, this service is another example of how Google appears to be serving the specific needs of genealogists worldwide. Google has worked with a range of content partners to provide content dating back nearly 200 years. Although the current base of historical content is

dominated by U.S. results, Google is working with other content providers throughout the world to ensure a global perspective on history over time. Accessed from the Google News page, the News Archive Search has both a basic and advanced interface. The basic input box (shown above) will accept many of the same commands and operators discussed earlier in this book.

Special Relevance for Genealogists

The content indexed within the Google News Archive represents a broad collection of free and fee-based content from historical newspapers and magazines, news and legal archives, as well as other sources. Our ancestors were often involved in many activities we may never think to search for—business transactions, probate and other legal proceedings, immigration and other international travel. Many of these items were newsworthy events when they occurred and a carefully constructed search of these archives may yield an unexpected find. As more historical content is digitized, it is reasonable to assume that Google will expand its partnerships with content providers and bring even more interesting data to our search result pages. A special time line feature discussed later in this chapter is an outstanding little-known feature offered by Google.

Advanced News Archive Search

Assuming you have already read chapters one through three, you should already feel confident in your ability to search the Google News Archive. As you learned in Chapter One, the better you define your query, the more likely your results will have true relevance to your research. Most commands and operators can be typed directly into the search input box, but there are a few notable exceptions that will require the Advanced News Archive Search form (shown at the bottom of page 124).

In October 2007, I began researching an old cemetery located just fifteen minutes from my home. My first few queries were using Google Web Search, but I quickly turned to the news archive to better filter unwanted results from other sources. The table below demonstrates the importance of using proper keywords and commands to filter results to a manageable list. Surprisingly, the **numrange:** command (e.g. 1880–1900) is not currently supported, but the Advanced Search form does provide a date range selection, which quickly limited my results to a single important find.

	Google Web Search Query	Results
1	cemetery	1,700,000
2	cemetery connecticut	59,800
3	cemetery bridgeport	34,900
4	saint augustine cemetery	35,300
5	"saint augustine cemetery" OR "st. augustine cemetery" bridgeport	83

Google News Archive Results Page Explained

As you can see from the image at right, this specialized content area within Google uses an already familiar interface and navigation to present results to your query. Building upon your foundation of Google Web Search, you can become proficient—if not expert—in using the Google News Archive Search in a matter of minutes. Numbered descriptions below correspond to the image at right. You may find it helpful to have your screen in full view as you read this chart.

1	The Google logo, primary text links, and the search input box are carried over from the primary News Archive Search page and are always visible in the upper left corner of your screen. Your search query is also carried forward enabling you to refine your original query or submit a new one as desired.
2	Two small text links to the right of the Search Archives button can be used to access an *Advanced archive search* or *Archive search help*.
3	A summary line showing the number of results found, the time it took Google to perform the search, and the original query definition. One of the most useful aspects of this service is hidden behind a simple *Timeline* text link. Clicking this link toggles from the *News Articles* view to a historical *Timeline* view. You can quickly navigate to a particular time frame using the graphic time line displayed.
4	A series of text links grouped into Recent (*Last hour, Last day, Past week, Past month*) and Archives, with various date ranges automatically appearing based on the natural results found. Click one to narrow your results to the time line indicated.
5	The primary element of Google's News Archive Search results is the content summary for each natural result found. As with Google Web Search, the default settings will display ten results per page. Each result has a layout similar to a Web Search result, but with slight variations. As always, understanding the layout of these results is critical to your success.
6	Depending upon the number of results for your query, you will see an expandable Google logo at the bottom of each page with links for Next and Previous, as well as individual page numbers representing another set of relevant results.
7	For your convenience, your original query is repeated in a search box at the bottom of the page so you can refine your query if desired.

Google News Archive Results Page

Google News   ① [augustine cemetery" OR "saint augustine c] [Search Archives]   Advanced archive search ②
Archive search help

News Archives   News Articles - Timeline   Results **1 - 10** of about 83 for **"st. augustine cemetery" OR "saint augustine cemetery" +bridgeport**. (0.11 seconds) ③

Browse Top Stories

Recent

Last hour
Last day
Past week
Past month

Archives ④

All dates
2005-07
2002-03
1989-90
1988
1891
Other dates

✉ News Alerts

MANY MONUMENTS DAMAGED.; DISGRACEFUL WORK IN ST. AUGUSTINE ...
New York Times - May 3, 1891
Great excitement has been occasioned here by the discovery of one of the most disgraceful pieces of vandalism ever known here. In the -centre of the city is ...
Related web pages

SOUTH JERSEY DEATHS
$2.95 - Philadelphia Inquirer - NewsBank - Sep 9, 1990
... Salvatore of King of Prussia, Pa., and William of **Bridgeport**, and three ... Jackson Road, Medford; burial, St. Augustine Cemetery, **Bridgeport**, Pa. ...
Related web pages

Edward J. Yates, 87, 'Bandstand' director ⑤
$2.95 - Philadelphia Inquirer - NewsBank - Jun 6, 2000
A Funeral Mass will be said at 11 am Burial will be in St. Augustine Cemetery, **Bridgeport**. Donations may be made to the Chester County National Alliance for ...
All 4 related - Related web pages

SOUTH JERSEY DEATHS
$2.95 - Philadelphia Inquirer - NewsBank - Feb 13, 1988
... Bernard of Somerdale and Francis of Washington Township; 12 grandchildren; six great-grandchildren, and a brother, Joseph Kulick of **Bridgeport**, Pa. ...
Related web pages

Philadelphia Inquirer, The (PA) and Philadelphia Daily News (PA)
$2.95 - Philadelphia Inquirer - NewsBank - Jul 19, 2002
OTTAVIANO On July 16, 2002, formerly of **Bridgeport**, PA., NICHOLAS, age 80 years; beloved husband ... Interment in St. Augustine Cemetery., **Bridgeport**, PA. ...
Related web pages

Philadelphia Inquirer, The (PA)
$2.95 - Philadelphia Inquirer - NewsBank - Aug 21, 1994
... Mass of Christian Burial, 10 am Tuesday, St. Mary's Church, Elm and Oak Streets, Conshohocken; burial, St. Augustine's Cemetery, **Bridgeport**. ...
All 2 related - Related web pages

PETER L. BRUNI, 50, COACH AT SHANAHAN
$2.95 - Philadelphia Inquirer - NewsBank - Jul 5, 1987
A funeral was held Monday at the Szpindor Funeral Home, Trooper, Montgomery County. Burial was in St. Augustine's Cemetery, **Bridgeport**.
Related web pages

Philip H. Crist
$2.95 - Philadelphia Inquirer - NewsBank - Feb 29, 2000
... followed by a Funeral Mass at 11 am at SS. Simon & Jude Church, Routes 3 and 352, Westtown. A private burial will be at St. Augustine Cemetery, **Bridgeport**.
Related web pages

John E. Maiden
$2.95 - Philadelphia Inquirer - NewsBank - Jan 6, 2007
Int. St. Augustine Cemetery, **Bridgeport**, PA. Memorial contributions may be made in John's memory to Make-A-Wish Foundation, One Valley Square, 512 Township ...
Related web pages

Philadelphia Inquirer, The (PA) and Philadelphia Daily News (PA)
$2.95 - Philadelphia Inquirer - NewsBank - May 26, 2002
Interment St. Augustine Cemetery, **Bridgeport**, PA. In lieu of flowers, donations in Mr. Figueroa's memory to The Gift of Life Donor Program, 2000 Hamilton ...
All 2 related - Related web pages

Goooooooogle ▶ ⑥
Result Page: 1 2 3 4 5 6 7 8 9   **Next**

⑦ ["st. augustine cemetery" OR "saint a] [Search Archives]

News Archive Results Page—Part 1

The header for News Archive Search results has a common look to other content areas within Google. Text links appearing above the Google logo provide quick access to major content types so you can access them with one click at any time during your research. The search input box shows a portion of your query, about 40 to 50 characters, but will scroll to reveal your full query definition up to 32 words or 2,048 characters, if needed. After your query has been refined, pressing the Search Archives button will instruct Google to perform your query but limits the search to within the News Archive content type.

News Archive Results Page—Part 2

To the right of the Search Archives button are two small text links, *Advanced archive search* and *Archive search help*. The Advanced archive search link brings you to a form-driven interface that enables you to build an advanced query for content indexed within the News Archive.

Google News — Advanced News Archive Search		Advanced archive search tips | About News archive search
Find results	with **all** of the words	10 results ▾ Search Archives
	with the **exact phrase**	10 results / 20 results / 50 results
	with **at least one** of the words	
	without the words	
Date	Return results published between	___ and ___ e.g., 1998 or 04/30/2004
Language	Return results written in	any language ▾
Source	Return results that come from	___ e.g., New York Times or NewsBank
Price	Return articles with the following price	all prices ▾
View	⦿ Search articles ○ Show full timeline ○ Show news timeline	

News Archive Results Page—Part 3

The results line, which runs horizontally across the page, reports on the number of results found, lists how quickly the search was performed, and displays the query being responded

News Archives   News Articles - Timeline   Results **1 - 10** of about **83** for **"st. augustine cemetery" +bridgeport**. (0.11 seconds)

to (or a portion thereof if the entire query cannot fit). One important difference in this results line is the appearance of a small *Timeline* text link. The default view is called the News Articles view, but you will appreciate the ability to view a time line graphic that can be used to further refine your query with a single click of the mouse. The three images below show how the *Timeline* graphic can be used to narrow search results to a more precise point in time, corresponding to your research needs.

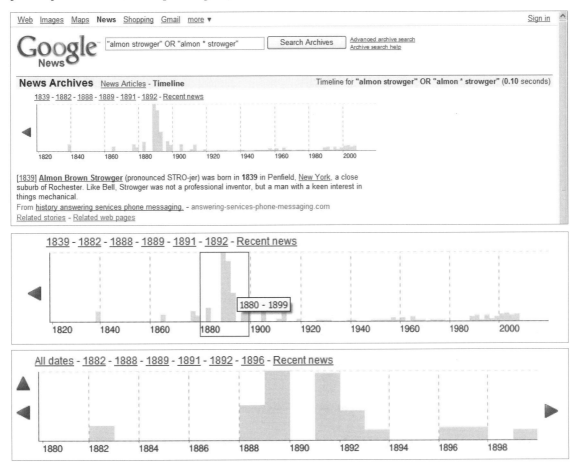

News Archive Results Page—Part 4

When viewing results in the default News Articles view (as opposed to *Timeline* view), the lefthand column of your screen will display a series of simple text links divided into two separate groups, Recent and Archives. As shown at left, the Recent results can be filtered based on those occurring in the last hour, last day, past week, and past month.

Recent

Last hour
Last day
Past week
Past month

Archives

All dates
2005-07
2002-03
1989-90
1988
1891
Other dates

✉ News Alerts

The Archives sub-group will have a series of dynamically generated text links depending upon the dates associated with the results for your particular query. By selecting the *Other dates* text link, you will access a feature whereby you can put a starting year and ending year to limit your results to within these parameters. This is similar to the **numrange:** command discussed in Chapter Three, but that command is not currently supported from the command line within this content type. (e.g., Instead of submitting a query including 1880..1900 as part of your query definition, you must use the advanced search form or refine your selection as a two-step process using the *Other dates* link.)

Free Content vs. Fee-based Results

As you search the News Archive, you will notice one distinct difference compared to other content areas within Google. Because some content within the historical archive is provided through third-party partnerships, some results may require a fee to view the full result. Most results should allow you to view a small summary for free and you are never charged for any item simply by clicking from Google's site to a third-party site. Sites such as the *New York Times* and Newspaper Archive may require payment to view the full text of a result found through the Google News Archive Search.

As you view results, you may notice that some results display a price as part of the results summary. You can still follow this link to the third-party site to view whatever portion of the result may be available free. If you determine it has value to your research, you may choose to respond to the trial offering.

News Archive Results Page—Part 5

The primary element of Google's News Archive Search results is the content summary for each natural result found. As of this writing there are no sponsored links appearing on the results page, but I can easily envision this changing in the future. If sponsored links do appear within the News Archive results, it is reasonable to assume that they would be introduced in a manner similar to the current Google Web Search results (see Chapter Two for details).

Assuming you have not modified your preferences, News Archive results will be displayed using the default settings of ten listings per page. Each individual result has a layout very similar to a Web Search result, but with slight variations. As always, understanding the format for these results is critical to your success in using this tool for research.

> ## MANY MONUMENTS DAMAGED.; DISGRACEFUL WORK IN ST. AUGUSTINE ...
> New York Times - May 3, 1891
> Great excitement has been occasioned here by the discovery of one of the most disgraceful pieces of vandalism ever known here. In the -centre of the city is ...
> Related web pages

In the examples above and below, you can see News Archive results following a familiar format—the title of an article followed by the source and date, a brief description, and a link to related pages. The image below is from the *Timeline* view and shows a slightly different format with the date as the lead item.

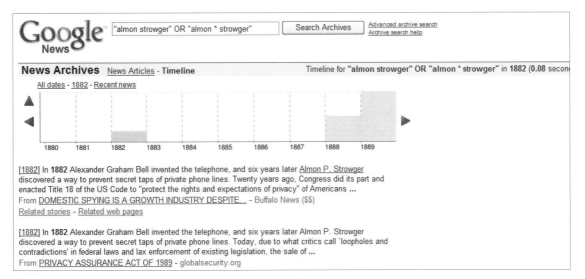

News Archive Results Page—Part 6

At the footer of each New Archive results page you will find a familiar navigation element that allows you to jump to a specific page of results or to click on links for *Next* and *Previous*. As of this writing, the results for this content type can only be displayed 50 listings per page (as opposed to a maximum of 100 per page for Web Search results). While your query may generate millions of results, Google will only display listings for the first thousand. This should not impact your research because if you've structured your query correctly, your most relevant results will appear within the first few pages of results.

News Archive Results Page—Part 7

The last element on your News Archive Search results page is the search input box with a button enabling you to refine and resubmit your query. This is placed here for your convenience and operates the same as the input box appearing at the top of your page.

An Example of News Archive in Action

Earlier in this chapter, I shared the details for a recent query submitted through the Google News Archive. A single result from a carefully structured query for a nearby cemetery led to a research breakthrough. Although this one result was a brief 1891 *New York Times* entry, the precise date was all I needed to search the microfilm at the local archives. This brief mention in the *New York Times* was major front-page news in several local papers published in Connecticut's largest city—just an hour by train to New York City.

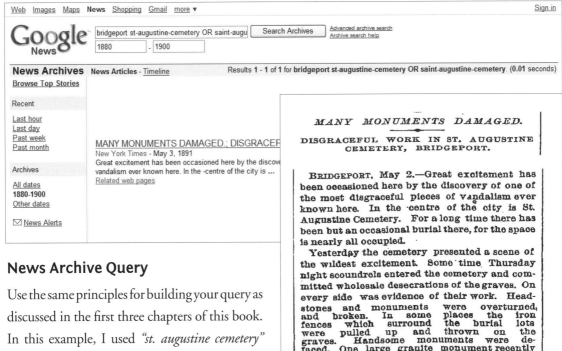

News Archive Query

Use the same principles for building your query as discussed in the first three chapters of this book. In this example, I used *"st. augustine cemetery"* OR *"saint augustine cemetery"* bridgeport. Since the word *Saint* is often abbreviated, my query helped capture both appearances. The date range 1880 to 1900 further filtered results to capture only those articles appearing within this twenty year time frame.

Using News Archive to Explore a Family Story

Throughout the world, there are just two types of genealogists—those who have hit a stone wall with their research and those who will. Having hit a stone wall with my Italian lineage (or should I say *muro di pietra*?), I recently thought I'd turn my attention to my Irish family lines. One aspect of my family history I've never researched is a long-standing family belief that we are closely related to Michael McGivney, founder of the Knights of Columbus. Unfortunately, in my entire family tree there are exactly zero entries with the surname McGivney. Time to visit the Google News Archive.

A simple search for ***michael mcgivney*** yielded nearly 1,400 results so I decided to refine my query slightly—***"michael mcgivney" waterbury***. I knew he was born in Waterbury, Connecticut, but didn't know much else. My results were now reduced to just eleven matching pages and the second listing was one I would have never considered researching

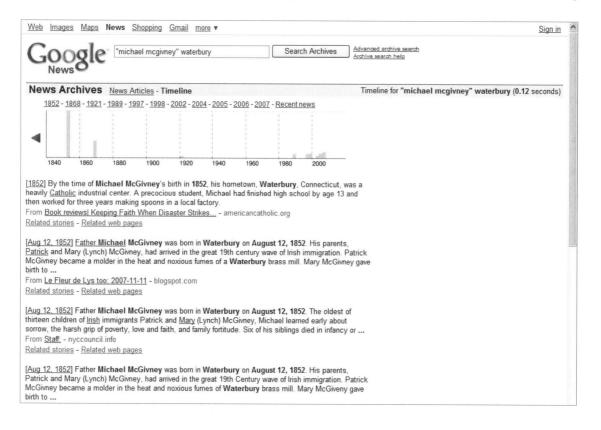

for a Connecticut-born ancestor. The *Dallas Morning News* (Jan 10, 1998) printed an article with the following snippet:

> *"Michael McGivney was born in Waterbury in 1852. He was the eldest of 13 children, six of whom died in infancy or childhood. His father, Patrick, worked…"*

Switching to the *Timeline* view, I quickly saw a possible connection. Without even leaving the News Archive results page, I learned that Michael McGivney was born on 12 August 1852 in Waterbury (New Haven County) Connecticut. The oldest of thirteen children, his parents were listed as Patrick McGivney and Mary Lynch, Irish immigrants. Other listings on this page report that Michael McGivney died of tuberculosis in 1890 at thirty-eight years of age.

So far, all of this information was obtained by submitting an initial search, refining it slightly, and then taking my hands away from the keyboard to carefully read the ten listings presented on the search results page. Some had prices next to them, others did not. I followed a link to the fourth entry, an article from <www.catholicweb.com>. The article included a portrait as well as a section on McGivney's roots in Waterbury. As interesting as this all was, none of it could be assumed to be correct. If I'm going to prove a family connection to a man who could very well become an American-born saint, I've got to pull a few vital records of my own for closer inspection. In less than ten minutes, however, I've collected some strong clues that can help me prove or disprove a family story that has persisted for several generations.

Statue of Father Michael McGivney, located in downtown Waterbury, Connecticut.

CHAPTER 7

Google Blog Search

Before I begin to describe how you can use the Google Blog Search in family history research, let me remove the mystery of blogs for those readers who may not spend as much time online as I do. A blog is simply an easy to maintain website, with regular entries that are usually displayed in reverse chronological order. Common types of blogs include electronic journals, diaries, or newsletters. The word itself, like many other computer terms, is an abbreviation of two other words—Web Log. Writing and computer technology have an interesting intertwined history. Shortly after the advent of the personal computer in the 1980s, word-processing software empowered many writers with the ability to produce professional-looking documents with relative ease. Shortly thereafter, more feature-rich page layout programs such as Aldus *PageMaker* raised the bar even higher for those wishing to publish more advanced books, catalogs, and magazines. Family historians were finally able to convert years worth of research into published works, but this wasn't the last advancement for would-be genealogical authors.

The widespread commercial adoption of the Internet, which started in the 1990s, provided a platform for many family historians to share different aspects of their research or to ask for help from others. Some researchers posted queries on message boards while others published lengthy volumes detailing every aspect of their family tree. In both cases, this content has become part of the growing online collection that Google helps access through its search tools.

Special software applications known as blogging software (e.g., *Blogger* or *WordPress*) enable novice computer users to share their thoughts on an unimaginable range of topics.

Interested in underwater basket weaving? Well, to my surprise, it turns out that there really is such a thing and there are people passionate about their craft who also maintain blogs on the subject. Who knew?

What Is a Google Blog Search?

A Google Blog Search is a query that limits results to only those online entries created as part of a blog. As you might expect, the volume of search results for this content type will be far less than a general Google Web Search, but it is this very filtering mechanism that may help you find a posting with greater relevance for your surname or place name research.

Most commands and syntaxes discussed in the first three chapters of this book are supported by Blog Search, but there are a few notable exceptions. An Advanced Blog Search form helps address these shortcomings, but I remain confident that Google will add support for additional commands over time.

Getting Started

To access the Google Blog Search from the homepage, you can either conduct a query for **blog search,** point your browser to <http://blogsearch .google.com>, or follow the steps below.

1. Point your browser to the Google home page <www.google.com>.
2. In the upper left corner, click the *more* ▼ text link.
3. Click the menu option for Blogs.

The Google Blog Search homepage (shown on the facing page) will look very similar to the main Google homepage. Using the techniques described earlier in this book, you can conduct your first query to see if any blog postings deal with topics of similar interest. Keep in mind that surnames, place names, and data types will help you obtain the most relevant results.

more ▼

Video
Groups
Books
Scholar
Finance
Blogs

YouTube
Calendar
Photos
Documents
Reader

even more »

Can I Start My Own Blog?

Although the focus for this book is on finding family history information already published online, you might also wish to share your findings through a blog of your own. While I won't discuss this in detail, you can access free blogging software at <www.blogger.com>, a company Google acquired in 2002. Another popular free service for blogging can be found at <www.wordpress.com>. Both are strong offerings and have a relatively painless registration and initial setup process. And while my favorite blogs are almost always genealogy related, these products work equally well for those with other areas of expertise and a willingness to share.

Advanced Blog Search

If your initial queries using the basic Blog Search command line are resulting in too many listings, you may wish to use the Advanced Blog Search form. You can access this form by using the text link to the right of the search input box on the Blog Search homepage. Although the appearance is slightly different, the functionality of this form is nearly identical to that described in Chapter Three. Given recent enhancements to the advanced search for Google Web Search, I expect this form will also undergo a revision in the near future.

any language ▼
any language ▲
Arabic
Armenian
Belarusian
Bulgarian
Catalan
Chinese (Simplified)
Chinese (Traditional)
Croatian
Czech
Danish
Dutch
English
Esperanto
Estonian
Filipino
Finnish
French
German
Greek
Hebrew
Hungarian
Icelandic
Indonesian
Italian
Japanese
Korean
Latvian
Lithuanian
Norwegian
Persian
Polish
Portuguese
Romanian
Russian
Serbian
Slovak
Slovenian
Spanish
Swedish
Thai
Turkish
Ukrainian
Vietnamese ▼

Input fields guide you through the formulation of an advanced blog query using any combination of AND, OR, " ", -, inblogtitle:, inposttitle:, inurl:, inpostauthor:, and options for selecting posting dates, languages, and SafeSearch filtering.

As with other aspects of Google, the company appears to be working hard to expand their language support. In the last few months while working on this book, I have watched the list of supported languages grow. The graphic at left shows the range of options you have as a researcher who may be searching for a blog posting in a foreign language. If you have a particularly stubborn family line you are researching, this may be especially helpful in connecting you to distant cousins working on the same family line from another country.

Feeding Blogs

You can leverage the power of blogs even if you don't have the time or desire to start a blog of your own. First, think about the family lines that you are most interested in researching. What ethnicity are they? What places do they connect with? Are there other special connections that exist relating to your primary family lines? Once you have a feel for the answers to these questions, you should begin a series of blog searches. Try to locate blogs that cover topics common to your ethnic, geographic or other special interests. Once you have located one or more blogs, bookmark them and visit often— looking for an opportunity to post a reply, letting others know of your interest in the topic. By including relevant details in your blog posting, you will leave a keyword trail that someone else may pick up on in the future when they conduct their search.

Keywords as Breadcrumbs

If you post messages on blogs or elsewhere, think about what you have learned in this book and how you can use this knowledge in reverse. Knowing that others can execute the same types of online queries, be sure to include variant spellings, place names, and other unique keywords that will lead a path to your virtual door. Message boards and blog postings have a long shelf life and you may be surprised just how effective this technique can be in helping someone else find you so you can collaborate on your research.

Targeted Blog Search

Keep in mind that there is one additional way to perform a blog search, but in this case you will be limiting your results to one or more named sites. If you have a favorite blog dealing with a particular subject, surname, or place name and want to know if the author has discussed a particular word or phrase, you can submit a query using the **site:** command from the Google homepage. In the example below, I search Dick Eastman's popular genealogy blog for any mention of New Haven County and am rewarded with two interesting posts.

site:eogn.com "new haven county"

Primary Elements of Google Blog Search Results Page

The numbers used in the summary below correspond to the graphic at right.

1	The Google Blog Search logo, primary text links, and the search input box are carried over from the homepage and are always visible in the upper left corner of your screen. Your query definition is also carried forward enabling you to refine as needed. Buttons enable you to Search Blogs or Search the Web.
2	The two small text links to the right of the search buttons provide access to the Advanced Blog Search and overall user preferences (called Global Preferences).
3	As with other content types, the Blog Search results line provides statistics on the number of results found, your query, and the length of time it took Google to perform your search.
4	In the upper right side of the screen, just below the results are two text links. These serve as toggles where Google will *Sort by relevance* or *Sort by date*.
5	As part of the left navigation, a series of text links allow you to narrow your Blog Search to results published during a specified time frame. Choices include Last Hour, Last 12 hours, Last day, Past week, Past month, and Any time (default).
6	Also located within the left-side navigation is a text link for *Choose Date*. When selected, this link enables you to specify an exact date range for query results.
7	The core element for Blog Search results, each listing is summarized very similar to that used for Google Web results (see Chapter Two). Listings include a title, date, source, snippet, URL, and other optional links.
8	At the bottom of each results page, Google presents three text links to help you automate future queries for your search topic. Each of these features is discussed in greater detail elsewhere in this book.
9	Navigation elements and an expanding Google logo allow you to select additional results pages—Next, Previous, or numbered pages.
10	As a user convenience, Google repeats the search box located in the upper left corner of the screen enabling refinement of the original query as shown.

Google Blog Search Results Page

The screen image below is a partial view for a Google Blog Search result for my command line query *"lynch" waterbury ~genealogy.* My initial query included *"eugene lynch"*, but returned no results, so I simply removed the first name. (The quotations would no longer be needed in this case, but I left them there out of habit.) The tilde command does not seem to be generating similar word results, but once again was left by habit (and the hope that it will work someday).

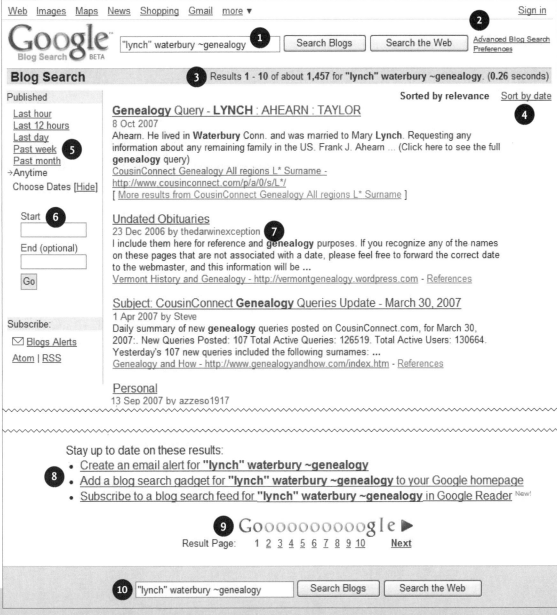

Beware of Blog Spam

Blog spam? And you thought it was hard keeping track of all the variant spellings of your ancestors' surnames! Blog spam, also called spam blog, comment spam, and spamdexing, is a technique used by blog posters—bloggers—to artificially enhance the visibility of their own website in search engine rankings. By submitting meaningless or automated comments to blog postings or creating one or more useless blogs, these individuals have unnecessarily cluttered search engine results with their self-promotion and bogus offers. While Google and other search engines have tried to stay a few steps ahead of these tech-savvy scammers, they have not yet found a mechanism to remove these postings completely.

As you use Google Blog Search, keep in mind that your search results may sometimes include strangely named pages. You may even click through a result and see an entry similar to the one shown below. This message will most often mean that the page or site has been identified as spam (useless content) and removed from the index.

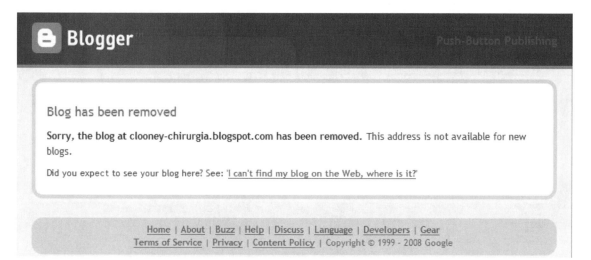

Special Relevance for Genealogists

Keep in mind that bloggers are simply people who are passionate about a subject and who take the time to share information through their online postings. Many good genealogy blogs cover a broad spectrum of sub-topics, but you can learn even more by visiting blogs that deal with niche topics specific to your research. Perhaps you're interested in learning about Polish research, Jewish genealogy, or the service of Lithuanians in the first World War. You can find blogs dealing with these topics and you can share your comments and questions almost as easily as sending an email. After all, blogging is often an online dialog.

Genealogy Blogs

In addition to using Google to search for genealogy blog postings of interest, you can also find a great collection online at the Genealogy Blog Finder < http://blogfinder.genealogue. com/>. This site by genealogist Chris Dunham is essentially a blog about other genealogy blogs. The site contains profiles for nearly 1,000 genealogy blogs categorized into areas of special interest.

Search Leading Genealogy Blogs

Although I'm happy to help you become expert at using Google to pursue your genealogical passion, I also recognize that some advanced commands are easier to use with an advanced search form. While Google comes close, I decided to create my own genealogy-specific search forms on the companion website for this book. You can access a flexible Blog Search exclusively for genealogy by visiting <www.GoogleYourFamilyTree.com>.

CHAPTER 8

Images and Video

Every genealogist has a collection of vintage family photographs. The size of the collection doesn't matter—it can be just a few faded prints or a well-organized collection of hundreds of photos. In either instance, these images serve as our special window into the past, as a way to meet the people, visit the places, and attend the events that represent our family story.

For decades, many of these images were stored in forgotten boxes or in dusty corners of old family homes. Genealogists were certainly among the first to recognize the importance of low-cost, high-quality digital scanners and personal computers. Technology that was once reserved for high-end labs is now commonplace among family historians, and many of these priceless images are being preserved and shared with a worldwide audience. Enter Google.

The proliferation of Web pages is made useful only because we have powerful tools for search and navigation—thanks to Google and others. Those same techniques can also be applied to searching what Google describes as "the most comprehensive image search on the Web."

There is no precise number available to quantify the volume of images being shared online, but it is certainly in the hundreds of millions, if not billions. It's increasingly rare to visit a Web page without at least one photograph, and this trend is likely to continue into in the months and years ahead. As with a general Web search, the challenge for family historians is to find a cost-effective tool for searching through a growing collection of online images. Well, that search has already ended. The same free tools and techniques you have learned for searching the Web can be directed toward a Google Images search, making your research more exciting and your finds more spectacular.

Google Image Search

Accessing a Google Image Search is a simple one-click process. From the Google homepage, click the *Images* text link located in the upper left corner of your screen. You will notice a slight change, but the page closely matches the look and functionality already described.

Primary Elements of Google Images Results Page

1	Nearly identical to the header as described in Chapter 2, the Google logo, primary text links, and search input box are carried over from the Home page and are always visible in the upper left corner of your screen. Your search query is also carried forward, enabling you to refine your original query or submit a new one as desired. The Image results page also includes a link to edit SafeSearch preferences.
2	A summary line showing the number of results found, the time it took Google to perform the search, and links to the primary keywords used for your query.
3	A drop-down box defaults to All image sizes, but enables the user to select from small, medium, large, and extra-large image sizes. Genealogists will appreciate the high resolution found in many of the extra-large images.
4	The primary component of Google Image results, a thumbnail of the image itself appears. Beneath the image is the image name or text descriptor, the image dimensions (expressed in pixel width x pixel height), the image size and format (e.g., .jpg, .gif, .png, etc.), and the address of the website where the image appears.
5	As with Web Search results page, the expanding Google logo, input box, and other basic text links appear at the bottom of the page as a user convenience.

Same Commands & Syntax

The first three chapters of this book discussed basic and advanced techniques designed to make you an expert Googler. Well, I've got some great news! Every command, every search tip, and every previous example can also be applied to a Google Image Search. Your overall mastery of Google will grow stronger as we explore this new content type.

Google Image Search—Results Page

As you can see in the screen shot below, the overall layout of the results page from a Google Image Search is very similar to that of a Google Web Search described in Chapter 2. The next few pages detail the unique elements for searching and viewing image results. You may find it helpful to execute a Google Image Search and refer to the results page as you review the next few pages of this chapter. The example query used in this section appears below.

Search terms: lynch connecticut ~genealogy ~vintage

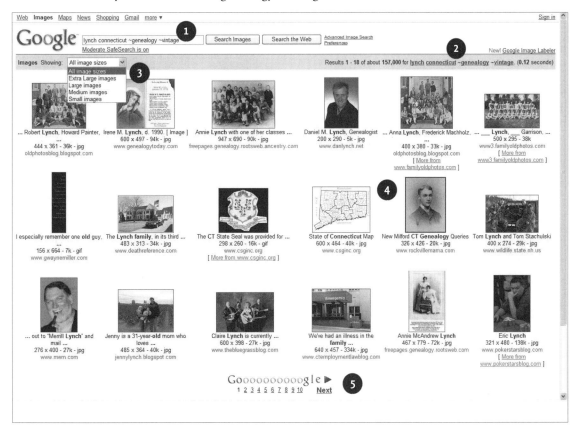

Results Screen Part 1—Results Header

As a convenience to the user, the top of each results page is essentially a miniaturized version of the Google homepage. The most important navigational links appear within close proximity to the Google logo. The logo itself is also a link and will take you directly back to the homepage where you can start fresh if you prefer.

One of the most useful items found within the results header is your original query, which is retained within the search box. This enables you to quickly refine your query as needed. If your query generated 12 million results, you may wish to quickly add quotations or another operator to filter out unwanted listings.

The dynamic links above the Google logo will switch you to another content type while retaining the subject of your search as the active query. The *Advanced Search* and *Preferences* links to the right of the Search button are described in more detail as part of Chapter 3.

Web	Click the *Web* link to be taken directly to the Web Search results page for the query shown in the input box.
Maps	Click the *Maps* link to be taken directly to the Maps results page for the query shown in the input box.
News	Click the *News* link to be taken directly to the News results page for the query shown in the input box.
Shopping	Click the *Shopping* link to be taken directly to the Products results page for the query shown in the input box.
Gmail	One click access to your free account on Google Gmail. (You can sign in here or register for an account if you wish.)
more	Links to Google Video, Groups, Books, Scholar, Finance, Blogs, YouTube, Calendar, Photos, Documents, Reader, and more.

SafeSearch Image Filtering

Immediately below the Search Input Box, you will notice a text link. (In our example it reads *Moderate SafeSearch is on.*) Google recognizes that some content available for online viewing may be considered inappropriate or offensive for certain audiences. Although Google can't control the content posted by others, it can and does provide advanced filters in an attempt to give you greater control over the types of results you receive. SafeSearch is part of the user preferences setting; it offers three options as shown below. The Google default is set to use moderate filtering, but you can change it to suit your own preferences.

SafeSearch Filtering	Google's SafeSearch blocks web pages containing explicit sexual content from appearing in search results.
	○ Use strict filtering (Filter both explicit text and explicit images)
	◉ Use moderate filtering (Filter explicit images only - default behavior)
	○ Do not filter my search results.

Results Screen Parts 2 & 3—Result Statistics & Image Size

The result statistics for Google Image Search function in the same way as described in Chapter 2 for Google Web Search. Our example query found 63,400 results in just 0.02 seconds and each of the terms appears as a blue hyperlink. Clicking on any keyword will direct you to <www.answers.com> and a variety of definitions for that keyword. As Google works on new features, it will often place links on various pages. I encourage you to explore any new link you find as this is the best way to expand your understanding of Google products and services. In this case, the Google Image Labeler is being introduced. (It will be discussed later in this chapter.)

Results **1 - 18** of about **63,400** for <u>lynch</u> <u>connecticut</u> <u>~genealogy</u> <u>~vintage</u>. (0.02 seconds)

Beneath the Google logo on the results page, a small drop-down box appears in the light-blue horizontal bar running across the page. This simple option allows you to select the image size included in your query results. In most cases, a larger image

Images Showing: All image sizes ▾
All image sizes
Extra Large images
Large images
Medium images
Small images

will contain more detail of definition (also called resolution). Very small images may look great on your computer screen, but will often not reproduce well in print.

Results Screen Part 4—Individual Results

As of this writing, the Google Image Results page is comprised entirely of natural listings (meaning no Sponsored Links are included on the page as they are with Web Search Results). Depending upon your computer's screen resolution, the number of miniature images (also called thumbnail images) displayed may be different than my sample screen shots.

After processing your query, Google presents the matching results in a grid pattern—evenly spaced rows and columns of miniature images with corresponding information appearing beneath each one. In the examples below, you can quickly see the value of an Image Search for family historians. Vintage photographs are common occurrences in search results, assuming you've properly structured your query to filter out unwanted images. In addition, you will easily find photographs of headstones; scanned images from family Bibles, old letters, vintage postcards; and a creative collection of family tree charts.

New Milford **CT Genealogy** Queries
326 x 426 - 20k - jpg
www.rockvillemama.com

BIBLE: Deacon **Family** New York.
Old ...
449 x 600 - 62k - jpg
familybibles.blogspot.com

Very **Old** German-language Bible ...
440 x 328 - 27k - jpg
familybibles.blogspot.com
[More from ancestorsatrest.com]

[Thumbnail]	Miniature image, click to view page containing full image
[Image Text]	Text assigned to the image file by the publisher of the Web page that contains the image (referred to as *Alt text*)
[File Statistics]	File width and height (in pixels), size of file, and graphic format
[URL]	Light green text appearing as the second or third line beneath the thumbnail image. Contains a full or partial Web address
More from...	Light blue text link indicating more relevant images may be found at this Web address, similar to executing the **site:** command

Evaluating Image Results for Genealogical Content

For some family historians, especially those new to the process of collecting information, it can be tempting to find a wonderful old photograph of an individual posted online and adopt it as your ancestor. As with any clue, however, you need to understand the context of where it was found, who posted it online, that person's connection to the photograph, and as much other information as you can obtain to reasonably conclude that the image belongs in your family scrapbook.

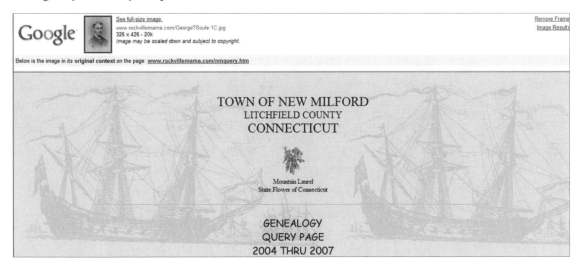

When you click on a thumbnail from the Image Search Results page, you will arrive at a target page similar to the example shown above and enlarged below. At the top of the page, you will see the Google logo next to summary information for the individual listing. By scrolling down the page, you should find the image in the original context of how it appears online. Carefully read the text describing the image and, if possible, look for information about the person who posted the image online. You may be able to confirm your legitimate connection to this particular image.

See full-size image.
www.rockvillemama.com/GeorgeTSoule-1C.jpg
326 x 426 - 20k
Image may be scaled down and subject to copyright.

Below is the image in its **original context** on the page: **www.rockvillemama.com/nmquery.htm**

Is This Your Great Grandfather?

In the example featured on the previous page, our query for a Connecticut ancestor led us to a page with an image of a young man. By visiting the Web page containing the image, we learn some fascinating details. The photograph was taken in 1882 by a Boston photographer. Writing on the back gives a possible identity—*George T. Soule, New Milford, CT.*

The most amazing part of this example is that the image was posted online by Gareth Watkins, a family historian living in Wellington, New Zealand. He came into possession of the photograph in late 2007, scanned the image, and posted a copy with supporting text online at a U.S. GenWeb page focused on the New Milford, Connecticut, region.

Despite his location on the other side of the world, Gareth has already researched the 1880 U.S. Census online for Litchfield County, Connecticut, and has shared the likely family connections for the man in the photograph. As of this writing, no descendants have been found, but perhaps someone reading this text may be in for a pleasant surprise, thanks to Gareth and Google Image Search.

Results Screen Part 5—Navigation & Page Footer

The footer of the Image Search Results page includes navigation elements very similar to those found on the Web Search Results page, modified slightly for Image Search. Functionality for each link is the same; refer to Chapter 2 to review in greater detail.

Gooooooooogle ▶

1 2 3 4 5 6 7 8 9 10 **Next**

| lynch connecticut ~genealogy | Search Images | Search the Web |

Special Genealogy Tip for Google Image Search

Earlier in this book, I described a technique for using synonyms to help expand search results, but within a reasonable scope of relevance (see page 29). For genealogists using Google's Image Search, this technique can be especially helpful in finding pictures likely to be of interest for your family history research. By using the technique described, I was able to determine that synonyms recognized by Google for the word *vintage* include: antique, classic, old, retro, used, and victorian. By using the *~vintage* qualifier as part of a Google Image query, you can greatly enhance your odds of finding relevant results.

Point your Web browser to Google Image Search and try the following queries. As discussed in earlier chapters, place names and surnames are both useful elements in structuring your query. Note the frequency of black and white images that appear in your results.

vintage	▶ ~vintage new york city
	▶ ~vintage "ellis island" immigrants
	▶ ~vintage Italian campobasso
	▶ ~vintage portraits WWI **OR** "world war one" **OR** "the great war"

Post Cards

If you are researching a city or town where your ancestors lived, you may find it helpful to look for post cards by using the Google Image Search. Conduct a search using the place name as the primary keyword, followed by "post card" or postcard. If your initial query produces too many unwanted results, try refining the query by adding ~vintage at the end and resubmitting.

You may also find it interesting to do more general queries (e.g., military, italian, etc.), using the resulting images to simply learn about the subject of your search through pictures and old postcards, which were popular for decades. The numrange command (see page 64) can be especially useful with postcards and photographs, allowing you to search for images from a particular era when your ancestor may have lived in a particular location.

> ▶ oswego ny **AND** "post cards" **OR** postcards ~vintage
> ▶ rochester ny 1890**..**1900
> ▶ ~vintage connecticut "post cards" **OR** postcards
> ▶ ~vintage +postcard +collection ~genealogy
> ▶ ~vintage ~military postcard

It is quite common to find images of richly colored post cards featuring churches, municipal buildings, city scenes, parks, and important monuments from an ancestor's

HOLYLAND — Waterbury, Connecticut U.S.A.

town. If you're lucky, one or more cards may be for sale. If you're extremely lucky, the card may have been sent to or by your ancestor or another name you recognize. Share your interesting image finds at <www.googleyourfamilytree.com>.

Google Image Labeler

As part of an effort to improve search results with help from a worldwide community of users, Google offers an interactive feature called the Image Labeler. By participating, you and an anonymous virtual partner are presented with a series of images for viewing and a two-minute countdown clock. As each image is presented on screen, you type keywords that describe the contents of the image while your partner does the same. The more you and your partner match, the more points you earn. While it may seem like nothing more than a simple game, it's a very clever and addictive means of "tagging" online images so they can be recalled later in response to a Google Image query.

The Photo Detective

Among the many things I have learned while researching my family heritage is that no one person can be expert in all aspects of genealogy. Some specialize in military records, some know every detail about one specific ethnic group, and others—but not many—have the ability to look at an old, faded photograph and tell you with precise detail when and where it was likely taken. That's the specialty of Maureen Taylor, The Photo Detective. In October 2007, the *Wall Street Journal* called Maureen "the nation's foremost historical photo detective." Through careful inspection of clothing styles, photographic techniques, mounting paper and size, image background, and any other visible clue that most of us would easily overlook, she can often help family historians connect the faces from a photo with the names in their pedigree charts.

It seemed only logical then to turn to Ms. Taylor to hear what tips and techniques she has found helpful while using Google or other Internet-based services to sleuth for family photographs. The next two pages will provide insights from the Photo Detective in her own words. Many thanks to Maureen for her willingness to share her expertise. For more information about her services, visit her website online at <www.photodetective.com>.

The Photo Detective 🅼🅶 Maureen Taylor

About the Photo Detective ▸

Photo Detective Services ▸

Recommended Resources ▸

Upload a Photo

Contact the Photo Detective

Ask the Photo Detective

Blogs ▸

A little man, c.1880, dressed like his father.

Professional Help for Family Photo Issues

Don't let heaps of unidentified, damaged, or disorganized family photos get you down. The Photo Detective can help. Maureen Taylor's expertise in photography, history, and genealogy can help you find missing photos, interpret unidentified pictures, and preserve and organize your precious photo collection.

"A family photograph collection is more than a random collection of images; each one is a story worth saving." *Maureen Taylor, Photo Detective*

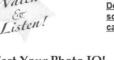

Watch & Listen!

Watch and listen as Photo Detective Maureen Taylor solves three example cases.

Test Your Photo IQ!

True or False: It's possible that your Revolutionary War-era ancestors were photographed.

And the answer is...

Using Google in Photo research

The Web is a visual medium which means that whether you're trying to find a "missing" family photograph, decipher the clues in one you own or just need more information on a photographic technique, Google is a tremendous resource. Here are four ways that I use this and other Internet search engines.

Locating Pictures

You can use Google's Image search to try to find family pictures or photographs of places your ancestors lived. Type in the family name, a specific first and last name or the town of residence then use Dan's tips for narrowing down the hits. While this works best with unusual names (first and last), if the person you're looking for was relatively well-known you could turn up hits on historical websites, family sites or even a museum page. In addition to finding photographic portraits you might discover a manuscript or artifact. It's an image search engine that covers all types of digital imaging from .jpgs to .tiff files regardless of whether the image is of a photograph or a piece of sculpture. For instance, a search for images of "Jesse James" results in 275,000 hits (as of May 1st 2008) including photos of the infamous outlaw, book jackets, wanted posters and a few contemporary men of the same name. If you thought you owned a picture of James you could compare your image to the ones found using Google.

Overseas Help

Whenever I'm confronted by a foreign phase or term in a document or on a family photograph I use the online translation services. Following the tips in Chapter 5, I can then discover the English translation for a place name in a photo caption or read the greeting on the back of a postcard. If I need more background on a place name, I'll begin by Googling it. See how I dated one woman's photo at <www.familytreemagazine.com/photos/apr13-06.htm>.

Photo Help

I recently used Google to help me connect with other users of an Epson scanner. I was having difficulty getting the slide scanning feature to work properly. Using the name of the scanner plus model number enabled me to find an online manual for the device. That was helpful, but expanding the search into blogs and tech columns on problems and solutions really paid off. The result—within minutes I had the answers I needed to make the scans and the advice I needed to fill in the issues not covered in the manual. I also use this basic search to locate professional reviews and customer satisfaction reports for any equipment I'm considering buying. It's a good way to avoid expensive equipment blunders.

Trivial Pursuit

Photo identification is all about adding up the clues in a picture from when a photographer was in business to what type of bicycle is shown in an image. Using the various tips and techniques profiled in this book, I'm usually able to acquire a bit of knowledge that leads me to a hypothesis. Each piece of the Google search engine helps in the pursuit of trivial facts all necessary to analyzing photographic evidence. From Google Books online library catalog help to Google Maps street level view each element offers me tantalizing data to close almost any photo case. It's not a single fact that identifies or dates a photo; the answer lies in the interpretation of all the facets of the problem—historical, pictorial, and genealogical.

Tips for Sharing Your Images Online

So where do all these images come from anyway? If other family historians hadn't preserved, scanned, and posted images online, think how few results would relate to our interest in old family photos. Whether you have already shared some of your photos online or are considering doing so some day, there are a few important tips to keep in mind.

Keywords are the primary ingredient for online success. That is not only true when you are searching, but it also holds true when you want to be found! When you scan an old photograph destined for the Web, don't accept the scanner default, which might name your file scan001.jpg or some other equally meaningless name. If the photo is an image of your great grandfather from a Civil War GAR Post, then use what you know to label the image: patrick_lynch_civil_war_gar_circa_1887.jpg. Think a few steps ahead when naming your images. Include the important keywords that might help someone connect with you and hopefully share additional details about this ancestor.

Miracles Do Happen!

In 1991, I found an old photograph among others in a box believed to be from the family of my maternal grandmother. The only obvious clue to my untrained eye was a photographer's stamp in the lower right corner that gave the location as Campobasso. That

coincided with the town in Italy where my family was known to have emigrated from, so it was a good start. After years of showing the photo to relatives with no success, it was posted online—like a net cast into the water just waiting for a bite.

Many months passed, but finally an email arrived. Several emails and phone calls later, I was able to identify each person in the photo with the help of my newly discovered Italian cousin living in England. And if that wasn't good enough, in 2006 I also met the little girl pictured in the lower right corner of the photograph holding the basket of flowers. When we met she was 95-year-old Luisa di Tota and she told me the story of the photograph, which included her mother and grandmother!

Google Video

While some may argue that Google Video and YouTube aren't tools for genealogists, I want to encourage you to think beyond typical research for ways these tools can help enhance your family story. Video has a unique ability to introduce you to people, places, and events from anywhere in the world. You can even learn how to become a better genealogist or computer user by watching one of the many free videos posted online by others.

One of my favorite videos on Google's YouTube service is an 8½-minute clip of Don Antonio Maione from Campobasso, Italy. Titled *Chiesa in crisi?*, the video features an Italian man in his sixties speaking to the camera in his local dialect about problems in the modern-day church. Having watched this video more than a dozen times, but not speaking a word of Italian myself, it's interesting to hear the native language from the village where my Italian ancestors were born. With each viewing, I seem to understand more.

Google Video Search

It is often said that a picture is worth a thousand words. For genealogists, that statement is especially true. What, then, is the value of video?

Google helped answer that question in October 2006 when it announced the acquisition of the popular video sharing site YouTube for $1.65 billion. Although relatively few family historians can boast that video recordings contain images of their ancestors, that will certainly not be the case in another generation. Today's parents and grandparents capture many family moments on

· 157 ·

film or disc with ease, and many of these moments are finding their way to the Internet for relatives to view from anywhere in the world.

Google's Video Search can be accessed from the Home page under the *more* text link. By now you should not be surprised to learn that you already have a certain degree of expertise in using this portion of Google—even if this is your first try.

The Google Video Search works in the same manner, using the same commands and syntax as Web Search and Image Search described previously. The results page (shown above) should also look strikingly familiar. The only real difference is the unique format used to display individual video results.

Although Google has two video services—Google Video and YouTube, I will focus my efforts on Google Video for one main reason. The Google Video service indexes and displays video results from any online source—including YouTube. The YouTube service, however, will only search and display results originally posted through the YouTube service itself. As a result, the Google Video results are more comprehensive that those found on YouTube.

Google Video Results—Page Header

A close-up of the Video Results header is located in the upper left of all Video Results pages. The now-familiar format operates as described in earlier sections. The table below provides a detailed description of header elements that are unique to this content type.

The dynamic links above the Google logo switch you to another content type while retaining the subject of your search as the active query.

[Radio Buttons]	Allows users to specify whether search results should be limited only to videos playable on Google or if results should represent all Web videos.
Advanced Video Search	Access to the Advanced Video Search page enables you to perform more precise video searches without using syntax.
Preferences	Access to the Global Preferences settings where you can specify a range of search and display options.
SafeSearch	Enables users to modify their SafeSearch settings. Google's default setting is for moderate filtering. Additional options exist to remove filtering or to implement strict filtering of explicit content.
[Layout Icons]	Select from one of three screen layout options by clicking on the icons located beneath the Google logo. Toggle between each view to select the one you prefer. The default used will show one main video, with summary results at left (as shown on the previous page).
Duration	A drop-down menu allowing you to filter video results to short (under 4 minutes), medium (between 4 and 20 minutes), and long (more than 20 minutes).

Google Video—Results Summary

The two examples below show the basic format for displaying Video Search Results.

Festa di Santo Marello a Riccia, **Campobasso, Italia**
4 min - Jun 7, 2007
, **Italia**...Nella domenica del Pentecoste: la celebrazione della festa del Santo Marello degli Oblati di San Giuseppe
http://www.youtube.com/watch?v=oXKjOnJKHls
⊞ Watch video here - Related videos

I'm My Own Grandpa
3 min - Dec 29, 2005 - ☆☆☆☆☆ (2 ratings)
Own Grandpa...That is just the cutest, funniest clip to wake up too lol. Nice animation.
http://www.metacafe.com/watch/54702/im_my_own_grandpa/
⊞ View thumbnails - Related videos

[Thumbnail]	Miniature image at left. Click on it to view video embedded in the page.
[Page Title]	The link on line one is featured in blue text and contains text from the title of the video and/or from the page containing the video.
[File Statistics]	Information about the length of the video (in minutes), as well as the date the file was posted. Typically appears on the second line in light-gray text. If the video is rated, a rating (1–5 stars) will also be shown, along with the number of reviewers who have rated the video.
[Summary Text]	Typically one or two lines of black descriptive text with content from the target Web page and/or a description added with the video.
[URL]	Light green text appearing as the fourth or fifth line of results summary, contains a full or partial Web address.
Watch video here	Light-blue text link indicating more relevant images may be found at this Web address—similar to executing the **site:** command.
View thumbnails	Light blue text link expands the results screen to display a series of thumbnail images captured from the video clip.
Related videos	Light-blue text link submits a new Google Video query using keywords found within the existing video results page.

Related Videos

As you are viewing an individual video result in the default results format, Google also displays one or more related videos in a thin strip along the right side of the page. Videos will appear here based on similarity of keywords in the title or description, and possibly other factors which Google may use to determine relevance. I have noticed that other videos posted by the same person are sometimes be displayed in this area.

Google Video—Expanded Summary

After conducting your search and viewing the summary results presented by Google, you will generally select one of the videos for viewing in your browser. Depending upon where the video is hosted (on Google or another hosting site), the screen may appear slightly different than the examples shown here, but they should be very similar to what you view on your screen.

While the video plays in an expanded window (as shown on the following page), the left-hand column will display other results relevant for your query as defined. As with other Google content features, a lot of information is packed into a small space. Your query definition, volume of results, title, length, date, rating, and target URL are all listed. Others who view this video can also rate the content, resulting in a rating between zero to five stars. This can help you more quickly decide whether or not to view an individual result.

vicoli,piazze e chiese di San Bartolomeo in Galdo
tra i vicoli le piazze e le chiese di **San** Bartolomeo
in **galdo** ...
▶ 6 min - ☆☆☆☆☆- youtube.com

Video View Screen Layout

The image at the bottom of this page features a full-screen view of an individual video result for the query ***galway ireland fiddler***. In this example, the video result summary (enlarged below) shows that a one-minute video was posted on March 3, 2007, entitled "Irish Fiddler in Galway, Ireland." On the left side of the screen are other videos that are suggested as relevant for this search term, while the right side of the screen includes a selection of videos that may be related, but have not been presented based on your keyword query. The related videos will often include other videos posted by the same person who shared the main video being displayed on screen at that moment.

In recent months, Google has made a few refinements to this page and I expect that effort will continue. If your video results page appears slightly different than described, don't worry—I'm certain that any changed made after this book prints will make the service even more intuitive and many of the screen elements will still be in use as shown. One other certainty is the underlying search technology which will enable you to obtain highly relevant results within your first few visits.

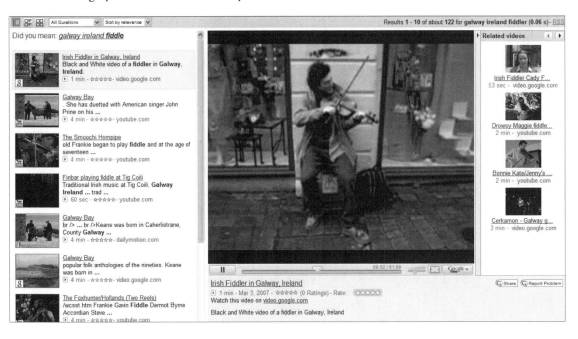

Roots Television

To this point, this guidebook has been focused on the services of Google. While discussing Images & Video, it seems appropriate to allow a brief diversion away from Google and toward another innovative online service created specifically for family historians.

Roots Television, located online at <www.rootstelevision.com>, is the perfect intersection of video programming and genealogy. Covering a variety of topics through its video programming, you can learn the basics of getting started or hear the details of the latest breakthroughs in DNA research techniques. I'm pleased to include commentary about this website since it will surely be of interest to every reader.

About Roots Television

Roots Television is an online television network focused on genealogy and family history. Because it is online, all of Roots Television's programs are available on-demand, 24/7, and nearly all of them are free.

The good news for avid genealogists everywhere—and that means literally anywhere around the world—is that Roots Television already offers twenty-four Internet "channels" focusing on everything from DNA, cemeteries, Hispanic roots, and how-to. Any aspect of

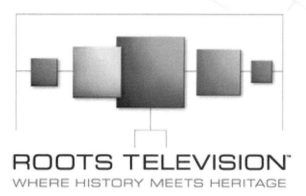

Featured Channels Include:
News & Featured
Conferences
DNA
RootsTube
Roots Books
How To
Dearly Departed
Immigration
Military
British Roots
African Roots
Roots Living
Preserving the Past
Kids
Irish Roots
Storytelling
Jewish Roots
Family Reunions
Hispanic Roots
Ancestors Series
Societies
Libraries & Archives
Roots Shopping
Pay TV

roots-seeking that is of interest to viewers has been covered. Roots Television has always tried to strike a balance between being a place for beginning genealogists to dip their toe in the water while offering advanced genealogists the latest and greatest information on their particular lines of research.

In addition to its popular conference coverage, Roots Television produces original series aimed at the genealogy crowd. In DNA Stories, roots seekers tell how they have used genetic genealogy to solve mysteries in their own family trees. It seems every family historian has a favorite cemetery and headstone, and in the newly-released series Down Under, you'll travel beyond the tombstones to learn about the stories of the people beneath the stones. And coming soon to Roots Television is Unclaimed Persons. In coroners' offices across the country are numerous remains of those who have been identified, but whose families have yet to claim them. How do these family ties sever in the first place, and can genealogists help to reunite the deceased with their loved ones?

My thanks to Roots Television, especially Megan Smolenyak Smolenyak and Samantha Butterworth who provided an insider's perspective for use within the pages of this book.

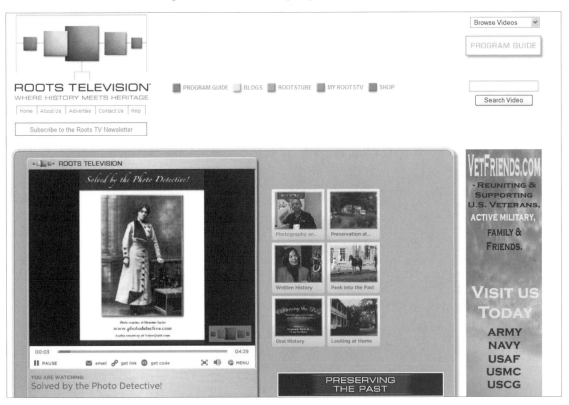

A Must See Video for Genealogists

If you're new to online video or genealogy, you may not have had a chance to enjoy the clever song by Ray Stephens titled "I'm my own Grandpa." Several animated versions exist online and you can see a sample screen shot below for a search that will help you find the version I prefer. Be sure to search for this video and have your volume turned up; you'll end up watching this one more than once to follow this clever family tree.

Advanced Video Techniques

The previous pages focused on techniques for finding video content online that can help add rich detail to your family story. If you have video of your own—either of family members or locations that may be of interest to other family historians, consider sharing them online.

In the months following publication of this book, I will be adding additional content on a free <www.GoogleYourFamilyTree.com> website. You can visit the video section for details on how to upload your video, as well as the best techniques for describing your content so they have the best chance of being found by distant cousins.

CHAPTER 9

Google Alerts:
Search While You Sleep

The Internet is certainly the most dynamic publishing medium that has ever existed. New pages are being published every minute and existing pages are being changed or retired. As innovative and thorough as Google is, even it can't keep pace with the exponential growth of the Internet. This growth is great news for family history enthusiasts as many local societies and individual researchers from around the world continue to publish their unique content via the Web. There is one thing better than a fresh supply of content—the Google Alert service, which helps automate the process of sifting through all these new entries round-the-clock.

Effective use of Google Alerts requires a basic understanding of the concepts discussed in Chapters one through three. The better your skills at defining a useful Google Web query, the more meaningful the updates you can expect to receive through Google Alerts.

Google™ Alerts   Google Alerts (BETA)   FAQ | Sign in

Welcome to Google Alerts

Google Alerts are email updates of the latest relevant Google results (web, news, etc.) based on your choice of query or topic.

Some handy uses of Google Alerts include:

- monitoring a developing news story
- keeping current on a competitor or industry
- getting the latest on a celebrity or event
- keeping tabs on your favorite sports teams

Create an alert with the form on the right.

You can also sign in to manage your alerts.

Create a Google Alert

Enter the topic you wish to monitor.

Search terms:
Type: Comprehensive
How often: once a day
Your email:

Create Alert

Google will not sell or share your email address.

What is a Google Alert?

Simply put, a Google Alert is an automated query that is executed on your behalf by Google using query definitions you have previously registered through Google's Alert service. As one or more items is found matching your search criteria, Google sends a very concise email summary to notify you that results have been found. The better your query, the more relevant your results will be.

For genealogists, this can be your most powerful tool because it harnesses the power of Google even when you don't have time to dedicate to your research. The Alert service would be the same as spending 15 or 20 minutes each morning submitting the same surname and place name queries for your various family lines. Certainly that's great when time allows, but letting Google do it for you is an even better use of your time.

No Spam

One concern with any online service offering to send email updates is the fear of receiving a flood of unwanted, overly commercial emails with little or no real content. I have been using Google Alerts for several years and can assure you that emails generated through this service are strictly no-nonsense notifications. As of this writing, Alert notifications don't contain any form of advertising—not even relevant sponsor links based on specified keywords.

more ▼

Video
Groups
Books
Scholar
Finance
Blogs

YouTube
Calendar
Photos
Documents
Reader

even more »

Getting Started

Setting up a new Google Alert is surprisingly simple. There are several ways to access the service, but I recommend the following:

1. Point your browser to the Google homepage at <www.google.com>.
2. In the upper left corner, click the *more* ▼ text link.
3. Click the menu option for *even more* ▶.

The resulting page contains icons, links, and brief text descriptions for a complete range of Google products. As of this writing, Alerts is the first item listed in the lefthand column. Click on the icon or text link and you will be taken directly to the simple setup page for Google Alerts.

Setting up Your Google Alert

The first thing you should consider when setting up your new Google Alert is how to define your query for best results. Be sure that you first submit your query manually using the Google Web Search to determine if the query definition is too broad (yielding too many unwanted results) or too narrow (yielding no matching results). The techniques described in Chapters one, two, and three can help you refine your query definition if needed.

 Alerts
Get email updates on the topics of your choice

Syntax

The syntax used in your Google Alerts is identical to that used throughout Google. Although the Search terms box may look small, it will accept just as many words and characters as the main input box featured on the Google homepage. In the example below, I am interested in receiving automatic notifications for free genealogy workshops being offered in Connecticut or New York during 2008 or 2009.

Syntax: "genealogy workshop" free connecticut **OR** new york 2008..2009

Type: Comprehensive ▾
News
Blogs
Web
Comprehensive
Video
Groups

How often: once a day ▾
once a day
as-it-happens
once a week

Create a Google Alert

Enter the topic you wish to monitor.

Search terms: _____

Type: Comprehensive ▾

How often: once a day ▾

Your email: _____

[Create Alert]

Google will not sell or share your email address.

Customize Your Alerts

After you have verified the syntax of your query, you can specify a content type (News, Blogs, Web, Comprehensive (default), Video, Groups) and the frequency for receipt of your notifications. At any point in the future you can edit all aspects of your Google Alert or delete it altogether if you wish.

Email Confirmation

After creating each new Google Alert, a confirming email will be sent to the address used. This is done to ensure that you are the one requesting the notification emails to follow. In the example below, a "google your family tree" notification has been created to monitor online postings about this book.

FAQ | Sign in

Google Alerts — Google Alerts (BETA)

Google Alert Created
Your Google Alert request ["google your family tree"] has been created and a verification email has been sent to ███████@gmail.com.

You will not receive Google Alerts on this topic until you click the link in the verification email and confirm your request.

Shortly after creating a new Google Alert, a message similar to the one displayed below will arrive in your inbox. Links allow you to *Verify* the request or *Cancel* the request. Following confirmation, you will begin receiving notifications according to the time frame specified. If no new content has been found matching your search criteria, you will not receive a notification.

To: ███████.com
Cc:
Subject: Google Alert - mattatuck

Google received a request to start sending Alerts for the search
["google ...] to ███████@gmail.com.

Verify this Google Alert request:
http://www.google.com/alerts/verify?s=EAAAADqMhQGOCeGm--KIM2ydeYw

Cancel this Google Alert request:
http://www.google.com/alerts/remove?s=EAAAADqMhQGOCeGm--KIM2ydeYw

Notification Format for Google Alerts

The email notifications sent by the Google Alerts service are organized by content type and contain summary results similar to those resulting from a Google Web Search. Each notification can contain one or more results. In the example below, a single result is highlighted in the notification email.

The subject line of the email includes the keywords from the query. The body of the email includes a hyperlinked headline in blue. Depending upon the source for this content, a line may appear below the headline with the name of the publication, blog, or news provider. The content is summarized with two or three lines of text with the keyword(s) appearing in bold text.

At the footer of each notification email, links to *Remove, Create,* and *Manage* Alerts are included as a convenience to users.

Manage Your Google Alerts

You can establish and maintain an unlimited number of notifications through the Google Alerts service. The best way to refine your query definitions is to establish your Alerts, then closely monitor the notifications as they begin to appear in you email inbox. If you receive few or no notifications, your query definition may be too restrictive. If, on the other hand, you are receiving notifications with multiple matching results but the results don't appear to be of any real value, you may need to refine your query to further filter out unwanted results.

Special Relevance for Genealogists

News alerts can be used for any topic you are interested in—genealogy or otherwise. All researchers are encouraged to establish a series of Alerts, one for each key ancestor or family line. Given the popularity of Internet genealogy, message board postings, obituaries, blog entries, and content pages are being published daily. Rather than wait until you have time to search, these carefully structured queries can generate useful notifications enabling timely follow-up for even the busiest family historian.

Word of Caution

You might be surprised how often the word *genealogy* is used online—on new Web pages, news articles, blog postings, and elsewhere. Unless you really like getting email, avoid establishing general Alerts for broad terms such as *genealogy* or *immigration* or *census*. They will all certainly trigger email notifications, but you will find that few summaries will be of particular interest to you. Think of each Alert the same way you would a carefully crafted query. If you get too many results from the query when submitting it manually, you will probably have the same experience with the notifications received through Google Alerts (See below).

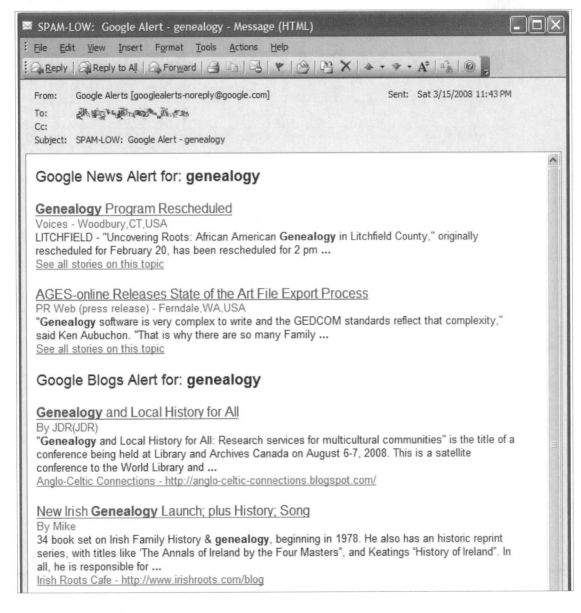

Google Alerts Worksheet

Use the following worksheet to formulate and refine your queries before establishing new Google Alerts. For type, I recommend accepting the default setting (Comprehensive), but you can also select only the following content types—News, Blogs, Web, Video or Groups. Frequency is either daily, weekly or as it happens.

Query Definition	Type	Frequency

Google Alerts Worksheet

Query Definition	Type	Frequency

CHAPTER 10

Google Maps

It's hardly a secret that genealogists love maps—the older, the better. Visit the vendor fair at any family history conference and you're sure to find attendees ogling over an old map or gazetteer, no doubt trying to figure out how they can justify the purchase when they get home. Many historic maps contain unique details documenting the development of an area long before our modern-day infrastructure. For most family historians, maps are part education, part nostalgia. Whatever the reason, there's little doubt that historic maps can help paint a clear picture of our ancestors' surroundings during the time they lived in a certain region—or even in a particular home.

But Google doesn't have historic maps, so why the fascination with Google Maps? The answer shouldn't surprise you, especially after learning about the innovative search features described earlier in this book. Google Maps combines the detail of a world atlas, the fascination of satellite imagery, and the utility of an online phone directory, and tightly integrates the package around Google's advanced search technology. And did I mention it's free?

Using Google Maps for Genealogy

This section will describe the various features and capabilities of Google Maps, but will do so with a focus on using these tools to further your family history research. There are certainly some aspects of Google Maps that will not be covered in depth. Though they're still useful for general mapping, we're trying to keep our focus on genealogy. Once you have a basic understanding of how Google Maps can help save you time in your genealogical pursuits, feel free to explore everything else the service has to offer.

If you discover a particular use of Google Maps that may benefit other family historians, contact me to share your find. Updates about the capabilities of Google Maps with a genealogical focus will appear on <www.GoogleYourFamilyTree.com>, our companion website.

Accessing Google Maps

From the Google homepage, you will see a series of links in the upper left corner of the screen. The default is *Web*, but one click on the *Maps* text link will take you to the Google Maps interface. You can also consult Chapter Two for additional details on how various Google Maps features can also be accessed through a general Google Web Search.

Using Google Maps

The three basic functions performed through Google Maps are highlighted below and discussed in greater detail on the following pages.

1	Search the Map—Navigate a detailed map by specifying either an exact or partial street address or simply the name of a city or town you are trying to locate for a particular state. (Note: If you provide just a city/town name, Google may take you on an unexpected journey. Typing *rome ny* will bring you to upstate New York, but entering simply *rome* will display central Italy.)
2	Find Businesses—Google's powerful directory search enables users to type an exact name or simply a business type and geographic qualifier to locate one or more businesses that may be of interest. Promoted as a separate feature called Google Local, this has since become an integral part of Google Maps.
3	Get Directions—Obtain step-by-step driving directions, as well as reverse directions from any point of origin to any destination.

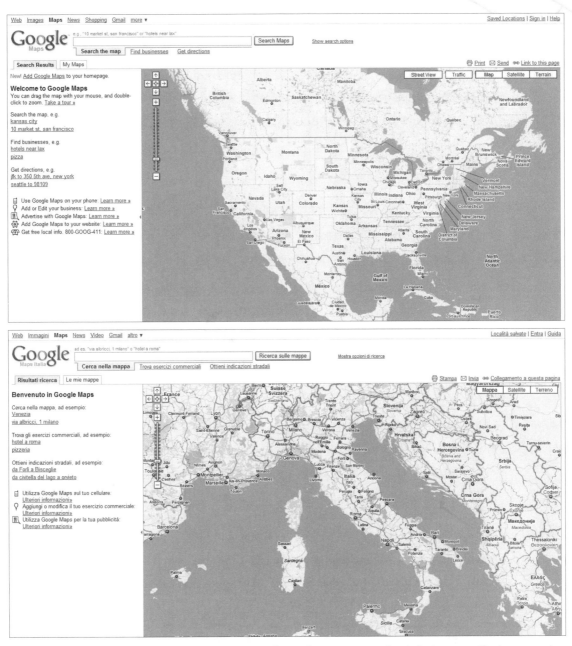

Google Maps—Depending upon the local version of Google you access, the default map will change. Using <www.google.com> will default to a U.S. map. If you are using an international version of Google, in this case <www.google.it>, your default will be the local country corresponding to your version of Google.

Sample Results Explained

In the example below, our query is for a general destination rather than a specific street address. Google Maps can often recognize a destination based on a name or will suggest the closest location based on the information provided. You can also use zip codes instead of geographic names. The keywords used in this query are ***new york public library***.

The default view for results is a traditional map view with major streets, highways, and landmarks labeled. Depending upon the number of results, an info window (item 3) will display details for one location. When your query has more than one result, they will be listed in the left margin (item 2) and also represented on the map as lettered icons corresponding to the listing.

You can navigate around the map and change the level of magnification using the controls superimposed over the upper left corner of the map (item 4). Depending upon the map, you may also have several alternate views available in the upper right (item 5, also shown enlarged below). The Map view and Satellite view will be of greatest interest to genealogists, as will photos accessible from the More / Photos box.

Anatomy of Google Map Results

The numbered descriptions below correspond to the sample map results displayed on the previous page. You may notice slight differences depending upon the geographic area being searched, as well as Google's ongoing efforts to enhance its service.

1	Google Maps Header—The header elements help maintain a common experience across content types, allowing you to quickly access Google Web, Images, News, and other services as desired. The three tabbed subsets of the Maps header include Search the map, Find Businesses, and Get directions. Use of keywords, commands, and syntax are consistent with other content areas.
2	Search Results—Text-based search results within Google Maps are displayed in the left column, with the actual map appearing to the right. Sponsored links, if any, appear above the natural listings, which are assigned a letter corresponding to a marked location on the map. These markers make it easy to compare the location of multiple entries. Clicking on a particular letter will bring an individual Info Window Bubble into view (see #3 below).
3	Info Window Bubble—A very useful content bubble provides a range of results for a location found through a Google Maps search. It can include street address, phone, Web address, a user rating, and quick links to a variety of mapping and directional features. For major cities, a Street view option provides a 360-degree view so you can take a virtual walk down the street.
4	Zoom & Directional Navigation—Along the left side of the map image, a series of arrows can be used to navigate up, down, left, and right. A center icon enables you to quickly return to the last result. Beneath the arrows, a sliding scale separates a plus and minus sign. Slide the scale up to zoom closer and slide it down for a view from further out. Depending upon the geographic area featured in the map, the zoom can range from 5,000 miles out to just 50 feet.
5	Alternate Map Views—In addition to the traditional map view, Google provides one-click access to several powerful tools. A Satellite view provides clear images from above, Street view (for some areas), Traffic view (for some areas), and Terrain view. A More box reveals options to display Photos and Wikipedia entries corresponding to your location. I expect that video and other options may be added here in the future. These are discussed in greater detail on the following pages and can be accessed by using the links located in the upper right corner of the map image (shown in close-up view at the bottom of the previous page).

Alternate Views—Map & Satellite Views

Map View appears at top. Satellite View with street labels visible is shown at bottom.

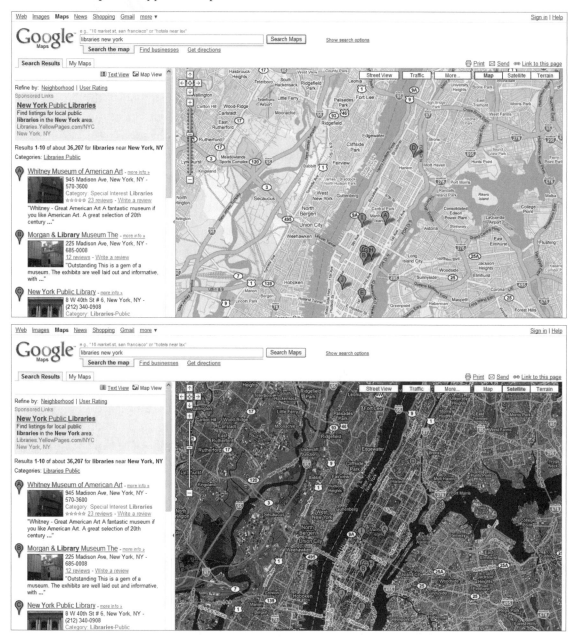

Alternate Views—Satellite Close-up & Text View

Closer Satellite View appears at top with Info Window. Text View results appear at bottom.

Text Listings

Below is a close-up view of the sample text listings that result from a Google Maps query. Results may sometimes appear with thumbnail photos as part of their description. You can determine the keywords used in the original query by looking for any words appearing in bold text. In this example, the query was ***new york libraries***.

Links within this section allow you to switch between a full-screen *Text View* or the default *Map View*, whichever you find more convenient for viewing.

Results can be refined via text links by *Neighborhood* or *User Rating*. Both links will expand the window with further options to reduce results to something you find more relevant.

Sponsored Links, if any, will appear highlighted in a light-blue background.

Typically, one link is placed above the natural listings and one or more may appear below the last natural result.

Each result is assigned a letter balloon that also appears on the map image. Clicking a letter or the result title will show an Info Window (an example of which is shown below).

Navigation and Magnification

The zoom and directional navigation icons, shown at right, help users move around the map, as well as zoom in for a closer view. Clicking on the plus sign will increase the magnification, while clicking on the minus sign will have the opposite effect. You can also use your cursor to drag the icon up or down anywhere on the scale of magnification. The closest zoom level is approximately 50 feet and the furthest is about 5,000 miles. This same navigational element appears in the upper left corner for most views—Street View, Traffic, More, Map, Satellite, and Terrain.

The more advanced Street View, currently available for select portions of more than half of the fifty states in the United States, provides a 360-degree virtual street-level tour of the corresponding map. This is an amazing addition to Google Maps. You can view a Google demonstration of Street View at: <http://books.google.com/help/maps/streetview/> or you can explore by clicking Street View and a camera icon.

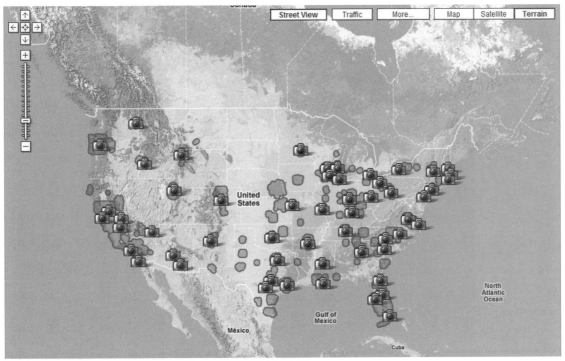

Street View Map—Each camera icon in the Street View map above indicates an area of the United States currently photographed and available through this engaging feature. Click a camera icon to explore.

Street View

The above image is from Google Maps Street View and shows the main entrance of the LDS Family History Library located in downtown Salt Lake City. The clarity of these images is so good that you can almost recognize individuals waiting to cross the street.

Panoramic City Views

To access a Google Maps Street View and take a panoramic tour of different parts of the world included in Street View, follow the steps below:

1. Access Google Maps by clicking the Maps link from the Google homepage.
2. For easiest viewing, click the Terrain box located in the upper right corner of the visible map of the United States.
3. Once the Terrain map is in view, click the Street View button found just a few boxes to the left of the Terrain button you clicked in Step 2. (While coverage is rapidly expanding, this feature is not available for all parts of the world, but keep checking.)
4. Click on a camera icon representing an area you would like to tour in the Street View mode. (A bubble window will prompt you to zoom in a bit closer.)

5. Roads highlighted in blue are those visible through Street View. The yellow man icon represents your current location on the map; you can click and drag him anywhere that you see a blue highlighted road.

6. A mid-sized box will appear on your screen displaying images of the road. Click the text link at the upper right to view the road at Full Screen.

7. Navigation controls in the upper left corner of the Street View box allow you to zoom and rotate. Arrows also appear as an overlay with a yellow line on the image itself; click or slide your cursor to begin exploring the Street View panoramic views.

Direct Addressing in Google Maps

Most genealogists will spend at least some of their time looking for their ancestors in census records. Although the information recorded varies from place to place and year to year, many census returns include a house number and street address, as well as a city or town name. Certainly the current map featured on Google will be quite different from when your ancestor lived there, but it may be helpful to search for the address and view the map and satellite image for the surrounding neighborhood. How far was it to their place of employment? How far away was their church? Don't forget, our ancestors weren't as mobile as we are today. Once you have located the address, you can obtain exact driving directions with approximate time and mileage from your location—or from any other location—with just one click of your mouse.

> Take a moment and point your browser to Google Maps. Using the search box at the top of the page, try to locate each of the places you have lived during your lifetime. Use both the Map View and Satellite View. This is one of the best ways to become familiar with the navigation of Google Maps—especially because you will already be familiar with the area being searched.
>
> **Google It!**

In the example shown below, you can see how using a direct address in combination with the Satellite view of Google Maps can help pinpoint a location of interest for your family. By using the zoom feature, you can clearly see that a cemetery is located in the lower right corner of this image. That corresponds exactly with the background image of several older black and white family snapshots taken from the front yard of the family home.

1930 Census Address—In the example pictured above, a street address was taken from the 1930 U.S. Federal Census for ancestors living in Waterbury, Connecticut. Although the home was taken by eminent domain in the 1950s to make way for an interstate highway, Google Maps still pinpoints the proper location where the home was once located.

Special Relevance for Genealogists

In addition to being an extraordinarily useful tool in general, several features within Google Maps can be used with a special focus for genealogists. Google's underlying technology called Google Local is perfectly suited for place-name research. Whether you are trying to identify cemeteries, churches, libraries, newspapers, or town offices in an unfamiliar part of the world, consider using Google Maps to generate a list of possible sources.

The following queries are examples of how you can use Google Maps to save time in locating one or more sources critical for your research in a particular geographic area.

- town offices hartford ct
- churches **in** rochester ny
- cemeteries **near** oswego ny
- libraries **loc:** boston ma
- vital records 06708

All five examples above can be used to find specific source types commonly used as resources for genealogists. If you know you will be traveling to another city for some other reason and wonder if there are any places of genealogical interest, you can submit the query shown below and explore the categories and results that follow.

- genealogy **near** boston ma

Local business results for **cemeteries** near **Oswego, NY**

A. Catholic **Cemetery** of St Peter - maps.google.com
379 E River Rd, Oswego - (315) 343-5002
Directions and more »

B. Sugar & Scanlon Funeral Home - maps.google.com
147 W 4th St, Oswego - (315) 343-6941
Directions and more »

C. Riverside **Cemetery** - maps.google.com
4024 County Route 57, Oswego - (315) 343-7691
Directions and more »

More results near **Oswego, NY** »

Customizing Google Maps

In addition to using Google Maps as a research tool, those of you who wish to explore this tool further will find an exciting range of customization features perfectly suited for family history. You can create either public or private maps tied to your particular family lines. To use these features, you will need a free Google account (as discussed elsewhere in this book) and must be signed in.

In the example shown below, I created a customized map corresponding to one of my family lines. I have chosen to share this map online, enabling it to be viewed by others with ties to this same family or region. The map allows you to mark locations with an electronic thumbtack, trace routes, or highlight an entire area. You can also append related photos or video that may already be stored online.

If you create custom maps for public viewing, be sure to remember the importance of keywords as discussed in earlier chapters. Use of proper keywords will enable others to find your map, so include surnames and place names that correspond to the topic of your map. More details for customizing your map for genealogy will be found online at <www. GoogleYourFamilyTree.com>.

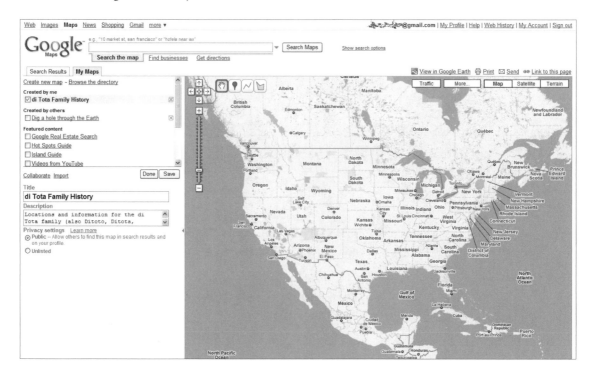

1-800-GOOG-411 (that's 1.800.466.4411)

What could be better than Google Maps on your desktop? Well, imagine a similar voice-activated feature for your phone and you've got the idea. Goog411 is a powerful voice-activated service available around-the-clock via a toll-free phone number (United States and Canada only). Simply place the call, specify the desired city and state, provide the business name or category and Google responds with matching results. So, whether you're looking for a genealogy library, hotel or restaurant, try Goog411.

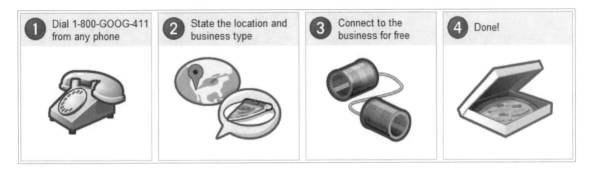

Goog411 Step-by-Step

1	**Dial 1.800.GOOG.411**—That's **1.800.466.4411** (The call is being recorded.)
2	**What City and State?** You can say a city and state (e.g., Boston MA), just a city (e.g., Boston), or say or type a five-digit U.S. zip code. You can clear this query and start over at any time with the voice command "Start over."
3	**What Business or Category?** You can say the name of a specific business (e.g., Ray's Pizza) or a general category (e.g., Chinese takeout)
4	**Searching › Top 8 Results**—Goog411 responds with the top eight results, reading names one by one. They give clear voice instruction; to select, you say or press the number corresponding to the listing you wish to explore.
5	**Selected Results**—Goog411 can either connect you directly or it accepts the voice commands for "Details" or "Go back." Details include address and phone read twice in succession. You can also have the details or a map sent to you by saying "Text message" or "Map It," if you are calling from a mobile phone.

Voice commands include: Start Over, Go Back, Connect, Details, Text Message, Map It. For a complete Q&A, visit <http://mobile.google.com/support/bin/topic.py?topic=12594>.

CHAPTER 11

Google Earth: The World on Your Desktop

In the previous chapter, I mentioned a fascination with maps shared by genealogists worldwide. With that fascination in mind, how can I possibly describe the reaction of family historians when they learn about Google Earth for the first time?

I first wrote about Google Earth in 2006, starting with both an apology and a confession. The confession was simple enough—I'm addicted to Google Earth. In contrast, the apology was a bit more complex—part encouragement and part warning, but also directed toward Google Earth. More than two years later, these same words of encouragement and warning hold true. If you have not yet tried Google Earth, you are missing out on one of the most extraordinary free applications available online! But be forewarned, you will quickly develop an addiction to virtual world travel, which may mean you'll have less time to pursue your family history. Certainly these comments are made tongue-in-cheek, but for genealogists, the only tools better suited for learning about any destination in the world are your passport and credit card.

Many of us know Google as the company that set the standard for how information is found on the Internet. Over the last few years, we've all grown accustomed to the sparse white homepage with simple search box and colorful logo. Type a few words and within seconds, we're presented with more results than we sometimes know what to do with—articles, photographs, news, video, books, blog postings, and much more. Google Web Search is just the beginning; I encourage you to also explore the dozens of products that are just a click or two away from that familiar Google homepage—a highlight of which is Google Earth.

What is Google Earth?

Google's description of this service is simple enough: "Explore the world from your PC." Also billed as "a 3D Interface to the planet," Google leverages the three-dimensional graphics capabilities of most computers to present a very visual and fun interface to the entire surface of the Earth, as well as a corresponding astronomical view of the sky. In genealogical terms, this is a free application that allows you to search for any location in the world where your ancestors may have been and then view clear detailed images of that place from your own computer.

Accessing Google Earth

As with Google Maps and other services discussed in this book, there are many different uses for Google Earth, but my focus will be on those features that add the most benefit to researching or documenting your family tree. The product is a powerful combination of satellite imagery, aerial maps, street maps, and Google's advanced search technology wrapped in a visual interface that truly puts the world at your fingertips. Adding the stars of the sky is just a bonus.

The basic version of *Google Earth* can be downloaded and installed free for use on most computers. Older computers or home computers with certain graphics cards may have difficulty running the application, but most will find the download, installation, and use to be an extremely easy process. If you have advanced mapping needs, *Google Earth Plus* ($20) adds support for GPS devices, as well as more powerful printing and other features. A high-end version called *Google Earth Pro* ($400) is available for professional and commercial use. This chapter will focus solely on the features available in the free application, but don't let the lack of a price tag fool you. There is a lot of power in this offering and we're lucky to have access to it for free.

Installing Google Earth

 **1**	**Google Earth Main Page**—You can access the main Google Earth page by searching for it from the Google homepage or by typing the address directly into the address bar of your browser software: <http://earth.google.com>.
2	**Download Application**—On the main Google Earth page, use the *Downloads* link located in the upper left corner of the page. A graphic download button may also appear elsewhere on this page; both point to the same download process. Follow the on-screen installation instructions through to completion.
3	**Launch Google Earth**—Click on the blue and white Google Earth globe icon that should appear on your desktop following installation.

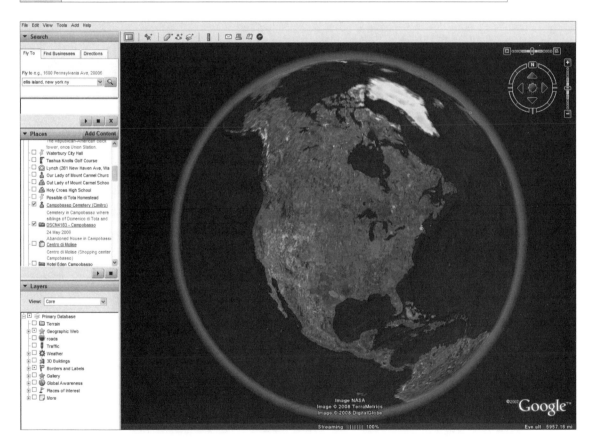

Getting Started

As you launch the *Google Earth* application on your computer, you should see a screen similar to the one displayed on the previous page. Before discussing the application itself, let's take a detailed look at the screen layout and navigation elements that will be your keys to successful travel.

The primary *Google Earth* screen is divided into two main sections. The search features and commands are organized in a left-hand column and the remaining larger portion of the screen is dedicated to a visual rendering of the earth itself. The width of each section can be changed as needed.

As with most software programs, there are several different ways to access most commands and features of *Google Earth*. A main menu appears at the top of the screen and each of six options expands to reveal related sub-commands. As your familiarity with the application grows, you will likely use many of the intuitive shortcut commands that have been built into the product. Just above the globe, a small toolbar also appears with icons representing certain frequently used commands (e.g., Hide/View Sidebar, Add Placemark, Print, Switch between Earth and Sky, etc.) The page displays a great deal of information; the trick is understanding the display layout.

Search (Fly To, Find Businesses, Directions)

It is not surprising that Search is the cornerstone of the *Google Earth* application. Located in the upper left corner of the screen is a search interface offering three basic options. Similar in functionality to Google Maps discussed in the previous chapter, you can search for an exact street address (e.g., 1600 pennsylvania ave, washington dc), a geographic location (e.g., rome italy) or in some cases just the name of a landmark (e.g., statue of liberty). The underlying search technology of Google Local also enables you to submit general queries, allowing you to select from a range of possible results found (e.g., hotels near boston).

In the example shown and enlarged at right, the query '***hotels near boston***' generates a number of natural and sponsored listings. Natural listings include address and phone and are assigned a letter corresponding to a marker, which appears superimposed above the Google Earth image.

In addition to a Search box, the left navigation column includes sections for Places and Layers. You can change the height of each column, as desired, by placing your cursor along the bottom edge of a section then dragging it up or down to achieve the desired view. Each section can also be collapsed or hidden entirely by clicking on the small downward triangle to the left of the section label. The triangle will change direction, pointing to the right to indicate that the content has been hidden from view. To expand, simply click again and the box will expand to reveal the hidden content.

Places

Below the Search box, you should see a section labeled Places. This is your list of saved places or favorites found while using *Google Earth*. Initially this section will be empty, but

Places   Add Content

- ☐ 🔺 Our Lady of Mount Carmel Church
- ☐ 🔺 Out Lady of Mount Carmel School
- ☐ 🔺 Holy Cross High School
- ☑ 🔻 Possible di Tota Homestead
- ☑ 🔻 Campobasso Cemetery (Cimitro)
  Cemetery in Campobasso where siblings ☐
  Domenico di Tota and others are buried.
- ☑ 📷 DSCN4183 - Campobasso
  24 May 2006
  Abandoned House in Campobasso
- ☑ 🔻 Centro di Molise
  Centro di Molise (Shopping center in
  Campobasso)
- ☑ 🔻 Hotel Eden Campobasso
- ☑ 🔻 Monforte Shopping Center
- ☑ 🔻 Nicola Gianfagna
  Home of Nicola Gianfagna, next to Tiberio

▶ ■

Layers

View: Core

- ☐ 📚 Primary Database
  - ☐ 📁 Terrain
  - ☐ ⭐ Geographic Web
  - ☐ 🛢 roads
  - ☐ 🚦 Traffic
  - ☐ ⚙ Weather
  - ☐ 🏢 3D Buildings
  - ☐ 🏴 Borders and Labels
  - ☐ ⭐ Gallery
  - ☐ 🌐 Global Awareness
  - ☐ 🏴 Places of Interest
  - ☐ 🗂 More

before the end of this chapter, you will learn how to add places to this list for quick access during future sessions.

You will certainly appreciate the ease with which a collection of links can be developed, marking the geographic locations of family homes, cemeteries, churches, libraries, and other destinations worldwide.

Layers

The third component on the left navigation column is a selection of labels and markers that can be applied as layers are superimposed above the Google Earth image. The simple checkbox toggles each layer on or off, depending upon preference. Markers include a wide variety of options, including banks, gas stations, golf courses, places of worship, roads, terrain, and much more. Take a moment to toggle one or more labels on and off to see how they work.

Google Earth Toolbar

Just above the Google Earth globe is a small toolbar with the following icons (from left to right):

- **Sidebar**—Toggles the sidebar elements on and off
- **Add Placemark**—Adds an icon to your Google Earth visual and saves to your Places
- **Add Polygon**—Defines an area on the map and saves a detailed description
- **Add Path**—Define a path on the map and saves a detailed description
- **Add Image Overlay**—Creates an overlay with detail for an area of the earth
- **Show Ruler**—Measures the distance between two points or along a specified path
- **Email**—Sends an email of your current location from within Google Earth

- **Print**—Prints search results, graphic view, or selected folders
- **View in Google Maps**—Launches Google Maps centered on the current image
- **Switch between Sky and Earth**—Toggles between Earth view and Sky view

Using Google Earth

While it may at times seem like you're looking at a real-time view of the earth, the visuals used in *Google Earth* are actually a composite of tens of thousands of individual photographs taken by satellite and aircraft. Each individual image is no more than three years old and the entire collection is digitally stitched together to present a comprehensive view of the earth. Individual images are updated on a rolling basis, so there is no reliable way to determine the precise date for any single point on the map. Currently, the entire world is represented by medium-resolution imagery and terrain data, but higher-resolution images are available for most major cities in the United States, Canada, the UK, and Western Europe. Even though Google does not currently claim to have high-resolution images for other locations, I was pleasantly surprised to find them for parts of Australia, South America, and elsewhere. This is great news for users because it is evidence that Google is continuing to improve its high-resolution coverage of the entire world.

The medium-resolution images are sufficient to see major geographic features—hills, mountains, oceans, lakes, rivers, and deserts—as well as man-made developments such as towns, although detail for individual buildings is lacking. The high-resolution images, however, will quickly reward you with amazing detail for buildings and other man-made objects. The resolution is clear enough to see cars on the road, but not individual people.

Compass Navigation

In the upper right corner of the screen, you will find a compass-like navigation element to control your movement around Google Earth. When not in use, it appears as a simple compass pointer, but when you slide your cursor nearby the full set of controls comes into view (as shown in the image on the next page).

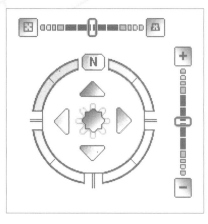

Sliding the horizontal control left or right changes the 3-D orientation of your image. A similar control along the right changes the magnification—slide up to zoom in, slide down to zoom back out. Arrows pointing up, down, left, and right will nudge the image in the corresponding direction. The object in the center of the circle acts as a joystick and can be maneuvered more precisely in any direction. Lastly, if you place your cursor on the outer edge of the circle and slide in any direction, you can rotate the image to any alignment you desire for better viewing. The image below shows an aerial view of the Australian Sydney Harbour Bridge (and shadow) as well as the famous Sydney Opera House (lower left corner of the screen).

Magnification / Zoom

One of the more exciting features of *Google Earth* is the ability to zoom in and out, allowing closer inspection of certain locations and landmarks. Once you become accustomed to an aerial view, you will enjoy inspecting world famous landmarks as well as the towns where your ancestors lived. Depending upon the location you are trying to view, the level of detail may vary. Google reports that most areas are covered to at least fifteen meters resolution (about fifty feet). Cambridge, Massachusetts, and Las Vegas, Nevada, are among the cities with the highest resolution available. These cities have images with resolution reported to be fifteen centimeters (approximately six inches).

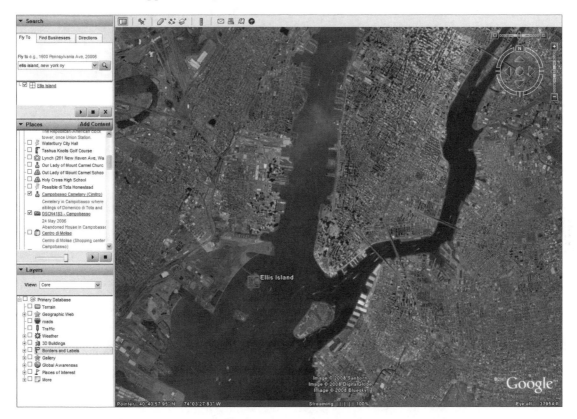

Zoom—The images on this and the next page show a view of Ellis Island in New York Harbor with different levels of magnification. In the image above, Manhattan is clearly visible with Ellis Island, Liberty Island, and Governors Island coming into view. The image shown on the top of the next page features a closer view with all three islands and ferry traffic visible. The third image, bottom of next page, has been rotated slightly to the east and is centered on Ellis Island.

As a genealogist, you will appreciate the ability to view cemeteries where family members are buried. In some cases, you will be able to mark the approximate location of individual graves.

Quick Tour

The quickest way to develop a familiarity with *Google Earth* is to simply type a location name into the search box located in the upper left corner of your screen. There are three tabs—Fly To, Find Business, and Directions. Using the Fly To tab, you can enter a specific location name (e.g., boston MA) or for some well-known tourist destinations, you can enter the name of a landmark and Google will go directly to that location. Try typing **empire state building** and press Enter, then sit back and enjoy a few seconds of virtual flight.

Visiting Landmarks with *Google Earth*—Many world-famous landmarks can be accessed in seconds using *Google Earth*. Type the name into the search box and the application will quickly bring you to the location in question (e.g., Empire State Building, Eiffel Tower, Red Square).

Google flies you to your destination and will simultaneously zoom in close enough for you to see details of your intended search target—in this case, the Empire State Building in New York City, between 33rd and 34th Streets and 5th and 6th Avenue. At first, it may take a while to become acclimated to the aerial view, but within a short time, you will easily navigate around this and other cities with the click and slide of your mouse.

The search results will often find several listings that match your query as entered and they will be listed in the space immediately below the search input box. Click on the first search result (letter A or the corresponding text link) for a more precise location and to view an Info Window with additional details for your listing. Use the compass navigation described on the previous page to zoom in closer or to rotate the image for better viewing.

Now that you've seen how easy it is to fly to the Empire State Building, take a few moments to explore other parts of the world. Try visiting any place you've lived or a few favorite vacation spots or the towns where your grandparents lived. The goal is to develop a basic familiarity with the navigation elements discussed to this point. Not only will you have fun doing this, but you will appreciate how quickly you master the zoom and pan features. These features will come in as you use *Google Earth* as a new power tool for your genealogy work.

When using any of the search features, you should keep in mind the good search habits discussed earlier in this book. For example, if you want to fly to Canton, Massachusetts, you must specify the state. If you don't, Google will have to guess and may fly you to Canton, China instead. Similarly, if you want to visit nearby Mansfield, Massachusetts, but simply type Mansfield, Google will present you with a range of possible search results from around the world (as shown in the sample graphic below right). You will then need to click on your choice and Google will "fly" you to where you want to go.

Google Local Integration

Google has done a very good job improving the integration between Google Earth and its overall search capabilities on its website. I have noticed many subtle changes for the better when compared with the capabilities I wrote about recently for *Internet Genealogy* magazine.

The greatest benefit you will realize from this tight cross-product integration is a greatly reduced learning curve. If you have spent time using Google Maps, you will already feel comfortable using the features of *Google Earth*. The more time you spend with either application, the better you will become at using both. These same principles will also help you become more proficient at general searches conducted through Google Web Search.

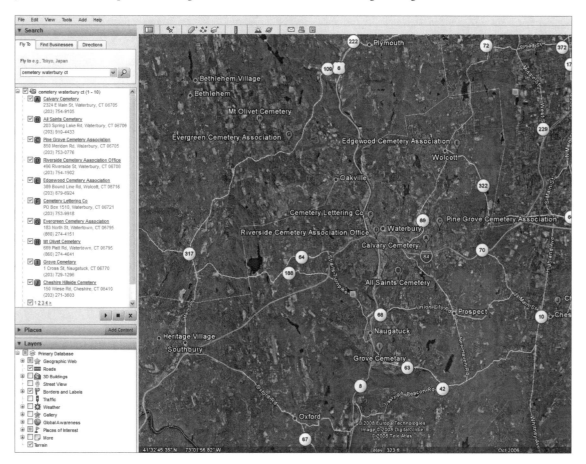

3D Buildings

One of the most impressive aspects of *Google Earth* is an optional layer that adds three-dimensional visuals to the buildings and other landmarks for many major cities throughout the world. Simply point your cursor to the lower left corner of your screen and click the 3D Building label on. Depending upon your computer's memory, you may notice a slower than usual response time as this application puts your graphics card to work.

While this feature is not likely to help you break through any of your genealogical brick walls, it presents the ultimate birds-eye view for any major city. When used in conjunction with the Street View feature of *Google Maps*, you can become familiar with the detailed layouts of certain cities long before you even book your flights.

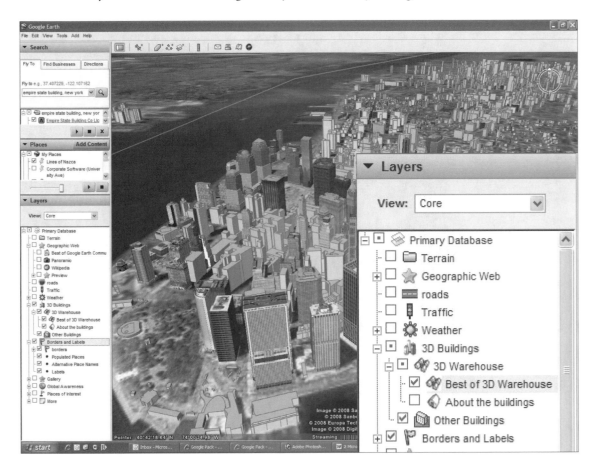

Rome, Italy—One of Rome's most notable landmarks is the monument to Italian King Vittorio Emanuele II who ruled from 1861 to 1878. The view shown above is that found through Google Earth in 3D. Compare that to a photograph I took while visiting the same monument in 2006.

Using GPS Coordinates in Google Earth

In addition to searching for locations on *Google Earth*, you can also input latitude and longitude coordinates from a GPS (Global Positioning System) or similarly equipped device. If you have distant cousins living in other parts of the world, have them send you the coordinates for any important family sites. Later in this chapter, I'll show you how to put place marks on these sites so you can have a customized map of the world.

Google It!

Try It Now!–Finding Palm Island, Dubai with *Google Earth*
Enter these coordinates into the search box located in the upper left corner of your Google Earth screen: 25 07'0.0N 55 08'0.0E . Now press enter. Once the island comes into view, use the zoom controls in the upper right to crop the image into view. Rotate the image slightly toward the northeast until you have a view similar to the one shown below. In the lower left, select the layer for Google Earth Community. Small icons will appear as layers over the image map. Click any icon to view community postings.

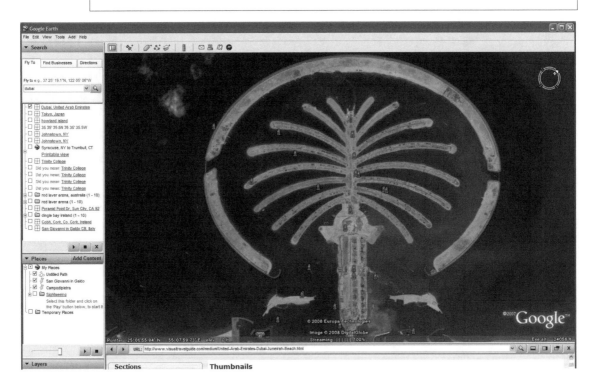

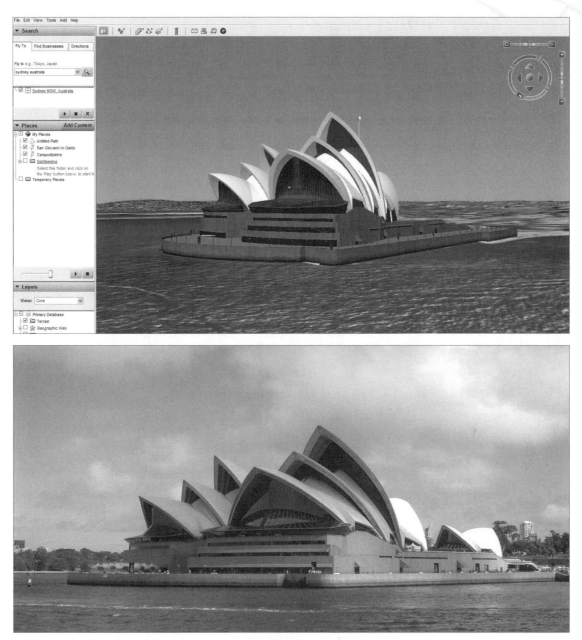

Sydney, Australia—The Sydney Opera House is one of the most recognizable structures in the world. The image above is a rendering from the Google Earth 3D overlay. When compared to a photograph I took in January 2005, you can see how realistic the views are within *Google Earth*.

Google Earth for Genealogy

While conducting genealogy research, we spend much of our time gathering names, dates, and places, but often we never get to visit these places in person. For decades, many genealogists have also been avid map collectors, especially of historic maps that show a town or village at the time their ancestors lived there. *Google Earth* can't step back in time (yet?), but it can bring your maps to life and help you appreciate more about the areas your ancestors called home.

You will also appreciate the integration between *Google Earth* and Google Local (not available worldwide, but surely Google is working on it). If you conduct a search for '*cemeteries near waterbury ct*', Google will "fly" to Waterbury and display lettered circles (representing balloons) for cemeteries and related businesses found nearby. Just below the search box in the left margin, you will see links corresponding to the lettered pins. By clicking on a given name, Google will adjust the image slightly and display a small Info Window with name, address, phone, Web address, and links to obtain directions to or from this location.

This feature can work equally well for finding churches, libraries, hotels, and restaurants. In fact, if you plan to travel to a city for something other than genealogy, but are curious if there are any special genealogical points of interest, you can simply execute a query for '*genealogy near hartford ct*' and *Google Earth* will fly you to Hartford and display locations of interest to genealogists. You could then choose from a number of libraries, historic sites, museums, or vital records offices.

Add Placemark—The image above shows the dialog box for adding a placemark to your Google Earth map. In this example, an approximate burial location was determined from close-up views of Calvary Cemetery, Waterbury, Connecticut. By using the Add Placemark icon from the toolbar, the dialog box collects a title and description as well as other information. The latitude and longitude are automatically populated based on the placement of a corresponding marker on the Google Earth image.

Calvary Cemetery, Waterbury CT—Although the shadows from large trees partially obscure the view, I can easily find the location of my paternal grandparents' gravesite using Google Earth. Many older cemeteries may not have maps available, so this can be a very effective tool to study before visiting a site in person. While a closer view was possible, I found it more helpful to have streets and other landmarks in the view to pinpoint the exact location of certain gravesites.

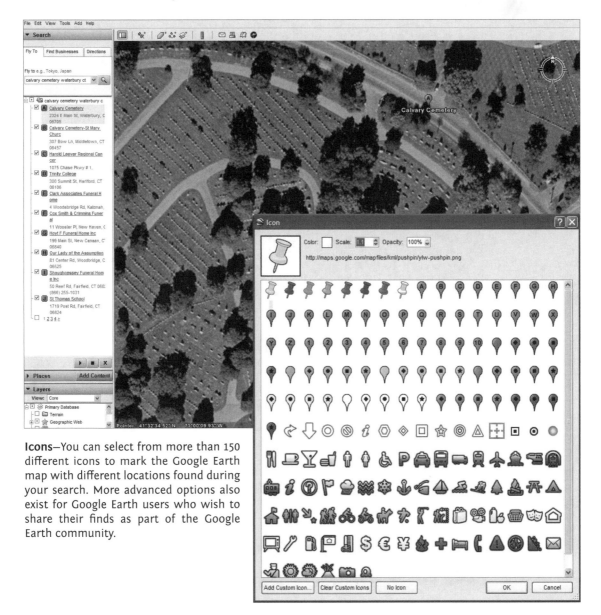

Icons—You can select from more than 150 different icons to mark the Google Earth map with different locations found during your search. More advanced options also exist for Google Earth users who wish to share their finds as part of the Google Earth community.

Sky View

In the same way that three-dimensional city tours take us beyond the genealogical uses of Google, it didn't seem right to ignore the capabilities of *Google Earth* that turn your attentions skyward. From the application toolbar located at the top of your screen (enlarged below), click on the button to the far right that will toggle between Earth and Sky views.

Google will launch a view of the night sky above the location where your computer is located. The navigation, rotation, zoom, and layers all work in the same way as the Earth view. Explore the constellations and keep in mind that this was the road map that Cristoforo Colombo used as he set out to discover the New World.

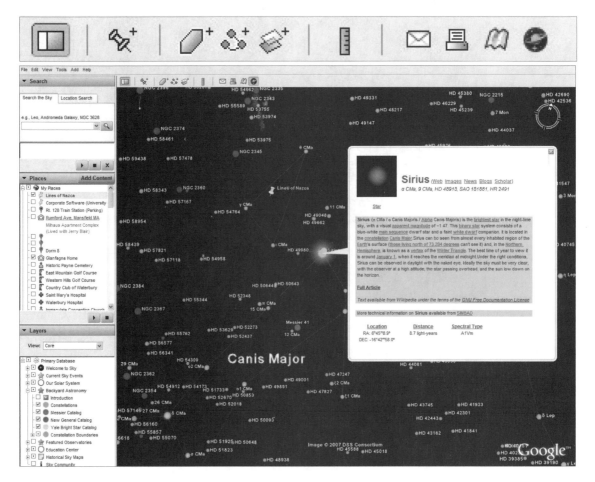

Genealogy Fun with Google Earth

Below is a table of interesting locations I found while playing with *Google Earth* during the preparation of this book. Type the coordinates directly into the Fly To search box to go directly to the corresponding location. Feel free to add some of your favorites coordinates to the list as well.

Location Description	Latitude / Longitude Coordinates	
NARA (New York City)	40° 43'50.38" N	74° 00'13.35" W
NARA (Washington DC)	38° 53'34.23" N	77° 01'19.80" W
The National Archives (Kew, England)	51° 28'51.28" N	0° 16'45.20" W
Statue of Liberty (New York Harbor)	40° 41'21.11" N	74° 02'40.47" W
Ellis Island (New York Harbor)	40° 41'56.96" N	74° 02'22.30" W
LDS Family History Center (Salt Lake City)	40° 46'13.25" N	111° 53'39.64" W
Allen County Public Library (Fort Wayne)	41° 04'40.00" N	85° 08'32.72" W
Coliseum (Rome Italy)	41° 53'24.74" N	12° 29'32.27" E
Great Pyramids (Cairo, Egypt)	29° 58'44.14" N	31° 08'02.09" E
Golden Gate Bridge (San Francisco, CA)	37° 49'07.60" N	122° 28'42.31" W
Yucatan Peninsula (Mixed Resolution)	20° 41'56.50" N	88° 35'48.83" W
Panama Canal	8° 57'48.70" N	79° 34'25.23" W
Easter Island (Chile)	27° 07'50.54" S	109° 20'34.93" W
Mt. St. Helens (Washington)	46° 11'28.26" N	122° 11'40.98" W
South Pole	90° 0'0.0" S	180° 0'0.0" E
North Pole	90° 0'0.0" N	180° 0'0.0" E

CHAPTER 12

Google Notebook

Browse, Clip, and Organize

Given all the new search techniques we've discussed throughout this book, it's no wonder that you are now finding more results online worth saving for further inspection. The trick to all this online research is keeping your results organized—regardless if your research sessions were conducted on your home computer or while visiting a local library or archive.

Once again, it's Google to the rescue. A relatively new service called Google Notebook provides you with the capability to browse, clip, and organize your online research in one central location that is accessible from any computer. This can be quite useful, particularly for those who frequently conduct research from libraries or archives offering subscription-based content not available from home. Think of the Google Notebook as your own central repository for storing, sorting, and sharing the results of your family history research.

A Google Account

Most services described in this book are available free of charge and do not require user registration. Many of the more robust features may require either a download or registration to tap their full potential. If you have not yet created a free Google Account, you may wish to do so now since it is required for access to the Google Notebook features described on the following pages. Creating a Google Account does *not* mean you need to create a new email address. While Google does offer users a free Gmail service (e.g., yourname@gmail.com), your account can be created using an AOL, MSN, Hotmail, Yahoo, or other address as desired.

Accessing Google Notebook

Once you have established and signed into your Google Account, the text links in the upper right corner of your page will display your sign-in email, as well as additional text links as shown below. To access your Google Notebooks, click on the *My Notebooks* link. This will bring your notebooks into view, as shown on the following page.

> ⬚@gmail.com | My Notebooks | My Account | Sign out

Note This & Duly Noted

Once you are signed in to Google Notebook, you can simply use the Internet and Google as you would normally. When searching for something on Google, there is one slight difference you should note. The default format for Google Web Search results now displays an additional link on the last line of each results summary. The text link reads *Note this*. One simple click and you have saved the summary listing as a link to your Google Notebook and the link automatically changes to read *Duly noted*. This enables you to quickly view whether or not you have saved a reference to this link at some point in the past.

In the example below, the top result has not been saved, so the *Note this* text link is visible on the fourth line, following the *Cached* and *Similar pages* links. (See Chapter 2 for more details on these links and the overall format of Web Search results.) Similarly, the second summary result listing has been saved to Google Notebook and the link now appears as *Duly noted*—and is no longer a hyperlink since no action is left to be performed.

> di tota :: Ditota :: **Campobasso** Italia
> Sunday, 02 Mar 2008, The di Tota families of **Campobasso**, Molise, Italy ... HOME »
> **Genealogy** & Family History Research for di Tota, Ditota, di Toto, Ditoto, ...
> www.ditota.com/ - 17k - Cached - Similar pages - Note this
>
> Province of **Campobasso** - Wikipedia, the free encyclopedia
> Map highlighting the location of the province of **Campobasso** in Italy ... Campobasso
> **Genealogy** & History Italian-American Surnames originating in **Campobasso** ...
> en.wikipedia.org/wiki/Province_of_**Campobasso** - 34k - Cached - Similar pages - Duly noted

My Notebooks

Your Google Notebook account resembles an email account in some ways. Folders appear to the left and your content appears in the main body of the page at right. Even those readers new to Google Notebook should have a general comfort level with the information being displayed on the page. The noted entries closely resemble Web Search result listings. Although the colors and format vary slightly, each entry is summarized with a headline, a link (if applicable), and a brief view of the content making up the full listing. To expand, simply click on the plus sign icon to the left of the title and your full listing will appear.

In the example shown below, I have saved an entry into a surname notebook—in this case the surname is diTota. The entry was saved while researching the World War I Draft Registration Cards on Ancestry.com (see image and details on page 219).

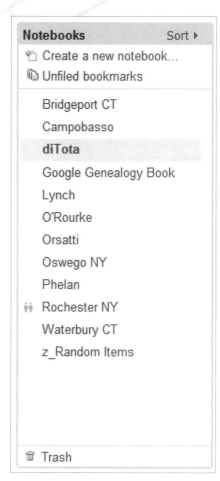

Notebooks   Sort ▸
- Create a new notebook...
- Unfiled bookmarks

Bridgeport CT
Campobasso
diTota
Google Genealogy Book
Lynch
O'Rourke
Orsatti
Oswego NY
Phelan
Rochester NY
Waterbury CT
z_Random Items

🗑 Trash

Tip—In computer applications, I often create "catch all" folders and label them with a leading 'z_' so they will sort to the bottom of an alphabetized list. You can see how this technique was used in Google Notebook to keep that folder separate from others.

Managing Multiple Notebooks

One of many useful features found in Google Notebook is the ability to create and manage multiple notebooks. For genealogists, this is especially useful since you can attempt to mirror the folders or binders you use at home to organize your physical documents and photos relating to your family history. If this is your first time using Google Notebook, take a moment to create a few individual notebooks based on surnames and place names that you frequently research online. To create a notebook, click the *Create a new notebook* text link found in the upper left corner of your page.

In the example at left, you'll note that I have set up several notebooks using surnames and place names. Folders can be sorted alphabetically or by date, depending upon your preference. As you search the Web and save items to your notebook using the *Note it* link described earlier, Google will place the item in the most logical folder unless you direct otherwise.

You will notice that the folder for Rochester NY (at left) has a small icon appearing before it. This icon represents two people and indicates that I have chosen to share the contents of this particular folder with one or more individuals. You can experiment with the sharing option as you become more comfortable with Google Notebook. You can limit viewing to just one other individual with whom you are collaborating on this aspect of your research, or you can choose to make the contents of the folder public via dedicated Web pages that you control. But don't worry; you won't need to know anything about building Web pages. Google will take care of that for you.

Pasting Content into Google Notebook

In certain cases, the content you wish to save to your Google Notebook will be found within the body of another Web page and not in a Google summary results listing. In the example below, where a user is accessing Ancestry.com while visiting a library with subscription access, he or she could highlight the results of a search and save the content to his or her Google Notebook. Simply highlight the desired text on the page, right click, and then select the *Note This* option from the menu that will appear. The content will be placed in your Google Notebook with an appropriate link to return to this page at some future point.

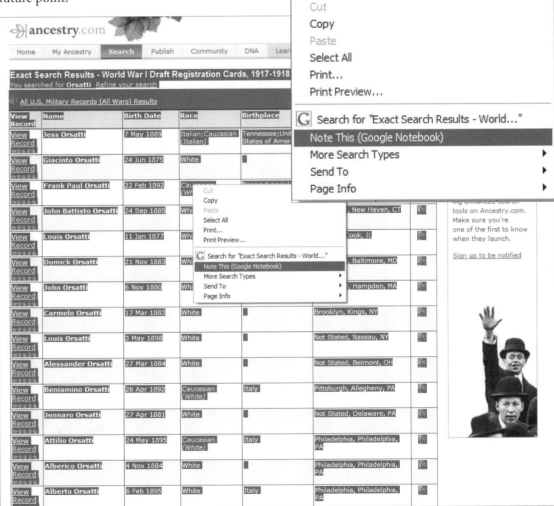

Miniature View of Google Notebook

While you are searching for content on Google, the Google Notebook application stands at the ready. As you add content to a notebook using the *Note this* text link, a small window will appear in the lower right corner of your screen. This is the miniature view of Notebook and will simply display the content being saved and the folder it was saved to. No further action is required. You can access all features of Notebook by clicking on the *Open in full page* text link, which appears in the header bar of this miniature Notebook view.

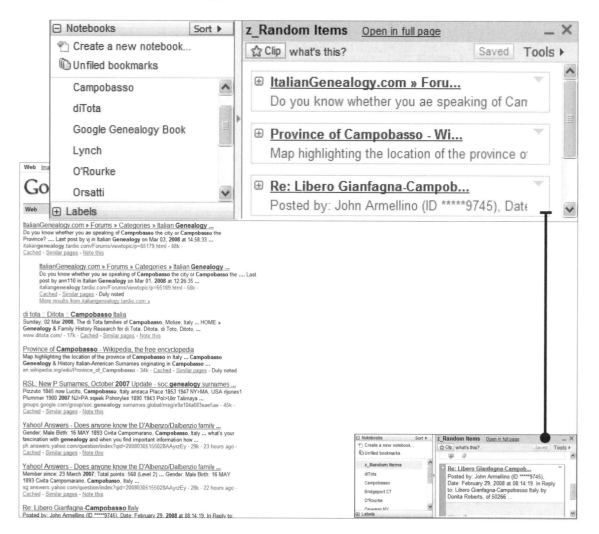

Sharing Notebooks

An optional feature of Google Notebook is the ability to share the contents of a folder with one or more individuals—both active sharing and passive sharing. Active sharing means that you invite others to join your folder as collaborators where they have permission to add, edit, change, and delete content just as you might do yourself. Passive sharing is simply publishing the information and allowing others to view it without collaboration—this is discussed in more detail on the following page. When considering active sharing, you should only invite individuals you know and trust to have collaborative rights to your folders.

Establishing and sharing notebooks is quite simple. In the upper right corner of your screen, click the *Sharing Options* text link. You will be presented with a window similar to the one shown at right. Simply enter the email address for one or more individuals you wish to invite as collaborators. I recommend also inviting yourself, primarily so you can see a copy of the email exactly as it will appear to the other invited guests.

Oswego NY: sharing options

This notebook is not currently shared.
Tip: this icon will appear next to a shared notebook.

Invite Collaborators:
Collaborators may view and edit this notebook. If you add someone who does not have a Google account, we'll help them set one up.

Separate email addresses with commas.

Publish this notebook (make a public web page)
⊙ No ○ Yes...

« Back to notebook   Save Settings   Cancel

Benefits of Collaboration

From a genealogical perspective, collaboration is a great feature when used with the right group of researchers sharing a common surname or place name interest. Rather than rely exclusively upon your own research, you can extend the depth and breadth of content by enlisting the support of others. This is especially useful when a great distance and several time zones separate you from another researcher.

Public Notebooks as Web Pages

If you have often thought it would be useful to have your own Web page for certain aspects of your genealogy but you have limited technical skills, the sharing feature of Google Notebooks may provide a rather simple solution. Google won't do your genealogy for you and can't write your interpretation of content, but Google can do the rest.

Seven Steps to Create a Google Notebook Public Web Page

1	Sign in to your Google Account to access Google Notebook as discussed on page 215.
2	Click the *Create a new notebook...* link in the upper left corner of your screen.
3	Specify a surname or place name that represents the subject of your research. Be concise but also descriptive as this will serve as both the name of your notebook and also the title of your Web page once it is created. After typing your name, click the OK button.
4	You can now type or paste from another application the content for this notebook entry. Keep in mind that you can have multiple entries in this notebook and that each entry will be treated separately on the resulting Web page. (See the example on the following page.) A text handling toolbar provides options for bold, italics, and underlining, as well as text size, font selection, and other formatting options.
5	Click the *Sharing options* text link in the upper right corner of the folder header. (This will initially appear as a light-blue background on your screen.)
6	On the Sharing options page, enter your email along with emails of any others you want to have access to your new Web page. Select Yes to Publish Notebook.
7	Click the Save Settings button, then check your email for the link that will direct you to the Web page you just created. Congratulations!

Viewing Public Notebooks on the Web

After you have successfully created and shared a notebook as a public Web page, Google will send emails to the addresses you specified during the sharing process. As mentioned, you should always include one of your own email addresses in this list so you can receive and save a copy of the email exactly as it will be received by others.

The email will include a long link starting with <**http://www.google.com/notebook/**>, followed by the word **public/** then a series of numbers and letters representing your unique placeholder on the World Wide Web. This is the Web address (or URL) that is needed to access the public view to your folder in the future. You will continue to edit the contents of this page using your Google Notebook application the same as you have done for your private folders. The image below is a sample page created for this example and is visible at the URL listed below.

http://www.google.com/notebook/public/10497925884533131274/BDRAtSgoQ5ZyrtYgj

CHAPTER 13

The Google Toolbar

Having worked in the technology field for twenty-five years, I have tested more than my fair share of software applications in nearly every product category imaginable. As a long-time family history enthusiast, nearly every one of these products has been subjected to my "How can this software help me with my genealogy?" test. It never mattered what the software was originally designed to do. Some of the best-selling genealogy software started out targeting other markets. Many of my first computerized family tree charts were produced using *OrgPlus* software and a very loud Oki Data dot-matrix printer. At the time, *OrgPlus* was the preferred product being used by corporate human resource managers trying to track their ever-changing employee population. Luckily for genealogists that software-maker Banner Blue actually listened to all those tech-support calls during which corporate customers asked questions about multiple marriages and maiden names. A version of that software product would later hit the market as *Family Tree Maker*, one of the most recognized tools in genealogy to this day.

Google may never publish a genealogy toolbar, but in many ways it already has. I strongly encourage installing this toolbar so you can get the most from your online research.

What is the Google Toolbar*?*

The *Google Toolbar* is an optional software application first offered by Google in December 2000 as a free download to help improve your overall online experience. From a genealogist's perspective, it saves time in searching, evaluating, and recording results, and even helping with foreign language translation. The *Google Toolbar* software is available free for both *Internet Explorer* and *Firefox* browser environments.

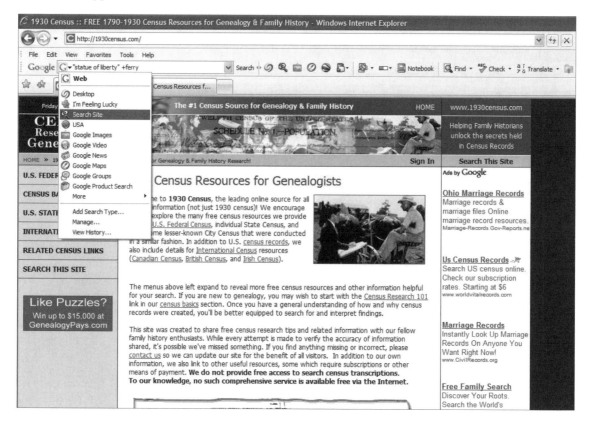

Once installed, the *Google Toolbar* appears at the top of your screen, typically below your browser software menu. Your screen may look different depending upon other software or preference settings you may have in place. An enlarged view of the toolbar appears above.

Downloading the Google Toolbar

Installation and configuration of the *Google Toolbar* is very simple and should take less than two minutes for most users. There are several ways to access the toolbar software. You can either search for **google toolbar** from the main search box and it will be your first result or you can point your browser directly to <http://toolbar.google.com/>. You can also follow these steps:

1. Point your browser to the Google home page at <www.google.com>.
2. In the upper left corner, click the *more* ▼ text link.
3. Click the menu option for *even more* ▶.

The resulting page contains icons, links, and brief text descriptions for a complete range of Google products. The toolbar is listed alphabetically under the Search section (currently the left-hand column). Click the corresponding text link and you will be transferred to the main *Google Toolbar* page.

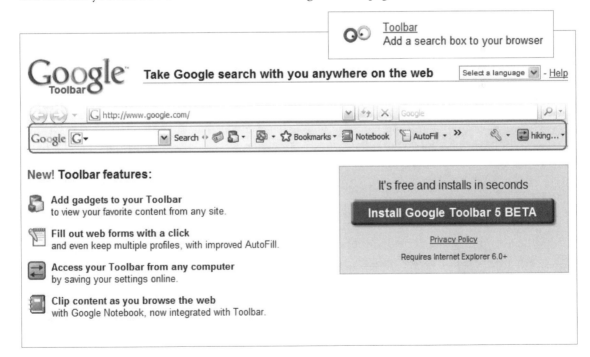

Setting Preferences

After you have successfully installed the toolbar application, you will see it as part of your browser software as shown on the opposite page. In the upper right corner you should see a small icon resembling a wrench. Click on this icon to reveal a menu of customization options. You can follow the recommendations in this book or choose your own, but there are certain tools that will not be covered in this text. My emphasis will remain on those tools most useful for genealogists or closely-related general productivity benefits.

The *Toolbar Options* dialog box, shown above, has a wide range of customization features that will be covered in detail. A quick summary appears below.

Search	In this section, you can customize main search features for the miniature Google search box that now appears in the upper left corner of your browser software. Features such as Search History and Google Suggest can save you some typing for repeat queries.
General	This section allows you to select a language as well as the button text that appears on your toolbar.
Custom Buttons	Here you can specify which search types and custom buttons you want on your toolbar. These can be easily added or removed with just a few clicks.
Tools	Select one of several tools. These are among the most powerful options you have in customizing your toolbar for genealogical use. The Pop-up blocker, Notebook, and FindBar are must-haves, and the Translate tool will help you become familiar with one or more foreign languages you may frequently research.
Auto Fill	This enables or disables the AutoFill capability and also includes a feature to require additional password confirmation for use of credit card information.

Google Search—One of the most popular reasons to download the toolbar application is to bring the Google search box right to your desktop. You will no longer have to go to the site to launch a search. Type your query the same way you normally would and click the desired button. Depending upon your settings preferences, Google can even save a history of your search queries for future use.

Toolbar Basics

The *Google Toolbar* is easily customizable and every user will grow fond of different tools for different reasons. I recommend certain settings based on several years of daily use, much of which has also involved genealogy research. If you decide that you'd like to change a setting, by all means do so. I'll even show you how in the following pages.

Google Suggest—Similar in appearance to your search history, the Google Suggest feature can be selected by checking this option from among those offered through the Search customization tab of Toolbar Options. As you begin to type keywords, Google suggests possible queries based on millions of other queries it has already responded to, starting with characters you have already typed. This can be a useful way to learn what similar words or phrases are of interest to other researchers.

Toolbar Options—Search

As of this writing, there are nearly a dozen customization options under this tab and they represent the most important aspects of how the *Google Toolbar* will work on your machine. Note that my recommended settings are underlined alongside each option below.

- Open searches in—[<u>current window</u>] [new window] [new tab]
- Use Google site—[list of countries...select yours]
- Suggest searches as you type—[<u>on/checked</u>] [off/unchecked]
- Store search history on my computer—[on/checked] [<u>off/unchecked</u>]
- Display Search button next to search box—[<u>on/checked</u>] [off/unchecked]
- Use Google as my home page—[<u>on/checked</u>] [off/unchecked]
- Google as the default search engine—[<u>on/checked</u>] [off/unchecked]
- Show a notification if this setting changes—[<u>on/checked</u>] [off/unchecked]
- Browse by Name in the address bar—[<u>on/checked</u>] [off/unchecked]
- Use Gmail for "Mail To" links—[on/checked] [<u>off/unchecked</u>]
- Up—[<u>on/checked</u>] [off/unchecked]

Toolbar Options—Custom Buttons

The third tab for customizing the *Google Toolbar* includes the selection of buttons to access major Google content types and functions with a single click from your desktop. Google will certainly add to this list as its offerings expand, so check back often to revisit your customization options. The options are enabled by clicking in the box to indicate an on/off position as desired. Additional buttons are available by clicking the *Add more buttons...* link in the upper right corner of your screen. I recommend setting the following to the on position:

- Search Site
- Google Images
- Google Video
- Google Maps
- Google Blog Search
- Google Books
- Google Earth
- Google Button Gallery

Toolbar Options—Tools

Extending the capabilities of the toolbar beyond content buttons, Google offers several special buttons to access applications or functionality ideal for genealogists. The selections I recommend are noted below:

- Pop-up blocker
- Notebook
- Find bar (see page 234 regarding the highlighter)
- Translate (select your desired language)

The PageRank option can also be useful for some users because it indicates how Google values the site you are visiting. PageRank is a proprietary score assigned by Google using a 0–10 scale with 10 being the most desirable. Sites such as <google.com> are a 10, <cnn.com> a 9, <weather.com> has a PageRank score of 8, <familysearch.org> and <ellisisland.org> both currently have a PageRank of 6, <1930census.com> a 5 and so on. Most website developers spend at least a portion of their time trying to improve their Google PageRank because it will help increase their site's visibility in the natural listings.

Toolbar Options

Tool selection

Choose and customize tools that will help you browse the web.

Search	
General	
Custom Buttons	
Tools	
AutoFill	

☑ Pop-up blocker — Stop websites from showing pop-up windows. ⊞ Edit About...

☑ PageRank — See Google's view of the importance of a page. Privacy...

☐ Bookmarks — Access your bookmarks from any computer. ⊞ Edit About...

☑ Notebook — Clip and collect information while surfing the web. About...

☑ Find bar — Find and highlight words on a web page. ⊞ Edit

☑ Spell check — Check spelling of text you type into web forms. ⊞ Edit About... Privacy...

☐ AutoLink — Turn text (addresses, ISBNs, and more) into useful links. ⊞ Edit About... Privacy...

☑ Translate — Translate English words by hovering over them. ⊞ Edit About... Privacy...

☐ Send to — Send part of a page using Gmail, Blogger, or SMS. About...

Help

Toolbar Options—AutoFill

Genealogists will most certainly want to keep the AutoFill setting in the "off" position (leaving the box unchecked). There are too many instances in genealogy where a site is seeking user input for an ancestor's first name, last name, and place of residence. The AutoFill option sometimes attempts to populate these fields with your own information.

The credit card feature can be useful in adding an extra level of security, but it is designed for those who have credit card information stored for use with online purchases. I prefer to not have this information stored, therefore I haven't made use of this Google feature.

If you share your computer with another person, you may wish to establish a profile by clicking on the *Add new profile* link. The profile records name, mailing address, phone, and other contact information typically collected as part of an online registration or purchase.

Highlighter

Among all the useful tools provided by the *Google Toolbar*, genealogists will almost always include the highlighter on their top three favorites list. Included as part of the Find button, the highlighter is an on/off switch that will immediately highlight all words on the current page that match the terms you are trying to find on a page. If you specify more than one word, the highlighter will use different colors for each word making it extremely easy to identify portions of the page most relevant to your search.

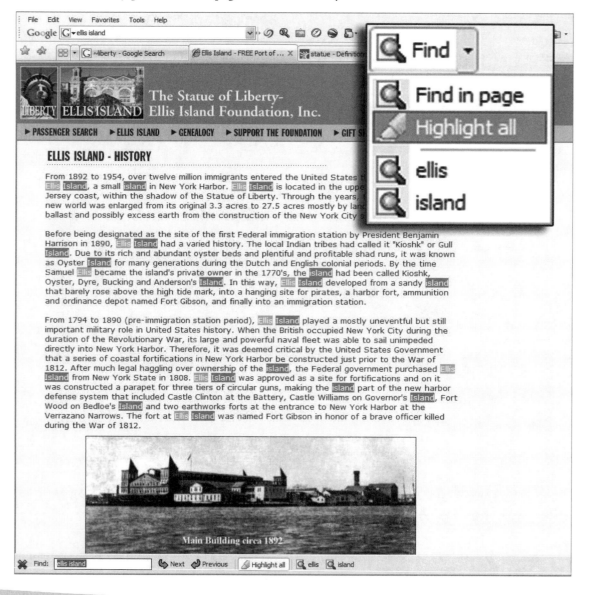

What is the Google Pack?

You may have seen links throughout Google's site promoting the *Google Pack*. This is simply a collection of software programs—some developed by Google, some developed by others and now owned by Google, and the rest developed and maintained by third-party developers. The important thing to know is that they are all free. Remember that Google is very careful about its reputation, so you can be sure the company wouldn't be featuring these products unless they provide real benefit to users.

Google has done an outstanding job of integrating various applications into one easy and seamless install program. If you don't see a text link promoting the *Google Pack*, you can point your browser to <http://pack.google.com/> or just submit a search for **google pack**. Your first natural result will be the link you're looking for. It's possible that you may have previously installed one or more of the software applications included in the *Google Pack*. For instance, the *Adobe Acrobat Reader* software is part of the *Google Pack* and is very popular among computer users—especially genealogists. The install screen should look similar to the one below.

Select the applications you are interested in by clicking the box so a check mark appears. Once you have the boxes selected, click the Install Software button to initiate the install process. Follow the on-screen prompts through to completion.

Which Google Pack Applications Should I Install?

Google has done a very good job developing software as well as selecting partners with products that deliver genuine utility for the user. Depending upon the age of your computer, your needs, and your comfort level in playing with and learning new applications, you may choose to install one or more of the products in the *Google Pack*. More offerings will certainly be added to this list in the future, so you should check back from time to time to see what else Google has to offer. I do not recommend checking every available box and starting the install just because the applications are free. If you don't have interest in an application, don't install it. You can always install later if your needs change.

Recommendations for Genealogists

Given that this book has dedicated chapters to two of the applications included in the *Google Pack*, you shouldn't be surprised that I'm recommending you download them to your computer if you haven't already done so. Following are my recommendations for those products that have special relevance to genealogy or are great general-use programs:

- Adobe Reader (*see Chapter Five—Google Book Search*)
- Google Earth (*see Chapter Eleven—Google Earth*)
- Google Toolbar (*see Chapter Thirteen—Google Toolbar*)
- Spyware Doctor

Google Chrome

As I was finishing the final edits for this book, Google made a somewhat surprise announcement that it was entering the browser wars—a longtime two-horse race between Internet Explorer and Firefox. Safari and others have also claimed a share of the Web browser market, but the two dominant products will now have to fend off an attack from Google's track record for true innovation online.

In less than a week, I have already found a number of features that most genealogists (and, in fact, most computer users) will quickly appreciate. If your primary use for your computer is the pursuit of your family heritage—then you should strongly consider switching to the Google Chrome browser software (sorry, but Chrome does not currently support the Mac platform).

One key element of Chrome is what Google calls the Omnibox—One Box for Everything. The address bar is a combination address bar and search box, with built in suggestions to help speed results. Launching a new tab will display your most recently visited sites, putting you to work quicker and in a more stable session. Check out our website at <www.GoogleYourFamilyTree.com> for more details on the benefits of switching to Google Chrome.

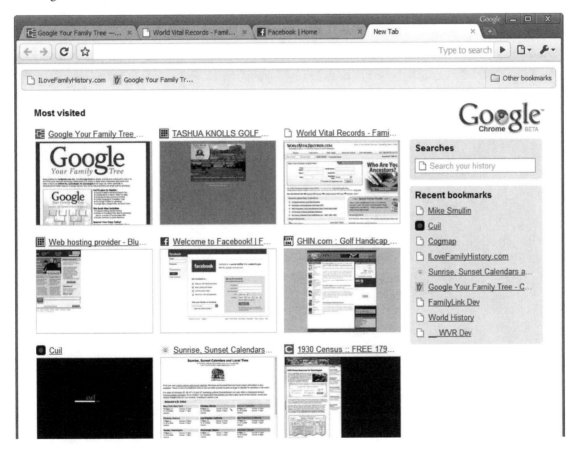

CHAPTER 14

Tips & Tricks

When I started working on this project, my goal was straightforward—to highlight only those features of Google most relevant for genealogy research. Somewhere along the way, however, I realized that I could find a genealogical use for nearly every Google feature if I stretched my imagination. The features, functions, and commands covered in this final chapter represent a combination of education, entertainment, and utility. Many of the topics will deal directly with aspects of family history research, but others may be just as useful in helping you save time in your everyday use of the Internet.

Features discussed on these pages will help you:

- Check the status of flights and airport delays
- View weather conditions and projections
- View the current time anywhere in the world
- Find capitals, currency, and population for places worldwide
- Search U.S. Patent filings
- View full info and links for Web pages
- Find details for movies showing in your area
- Track shipments from FedEx, UPS, and USPS
- Check Vehicle Identification Numbers
- Track stock prices
- Customize your Google homepage

Check the Status of Flights

If you're on your way to a genealogy conference or a family reunion, you'll find these travel-related commands helpful. Type the airline name and flight number for a flight into the main Web Search box and press Enter. If it's a valid flight number, Google will display the most up-to-date flight results using a special result format. Other relevant results may also follow using the standard *Web Search Results* format described in Chapter Two. You can simply type **AA167** (for American Airlines, flight 167, New York to Tokyo) or an abbreviation like **United 210** or **UA 210** (for United Airlines, flight 210, Los Angeles to Washington).

Airport Conditions

To quickly access information concerning delays or weather conditions for a specific airport, type the three-character airport code followed by the word ***airport*** in the search box. Google will provide a specially formatted link followed by other relevant search results. In the example below, a query for ***jfk airport*** checks overall conditions at John F. Kennedy International Airport in New York, New York.

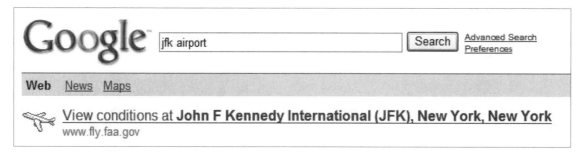

Weather Projections

Now you're hosting the next family reunion and trying to decide if you need to start searching the Web for tent rentals? Weather projections certainly aren't new to Internet users. In fact, the website for The Weather Channel at <www.weather.com> is consistently among the most popular sites online. Google provides its typical quick, no-nonsense approach to getting at the content users want. Simply type the word ***weather*** followed by a zip code or location (worldwide) and you'll be presented with a five-day summary (today, plus a four-day outlook).

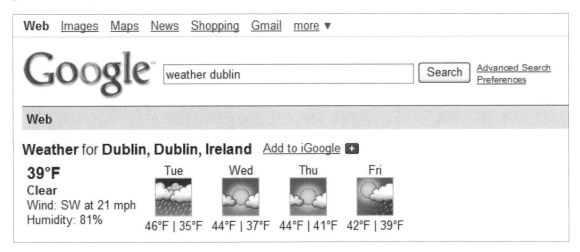

In the example above, a search for the weather in Dublin, Ireland, as conducted from the U.S. version of Google shows the current temperature as 39 Fahrenheit. Using the Google command line as described in Chapter Three, you can enter ***39 degrees F in Celsius*** into the search box to determine the corresponding temperature in Celsius. Another option is to use <www.google.ie> to view weather results as they would be presented in Ireland (using Celsius in this case).

View the Current Time for Any Place in the World

Need to call a cousin in Rome, but not sure of the time difference with daylight savings? Simply enter *time in rome* into the search input box. Once again, Google is one step ahead of you. Unless you specify a more precise location, Google will respond with various locations and times that meet your search criteria, but will list the most likely result at the top of the results page in a larger typeface. If it is Rome, New York, you're interested in, you could also type *time in rome new york* or *time in rome ny*.

2:53pm Friday (CET) - **Time** in **Rome**, Italy
Rome, New York 8:53am EST
Rome, Illinois   7:53am CST

9:51pm Friday (CST) - **Time** in **Canton**, China
Canton, Massachusetts 8:51am EST
Canton, Illinois   7:51am CST

1:49pm Friday (GMT) - **Time** in **London**, United Kingdom
London, Ontario   8:49am EST
London, Arkansas 7:49am CST

Need to set your watch or check the correct time on your computer? You can enter the word single keyword *time* into the search box and press enter. Google will recognize this keyword and present a specially formatted result above the natural results.

Web Images Maps News Shopping Gmail more ▼

Google | time | Search Advanced Search Preferences

Web

12:57am Tuesday (EDT) - **Time** in Berlin, Connecticut
Washington D.C. 12:57am   EDT   Chicago   11:57pm -1 day CDT
Denver   10:57pm -1 day MDT   Phoenix   9:57pm -1 day MST
Los Angeles   9:57pm -1 day PDT   Anchorage   8:57pm -1 day AKDT
Honolulu   6:57pm -1 day HST

Country Capitals

Whether you're working on your genealogy, helping your children or grandchildren with their homework, or watching Jeopardy, type ***capital of armenia*** into the search box and Google responds with a specially formatted answer along with your list of relevant results. Type the name of the country your ancestors were from to view similar results, but keep in mind that Google will provide the current capital, not historic capitals or details for historic countries.

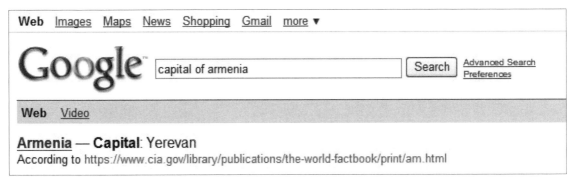

State and Regional Capitals

This technique works equally well for many state and regional capitals worldwide. In the example below, simply enter ***capital of abruzzo*** to obtain the capital of this Italian region. The specially formatted result is followed by ten relevant listings in the typical results format.

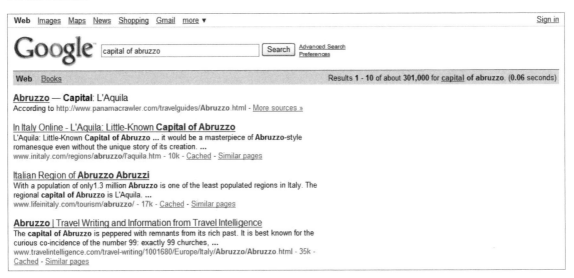

Foreign Currency

Are you planning a trip to the home of your ancestors? Perhaps you're simply curious what currency is used in another part of the world. Google provides a specially formatted response to this query which will appear as the first listing, above the ten natural listings that will follow. Using the main search input box, type ***currency of kazakhstan*** using any country name in place of Kazakhstan. The results will state the name of the currency and an equivalent value in relation to the U.S. dollar. Testing this command using International versions of Google still yields U.S. Dollar comparisons, but it is possible that Google detects the actual location where the query originates from and responds with a currency equivalent in that country.

Foreign currency conversion and other conversion types are discussed in greater detail as part of Chapter Three—Advanced Search Techniques.

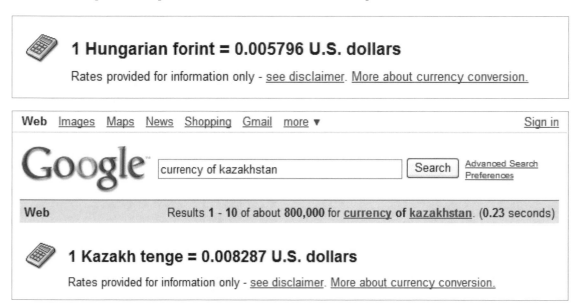

Population Statistics

You can use Google to provide quick estimates for countries throughout the world. Simply type ***population of italy*** into the main Google search box and the leading result will be specially formatted as shown in the various examples below. Other relevant listings will also follow for your query, but if a quick number is all you're after, your search has ended in less than a second.

Italy — Population: 58,147,733 (July 2007 est.)
According to https://www.cia.gov/library/publications/the-world-factbook/print/it.html

Web   Images   Maps   News   Shopping   Gmail   more ▼

Google™ | population of poland | Search   Advanced Search / Preferences

Web

Poland — Population: 38,518,241 (July 2007 est.)
According to https://www.cia.gov/library/publications/the-world-factbook/print/pl.html

Web   Images   Maps   News   Shopping   Gmail   more ▼

Google™ | population of the united states | Search   Advanced Search / Preferences

Web

United States — Population: 301,139,947 (July 2007 est.)
According to https://www.cia.gov/library/publications/the-world-factbook/print/us.html

Web   Images   Maps   News   Shopping   Gmail   more ▼

Google™ | population of the world | Search   Advanced Search / Preferences

Web

World — Population: 6,602,224,175 (July 2007 est.)
According to http://kids.yahoo.com/reference/**world**-factbook/country/xx--**World** - More sources »

Google Patent Search

Did your ancestor have a patent? Maybe one or more of them did, but how would a genealogist ever know without some easy way to search through the archive of patents maintained by the United States Patent and Trademark Office (USPTO). All patents issued in the United States are public-domain government information, so it was only natural that Google would put its considerable talents to work making them searchable online.

Google Patent Search is the specialized tool that enables any user to freely search over 7 million patents—some dating to the 1790s. As of this writing, the collection is current through mid-2006 and includes all patents awarded, but not applications, International patents, or the most recent awards. In the Frequently Asked Questions for this service, Google notes that it is looking to expand its coverage in these areas, so you can expect that functionality described within these pages will represent only the minimum.

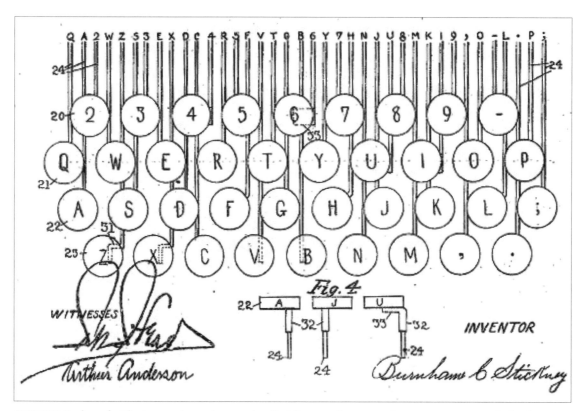

QWERTY Keyboard —The image above shows a detailed diagram from one of many patents awarded to inventor Burnham C. Stickney and the Underwood Typewriter Company. Note the QWERTY keyboard layout common on most computers to this day.

Special Relevance to Genealogists

While patent documents will never have the broad-based appeal that census records, military records, or passport applications have, they can be a tremendous find for those family historians searching for these detailed records. To access this collection, point your browser to <www.google.com/patents> or simply type *patent search* into the input box. One of the first listings will likely be the U.S. Patent and Trademark Office located online at <www.uspto.gov> with the *Google Patent Search* link not far behind.

Google Patent Search employs many of the same commands and syntaxes described earlier in this book, but one surprising exception is a lack of support for the **numrange** command. A special Advanced Patent Search does provide this capability, but it is logical for an experienced Google user to type *strowger telephone 1870..1900*—seeking any patents where the surname **Strowger** and the keyword **telephone** appear for any year from **1870** to **1900**. Google—if you're reading, can you please add this?

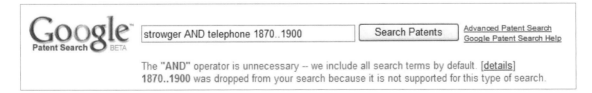

A Family Story Involving a U.S. Patent

In the early 1990s, I drove to southern New Jersey from Connecticut to interview an eighty-year-old relative who had been active in genealogical research for much of his life. His work was done years before the advent of the personal computer. Though his memory and attention span were both limited, he did share some handwritten notes and copies of old documents that hadn't been touched for decades. Several times during our discussion, he became upset and said his family had been "screwed by the phone company," but he didn't say how or why. Pressing too hard for details seemed risky for a first meeting so, rather than get lost on that one comment, our conversation took another direction. He never did elaborate, nor did it seem important enough to include in my notes from the interview, but years later it all made sense—thanks to information found through inspection of documents on file with the U.S. Patent and Trademark Office.

Almon Brown Strowger

Almon Brown Strowger was born in 1839 at Penfield (Monroe County) New York, a town just outside Rochester. He was a schoolteacher, served in the Civil War, and following the war moved to Kansas City, Missouri, where he was an undertaker. It seems that Strowger became suspicious of the local telephone operators, fearing they were directing his calls to a competing company whose owner was married to one of the operators. Although he knew relatively little about electricity or mechanics, Strowger set out to create a mechanical device that would connect phone calls to their intended destination without the need for phone operators as intermediaries.

On 12 March 1889, Almon B. Strowger, a resident of Kansas City (Jackson County) Missouri, filed a patent application for an Automatic Telephone Exchange. Nearly two years to the day, Strowger was awarded patent number 447918 (on 10 March 1891), the first of several patents he would receive for devices dealing with the relatively young telephone industry. In October 1891, Strowger and several partners formed the Strowger Automatic Telephone Exchange Company. Many of the technologies invented by Strowger were still in use until the fairly recent conversion to digital technology.

Although I couldn't keep track of all the buyouts along the way, it appears the technology and patents originally developed by Strowger wound up in the hands of Automatic Electric Company, then GTE, then a joint venture of AT&T and GTE called AG Communications, and most recently Lucent Technologies. In 1896, Strowger had sold his patents for $1,800 and two years later also sold his shares in the Automatic Electric Company for $10,000. Strowger retired to Florida where he died in 1902. In 1916, his patents sold for approximately $2.5 million. Strowger—where had I heard that name before? Oh yes, the relative from New Jersey had been born in Rochester and his mother's maiden name was Strowger. So, it would seem as though his descendants did feel they were screwed by the phone company!

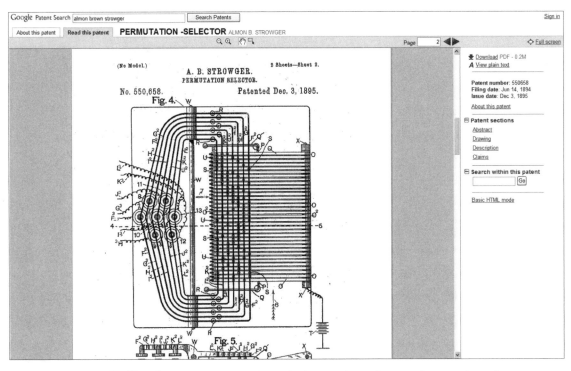

Patent Documents filed by Almon B. Strowger, 1894—The image above shows a close-up view of a drawing submitted as part of the patent filing.

movie:

Let's assume you're heading to another city to attend a genealogy conference and have the evening free. (There, now I've connected genealogy to this very clever and useful command.) The **movie:** command directs Google to obtain up-to-date listings and information for a specified movie in a particular geographic area (U.S. cities or zip codes). The movie name is placed in quotations immediately following the command with the location specified as either a zip code or city/state. Google results provide show times, total viewing time, rating, genre, as well as theater names and links to Google Maps, movie trailer, and the Internet Movie Database (IMDb).

Syntax

movie: "no country for old men" 10017

movie: "no country for old men" rochester ny

Sample Results

The two partial images below show an enlarged view of sample movie results. Note that Google provides results for "today" (the day you search) along with one-click access to view details for tomorrow, the next day, and the day after that—a very simple, but intelligent user interface. This feature is enhanced frequently, so experiment often!

Find Movie Times and Info on Google

The results page shown below includes links to view information on the same movie and location, but for each of the next three days. Aggregate ratings and individual reviews from the Google community are also included (in this case 4.5 of 5 stars).

In the image below, Google presents specially formatted movie information in response to a query for information concerning a movie that is no longer playing in theatres. The syntax is simply *movie: "the green mile"*

Tracking Parcels (UPS, FedEx, and U.S. Postal)

From the Google homepage, you can enter a UPS, FedEx, or U.S. Postal Service tracking number and receive a direct link to details about the status of your shipment. No special command or syntax is required. Follow the link directly to your package tracking page.

Research Vehicle Identification Numbers

Google enables you to enter a Vehicle Identification Number (VIN) into the input search box from its homepage. No special command or syntax are required, simply type the VIN in and press enter. Google will recognize the string of characters as a VIN and will provide a link to basic CarFax results. If any information has been posted online about this vehicle, those results would follow in the basic Web Search results.

Following the link provided by Google, you can obtain free summary results including year, make, model, body style, engine type, and location of manufacture. Additional details are available for a fee.

CARFAX RECORD SEARCH RESULTS

VIN	WVWGA0160FW254781
Year/Make/Model:	1985 VOLKSWAGEN JETTA DELUXE
Body Style:	SEDAN 4 DR
Engine Type:	1.8L L4 FI
Manufactured In:	GERMANY
Search Results:	3 records found in our database What is a Record?

IMPORTANT! The 3 records on this 1985 VOLKSWAGEN JETTA DELUXE may confirm a clean title history or uncover potential problems. Find out by ordering the complete CARFAX Vehicle History Report.

Check Stock Prices

Google provides access to stock information directly from the main search box on its homepage. No special syntax or command is required; simply type a stock symbol into the search box and press Enter to view a results summary like the one featured below. With one click on the *Google Finance* link (above the line graph in the image below), Google directs you to a page with much more detailed news, information, and financial analysis for the subject of your query.

View Web Page Information

In Chapter Two we provided a detailed look at Google Web Search results. From time to time, you may wish to obtain a summary view of all information available for a particular Web page. Google provides an **info:** command that includes the following:

- Access to Google's recent snapshot of the specified page (see **cache:**)
- Link to pages with similar overall content (see **related:**)
- View other pages in Google's index that link to the specified page (see **link:**)
- Listing of all pages in the Google index for this site (see **site:**)
- Google Web Search results for all pages including the page name (see " ")

Web   Images   Maps   News   Shopping   Gmail   more ▼

Google™ [info:www.1930census.com/1930_census.php] [Search]   Advanced Search
Preferences

Web

1930 Census :: 1930 U.S. Federal Census :: 1930 Free Census Resources
1930 Census and other Census information for family history, genealogy, and general research. If you're researching the 1930 Census, we have FREE Census ...
www.1930census.com/1930_census.php

Google can show you the following information for this URL:

- Show Google's cache of www.1930census.com/1930_census.php
- Find web pages that are similar to www.1930census.com/1930_census.php
- Find web pages that link to www.1930census.com/1930_census.php
- Find web pages from the site www.1930census.com/1930_census.php
- Find web pages that contain the term "www.1930census.com/1930_census.php"

Customize Your Google Home Page—iGoogle

In less than sixty seconds, even the most novice computer users can customize their Google homepage to feature content of particular interest. A simple text link in the upper right corner of the page can always take you back to *Classic Home*.

But Wait... There's More!

Click the *Add a tab* text link on your new iGoogle homepage and, when asked for a name, enter ***Genealogy***, then press enter. Google will create an entire tab of family history favorites including *Eastman's Online Genealogy Newsletter,* from Dick Eastman. In less than two minutes, you've customized your homepage and added a genealogy-specific tab full of great information! Now you can tell fellow genealogists that you truly are a Google power user. Happy hunting.

Google Gadgets

In addition to all the tools and commands discussed previously, Google offers an ever-growing collection of Google Gadgets that you can use as part of iGoogle, your Google Desktop, or, if you have a website or two of your own, you can even place the Google Gadgets on your family website for all to enjoy. Some of my favorites are the Google Site Translator, World Clocks, and Birthday Countdown Clock. I find at least one new favorite every few days.

Google Gadgets are developed by a worldwide community of developers so they represent a wide assortment of utility, education, and just plain fun.

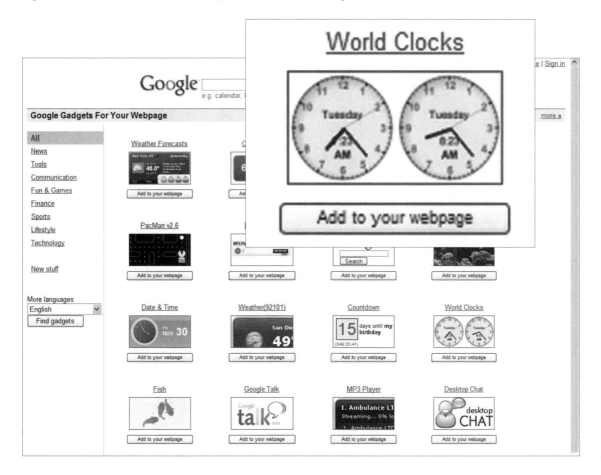

Getting Started In Family History

For those of you just starting to explore your family heritage, you should know there has never been such an exciting time to begin your journey of discovery. The availability of content and tools for genealogy research is better than at any other time in history. As a result, research that once took years to complete can now be accomplished within a much shorter time frame. Your personal computer can help you research and record details about your family, but it can also be used to communicate with others who share your newfound interest.

By A. Smith

I am often asked when I first started working on my family history—and each time I struggle to give an accurate answer. Was it the first time I recorded names and dates on a pedigree chart? Perhaps it was the first conversation with my maternal grandmother about her parents' arrival in America? Or maybe it was my eighth-grade school project during the American Bicentennial? I'll never be able to answer this question with any certainty, but I'm certainly glad I started my journey early in life!

Even if you are "just starting out," odds are good that you already have the basic experience needed to make great progress. After all, it's your own curiosity that will drive continued success in your research. The more you learn, the more questions will be raised, and the more you will want to know.

Genealogy can be a pastime, a hobby, an addiction, a profession, or all of the above. That is entirely up to you. There are no rules other than to enjoy yourself. On the following pages, I'll share some important concepts as well as step-by-step instructions and recommendations for getting started. Before you know it, you will be several generations back and wondering why you waited so long to get started.

Enjoy your journey!

Genealogy Step-by-Step

There is more than one right way to begin researching and building your family tree. While certain activities are easier if they are performed before others, all will help you achieve your goal and can be reordered if you prefer. The following are basic activities that will serve as your foundation for all future family history research:

- Record basic facts that you know about yourself, your parents, and your grandparents. Where possible, also include siblings.
- Try to verify what you have recorded by using information from source documents to compare details.
- Search for additional clues in various sources within your home.
- Interview relatives to capture additional details and family stories that may provide valuable clues in the future.
- Organize and record your findings.

What Do I Need to Get Started?

In many cases, you have everything you need already—a pencil or pen, some blank paper or a notebook, and folders or three-ring binders. I have also found index cards to be helpful in the early stages of gathering information. This next statement may surprise you, but I often recommend staying away from your computer until you have performed some very basic research offline. Once you have completed some preliminary research offline, your time spent researching online will be much more productive.

Over time, you may wish to expand your list of tools to include a digital camera, an audio or video recorder as well as a personal computer, scanner, and printer. If you do not have a computer or scanner of your own, many public libraries are now equipped with a range of technology and knowledgeable staff members who can help you get started.

Who, What, When, and Where?

As you step into the role of family detective, you need to ask at least five questions for each person—who is it, what is the person's connection to your family, when did he or she live, where was he or she from, and where did he or she live? The more detail you can capture in response to each question, the better equipped you will be to round out the story of your family.

Stepping Backwards

An important concept in tracing your family history is to step backward through time. The reason for this is that more recent records for an individual will often provide clues that allow you to find older records more easily. A headstone or an obituary may give a date of death and age, and from there you can estimate a date of birth if none is given. Passenger records may record a date and age at arrival, enabling you to once again establish an approximate year of birth. You may be surprised at just how many events you can chronicle for the lives of each of your ancestors.

What's in a Name?

Names are among the most basic facts you will collect as you begin your research. It certainly sounds easy enough, doesn't it? You will quickly learn, however, that names present some of the most difficult challenges to genealogists. Your search for names will involve two basic types—people and places. Each has its own distinct set of challenges and will yield its own set of unique clues.

Place Names

No matter where you live, I am certain you already have all the experience you need in researching and understanding place names. Have you ever gone on vacation in another country or somewhere far from home? If you have, think about how you answer the question when someone asks, "Where are you from?" If you're in Australia, you may simply say, "I'm from the United States." If that person seems familiar with U.S. geography, he or she may inquire further, "Where abouts?" "Massachusetts," you reply. To your surprise, the person from the other side of the world replies, "My son lives in Lexington, just west of Boston." You smile knowingly and say, "I live in Bedford, just over the Lexington town line!" You can see how many place names can be used to describe a location; it just depends upon the circumstances how the place may be described in words or in print.

One of my great-grandfathers was born in southern Italy. The region is named Molise, the province is Campobasso, which is also the name of the capital city of that region. Within the city (called a *commune*), there are also different sections and the family home was located in an area known as Calvario. Consider the following examples—one from Italy and one from the United States.

	Example 1—Italy	Example 2—USA
Country	Italia	United States
Region/State	Molise	Connecticut
County/Parish/Province	Campobasso	Fairfield
City/Town/Village	Campobasso	Fairfield
District/Ward/Neighborhood	Calvario	Black Rock
Street/Road	Strada Comunale Lazzari	Stillson Road
House Number	50	1234

In the examples above, note how the county/parish/province and city/town/village have the same name in both cases. This will not always be the case, but when it does happen it can present challenges in locating records. This underscores the need to become generally familiar with the geography and history for the places your ancestors lived.

People's Names

In most cases, your ancestors will have at least two names—a first name or given name and a family name or surname. As you begin recording names, you should also try to determine any middle names, nicknames, or alias names used. For your female ancestors, obtaining their maiden names is often one of the first obstacles you will encounter in your research.

Surnames, also called family names or last names, generally have their roots in one of four main areas—occupation, geography, patronym (based on a father's name), and physical features or nicknames. Many surnames also have numerous spelling variations, either intentional or unintentional. In other cases, your family may have changed its surname out of a desire to assimilate to new surroundings. Many European families immigrated to North America, South America, and Australia, and some changed their surnames upon arriving in their new home.

Type of Surname Origin	Examples
Occupation	Cooper—A barrel maker Fisher—A fisherman Schneider—A cutter or tailor Smith—A metal worker, blacksmith, silversmith, etc.
Patronyms/Patronymic	Peterson—Son of Peter McHenry—Son of Henry di Cesare—Son of Cesare Fitzwilliam—Son of William O'Rourke—Son of Rourke
Geography	Churchill—Resides on or near the hill by the church Eastman—From the eastern part of town Rivers—Lived near the river
Descriptive Names	Armstrong—One with strong arms Small—Of small stature Goodman—A good man Broadfoot—A large or broad foot

While this chapter is designed to give you just the basics of getting started, you may have unique challenges with your surname from the very beginning. If your family name is often misspelled, you may wish to become familiar with Soundex, a system developed to help compare names based on how they sound. Conduct a Google search on the keyword *soundex* and you will find many helpful resources included in the first page of results.

Recording Dates

In addition to recording the names of your ancestors and the places they lived, you will also need to record dates of various events that occurred from birth through burial. In some cases you will be able to document an exact date, but use an approximate date until you can verify a more precise date through continued research. Record dates as follows:

- Use the International date format (e.g., 18 May 1884).
- If you are unsure of the exact date, use ABT (e.g., ABT 1884 meaning about 1884).
- If you're sure an event happened before a certain date, use BEF (e.g., BEF 18 Jan 1911).
- If you're sure an event happened after a certain date, use AFT (e.g., AFT 10 May 1908).
- If you believe an event happened between two dates, use BTWN (e.g., BTWN 1880–1890).

As you conduct your research, you will often have dated documents that also include an age for your ancestors. If you don't already have an exact date of birth, you should subtract the age from the year of the document to determine an approximate year of birth.

> *In loving Remembrance*
> *of our Dear ones,*
> *Eliza Phaelan.*
> *Died. Apr 11, 1892. Age 55 years.*
> *Kate Phaelan.*
> *Died. May 14, 1892. Age 32 yrs.*
> *Robert Phaelan.*
> *Died. May 22, 1894. Age 65 years.*
> *Robert Phaelan.*
> *Died. July 29, 1895. Age 3 mo. 14 ds.*
> *John Phaelan.*
> *Died Apr 6, 1901. Age 35 years.*
> *John Francis Phaelan,*
> *Died. Dec 18, 1900. Age 1 yr. 6 mo. 14 ds.*
> *Martin Phaelan,*
> *Died. Nov. 28, 1901. Age 14 years.*

Working with Dates—The image above shows a small slip of paper found among my uncle's possessions after his death. The names and dates provide clues, but so does the handwriting and the fact that all entries appear to have been written by the same person at the same time.

What Are Sources for Genealogy Information?

A source can be almost any person, place, or thing that can provide a clue about some aspect of your ancestors' lives. In nearly every case, you already have one or more sources available to you but you may be unaware of the value they hold from a genealogical point of view. Some sources of family history information include the following:

- Birth certificates
- Business cards
- Cancelled checks
- Census records

- Citizenship / Naturalization documents
- City directories, phone books, social registers, member lists
- Court records (probate, business transactions)
- Death certificates
- Deeds and land records
- Drivers license
- Family Bibles, journals, and other papers
- Headstones and cemetery records
- Letters, envelopes, postcards
- Maps and gazetteers
- Marriage certificates
- Memorial cards, funeral cards
- Military records (draft cards, pension files, veteran lists)
- Newspaper clippings (birth/death notices, social pages, obituaries)
- Passenger lists (emigration and immigration records)
- Passport
- Personal interviews with relatives, friends, and neighbors
- Photographs, portraits, paintings, photo albums
- Published family and local histories
- Religious records
- Resumes
- School records
- Scrapbooks
- Web pages
- Wills
- Yearbooks, alumni directories

Evaluating Source Documents

Certificates of birth, marriage, or death—often abbreviated as BMDs and known formally as vital records or vital statistics (in the United States) and civil registrations (in Canada, Europe, and Australia)—are among the most well-known source documents used in genealogical research. Take a moment to look at your own birth certificate and carefully review all the information recorded about your family at the time of your birth. A birth record will almost always include the parents' names, ages, and places of birth; address;

father's occupation; mother's maiden name; the number of other children born to this mother and the children still living; and other facts.

The vital record shown above is an 1896 Certificate of Death for my great-grandfather. If you review the document carefully, you can find nearly thirty individual elements that serve as clues for some aspect of genealogical research.

Using information obtained from a birth, marriage, or death certificate, you can then check other sources for additional detail. In the example above, the date and cause of death led me to search microfilm records of the local newspaper. The front-page article reported the story of an accidental death under the headline "Falls Four Stories."

It's All about You

Now that you've learned the basics, it's time to get started. Refer to the table on the following page, and the corresponding sections of the pedigree chart. Record your complete name in the space provided as it appears on your birth certificate as well as the date and place you were born. If you are married, you'll record that information as well. If you have siblings, you'll note their names from oldest to youngest. Once you're finished, you'll step back a generation and record this same basic information for your parents, and then for your grandparents. Additional charts are available online for free download at <www.GoogleYourFamilyTree.com>.

1. _____

born: ....

place: ....

wed: ....

place: ....

siblings: ....

....

1.	Record information about yourself in this first section (above). If you are married, consider having your spouse record a similar set of family history information for his or her side of the family.
2.	This is information for your father—also called your *paternal* line. If he has siblings, you should also try to record their names and the order of their birth. The eldest child of this group will be of special interest later.
3.	This is where you record information for your mother—also called your *maternal* line. If she has siblings, also record their names and birth order here if possible.
4.	Information for your father's father (also called your paternal grandfather).
5.	Information for your father's mother (also called your paternal grandmother).
6.	Information for your mother's father (also called your maternal grandfather).
7.	Information for your mother's mother (also called your maternal grandmother).

Parents

Grandparents

4.
born:
place:
wed:
place:
died:
place:

2.
born:
place:
wed:
place:
died:
place:
siblings:

5.
born:
place:
died:
place:

6.
born:
place:
wed:
place:
died:
place:

3.
born:
place:
died:
place:
siblings:

7.
born:
place:
died:
place:

Stepping Back Even Further

Depending upon your age and the profile of your extended family, you may have been able to complete the pedigree chart on the previous page without difficulty. If you are in your twenties or thirties and both parents and all or most grandparents are still living, it's a far easier task compared to the effort required by someone in their sixties or seventies.

Once you have gathered as much information as possible for your grandparents' generation, select a family line you are most interested in researching and step back one more generation. Who were your grandparents' parents? Although you may never have known your great-grandparents, you have eight of them. If you can name all eight without much difficulty, you're in great shape already, but in reality, few beginners can accomplish this task without some work.

The following questions are designed to help you understand the process you should use in identifying another generation of ancestors. You should work backward and assume that a generation spans about twenty-five years. (This is only an approximation.) Think about the answers to each question as they pertain to each of your great-grandparents:

- Do you know where this ancestor is buried?
  - —If not, who in your family is most likely to know?
  - —Did your grandparents have siblings? One of them might know.
- If there is a headstone, do you have a photograph or notes detailing the inscription?
  - —If not, can you easily travel to the burial site or is there someone who can help get this information for you?
  - —Note other family members who may also be buried nearby.
- If you have a date of death (from a headstone or otherwise), do you have a copy of the death certificate and obituary?
  - —If not, try contacting local libraries, newspapers, and the town hall to see if copies of either document are available.
- Do you know when and where this ancestor was married?
  - —Do you have or can you obtain a copy of the marriage license?
  - —Can you identify the first-born child of this marriage?

- Do you know when and where this person was born and where they lived?
  —You can estimate their birth based on death or marriage data.
- What other facts, stories, suspicions, or assumptions do you or other family members have pertaining to this ancestor?
- Do you or any of your relatives have a photograph of this ancestor?

Example of an Official Source Document

The certificate of baptism at right includes the date and place of birth, names of both parents, and other possible clues. This copy of the original entry is dated sixty years after the event occurred.

Interviewing Relatives

One of the quickest ways to gather family information is through personal interviews—either by phone, personal visits, letters, or email. As you tried to complete the Pedigree Chart earlier in this chapter, you may have already called a brother, sister, parent, aunt, uncle, cousin, or other relative for a quick check on one or more facts. Congratulations! You're following your instincts and already tapping an important pool of source material.

To help you get the best results from your conversations with relatives, I recommend the following techniques:

- **Be prepared**—Before each conversation, determine the three most important facts you are searching for and, when possible, try to steer the discussion accordingly.

- **Be thoughtful**—When contacting relatives with research in mind, always work to accommodate their preferences, rather than your needs. If they prefer letters, write a letter. If they don't want to discuss a certain topic, change the subject.

- **Pre-announce yourself**—If you wish to discuss your family history with an older relative whom you have not seen or spoken with for a long time, send a letter or post card to pre-announce a phone call or visit and be sure to mention your reason for calling. This will give them time to prepare for your call.

- **Pace yourself**—You will not finish your family history in a few weeks no matter how hard you try, so pace yourself. Older members of your family may need time to warm up to the concept of sharing some of their long-held family memories. Your patience and polite persistence will serve you well over time.

- **Share**—When possible, share some of what you already know or share copies of documents or photographs. This will generally get a discussion moving along more quickly than a simple question and answer session.

- **Listen carefully**—Don't challenge your relatives' recollection of facts. Let them talk, and listen carefully as you write or record what they say. Remember that there is generally an element of truth behind even the most far-fetched family story.

- **Record conversations**—Always makes notes of your conversations and meetings and, whenever possible, try to get permission from the participant to record your discussion with either audio or video equipment. Make detailed transcriptions of your notes within twenty-four hours of your meeting while your memory is fresh.

- **Send a thank-you note**—Yes, it's a basic courtesy, but a simple thank-you card following a phone call or visit will stress the importance and value of your discussion.

Investigate Family Stories

As you speak with other family members about your common ancestry, it won't be long before you begin to hear family stories. They will vary in length and accuracy, but listen carefully because you will eventually be able to use these stories as research source material. Little was known about my great-grandfather whose surname I share. I had heard the story a few times while in grade school—that Grampa Lynch had been telling jokes with friends, lost his balance while laughing, and fell to his death from a fourth-floor porch. As I began to conduct my formal research years later, this story was one of the first things I searched for. His date of death was fairly easy to find and the death certificate (shown earlier in this chapter) certainly seemed to verify something close to the story. The cause of death was listed as *fracture of skull* and *shock*.

The following entry appeared under the headline "Dashed to Death" in the August 10, 1896 edition of the *Waterbury Evening Democrat*.

Eugene Lynch Instantly Killed By a Fall early This Morning

Eugene Lynch, aged 48 years, fell from the top verandah of the four story block owned by Mrs. Maurice Walsh, 10 Fuller street, at 1:30 o'clock this morning, and was instantly killed. It is not known how he happened to fall. During the early part of the evening he had been visiting with the family of John Leary, who lives on the top floor of the building, and at midnight the family left him sitting in a chair on the verandah. It is quite probable that later he rested himself upon the railing, and losing his balance fell to the ground.

Richard Galway was sitting on the step of his residence at the time and hearing the unusual noise he called over to see what had happened and found the man dead on the concrete walk. Soon others arrived and Attorney Carmody, who lives opposite the scene of the accident, notified Medical Examiner Axtelle, who ordered the remains removed to Mulville's morgue, where he conducted an examination. The victim had a deep gash cut in his head and some of the bones in his body were broken by the fall. The deceased was a widower and leaves four children.

The dead man was a cousin of Mrs. Walsh. The remains will be taken to her house this afternoon, and the funeral will be held at 2:30 o'clock tomorrow afternoon.

Learn to Look beyond the Obvious

In the 1896 news article about my great-grandfather's death, there is more information available than may be obvious at first pass. Whenever you read a news clipping or other source document, read it first to digest the general content, then read it at least one more time to extract all the possible clues you can find. This will take some practice, but you will develop a keen eye for detail over time. The following points are either stated in or inferred from the article:

- Eugene Lynch was born about 1848 (died in 1896 at the age of 48).
- Mrs. Maurice Walsh was a cousin (it might be first cousin, second cousin, etc.).

- Eugene was friends with family of John Leary (who resides at 10 Fuller Street).
- Eugene's wife had predeceased him.
- Eugene had at least four children.
- It's probable that Eugene married in the 1870s or 1880s based on his age and information stated. (Marriage may have been in either Ireland or United States.)
- Likely living in Irish section of town (note surnames Lynch, Walsh, Leary, Galway, Carmody, and the undertaker Mulville).

By looking at local maps for the city of Waterbury from 1896 and also using a city directory to determine which churches existed at the time, it is not difficult to establish the church where the marriage may have occurred. After contacting the Immaculate Conception Church, I was able to verify my assumption that Eugene's marriage had indeed occurred in Waterbury, Connecticut. Eugene wed Elizabeth O'Rourke on 25 June 1882.

Using the 1882 marriage date and knowing that Eugene was a widower at the time of his death in 1896, I now had bookends for a ten-year span to search for a death record. Normally, I would also look to census records, but since the 1890 U.S. Federal Census was destroyed, this isn't an option. A review of the local death records yielded an entry for Elizabeth (O'Rourke) Lynch who died on 06 March 1892. I then turned to the local newspaper and found this entry:

> *The funeral of Mrs Eugene Lynch of 125 Scovill street, took place at 9:30 this morning from the church of the Immaculate Conception. The deceased was a sister of Timothy O'Rourke. The pallbearers were: Edward Flaherty, James Fitzmorris, William Sweeney, Thomas Lynch, John O'Rourke, John Fitzmorris.*

Hopefully, you can see the value of using several sources in conjunction with one another. A headstone may provide a clue leading to a death certificate which in turn provides a clue that can be verified by a news clipping. The news clipping may mention another family member leading you back to vital records, and the cycle continues.

The image above is a copy of the original death certificate for my great-grandmother, Elizabeth (O'Rourke) Lynch, wife of Eugene Lynch. The information from the certificate confirms some of what was found in the news clipping, but also provides an age at death which can be used to approximate a year of birth as 1860. The certificate also includes the names of my great-great-grandparents, John O'Rourke and Honora McElligott.

While vital records (also called civil registrations or simply birth, marriage, and death records) are a common source used in family history research, you should also keep in mind that even these "official documents" can contain errors. An original birth record created shortly after the birth may contain different details than an official extract obtained twenty, thirty or more years after the fact. Even the best of clerks make their mistakes—a letter or number could be transposed, some details appearing on the original may be overlooked when creating the transcribed copy and any number of other possible errors.

Also, if an alphabetized or chronological index was created after the fact, it's possible that your ancestor's record was overlooked during the indexing project, but the record is contained within the ledger.

When reviewing death certificates or obituaries, you need to keep in mind that in most cases, the information being provided about the deceased is being provided by another family member or close friend. In some cases, and individual might write their own obituary prior to their death, but most times the details you will read in a death certificate, funeral notice or obituary will require further verification. A family member may—unintentionally or otherwise—provide facts about the deceased that become part of the official record. These facts can often be verified (proven or disproven) by reference to other source documents. The decedents name may be spelled incorrectly, their age may be wrong—suggesting an incorrect year of birth, and any other number of possible errors. The main thing to keep in mind is that while you may be looking at an official document with fancy script and a raised seal—there is still a chance it may contain incorrect information. Always consider all the facts before drawing important conclusions about your family lineage. If you're not certain, but need to be—then check with a professional. You may need to pay them for an hour of their time, but it can also save you from years of climbing someone else's family tree.

Enjoy the Journey

I certainly hope the guidance shared within these pages will enable you to enjoy your journey as much as I have enjoyed mine. Genealogy is not just about the destination or about completing a pedigree chart—it's about learning the stories that make up the truly unique story of your own family heritage.

Top Genealogy Sites

Who doesn't like free? In this world of "you get what you pay for," the online genealogy market offers a few noticeable exceptions. Before discussing the list itself, let me clarify a few things about free websites versus fee-based commercial sites. The current landscape for online genealogy offers an amazing variety of sites—some free, some partially free, and others available through paid access. It's not the price tag that makes a site good or bad, it's the content contained within as well as the ease with which the content can be found. The process of finding, evaluating, scanning (or digitizing), and transcribing collections of original records represents a significant investment of time, technology, money, and expertise. Add to that the costs associated with creation, ongoing maintenance, and hosting these high-traffic websites and you can understand the need for financial support.

Companies including The Generations Network (Ancestry.com), FindMyPast.com, FamilyLink.com, Inc. (WorldVitalRecords.com), Footnote, and others have a for-profit model with the necessary expertise to bring quality products to market for your use. While free is always good, for-profit isn't a bad thing by any stretch of the imagination. Each of us must judge for ourselves the value of the content based on our personal research needs. But it's important for all family historians to know where they can find some great content and tools online that are freely available—often thanks to the volunteer efforts of other family historians. The list that follows is a Top Ten in alphabetical order. It was hard enough to select just ten sites; I wasn't going to endure the self-torture of trying to prioritize the list too. They're all great, but for their own unique reasons!

Top Ten Free Sites for Genealogy (Alphabetical Order)

- Eastman's Online Genealogy Newsletter   \<www.eogn.com\>
- Ellis Island Passenger Arrival Records   \<www.ellisisland.org\>
- FamilySearch (LDS Church)   \<www.familysearch.org\>
- Immigrant Ships Transcribers Guild   \<www.immigrantships.net\>
- One-Step Search Tools by Stephen Morse   \<www.stevemorse.org\>
- Random Acts of Genealogical Kindness   \<www.raogk.org\>
- Wayback Machine (Archive.org)   \<www.archive.org\>
- Wikipedia   \<www.wikipedia.org\>
- WorldGenWeb   \<www.worldgenweb.org\>
- [insert your favorite here]   \<www._____.com\>

In addition to the sites listed above, I have included additional mention of more than twenty free sites that are sure to be of interest to family history enthusiasts throughout the world. Several fee-based sites are also previewed with Web addresses for your reference.

Be sure to visit the companion website for this book at \<www.GoogleYourFamilyTree. com\> to view updates and additional links to some of the other important sites that may emerge after the printing of this text.

Eastman's Online Genealogy Newsletter

Long before the days of bloggers, Dick Eastman was writing about different aspects of genealogy. A long-time family history enthusiast and technology addict, Dick used his professional background in technology to help organize his family records. As he discussed this fascination with others, he realized he wasn't alone. By the mid-1980s, he was sizing up the new personal computers to determine their usefulness as tools for genealogists.

Over time, Dick began to share his genealogy and technology observations via email with a growing list of followers—including me. And I could always be sure of one thing—Dick was going to call it as he saw it. As technology advanced, so, too, did the newsletter. Today, it's available via email, RSS feeds, or by visiting the blog itself. You can keep tabs on new content, software, events, gadgets, research techniques, scam sites, and much more.

This site can be easily found by conducting a Google search for **_Dick Eastman_** or by pointing your browser to <www.eogn.com>.

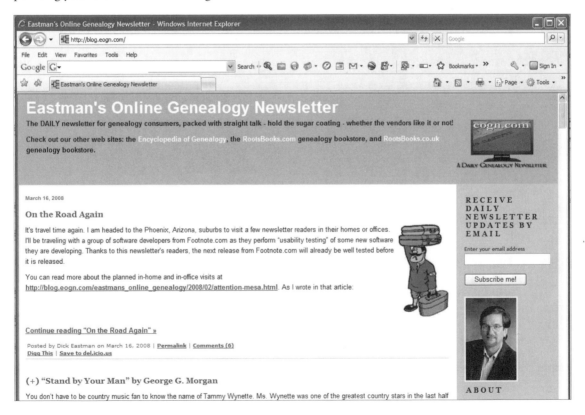

Ellis Island Passenger Arrival Records

This site was officially launched on 17 April 2001 and has been a staple of online genealogy research ever since—with good reason. The site contains passenger list details for 24.1 million arrivals occurring from 1892 to 1924. Passengers included immigrants, traveling U.S. citizens (including several U.S. Presidents), international travelers, and ship crew. An electronic index of names can connect you with digitized versions of the actual passenger manifest as well as ship images and other details. Use of the site and access to all images is free, provided by The Statue of Liberty-Ellis Island Foundation, Inc., a nonprofit organization based in New York City.

Access this site online by conducting a Google search for ***ellis island*** or by pointing your browser to <www.ellisisland.org>. (Note the .org extension.)

FamilySearch

A website hosted by The Church of Jesus Christ of Latter-day Saints (often abbreviated to the LDS Church or the Mormons), this online destination is a must-have bookmark for all researchers, regardless of geography, ethnicity, or religious affiliation. Based in Salt Lake City, Utah, the LDS Church has been preserving and sharing records on microfilm worldwide for decades and continues to make progress in placing its content online.

In addition to the website content, FamilySearch offers a free software application for organizing and charting your ancestors. *Personal Ancestral File (PAF)* is available through a free download and is very easy to learn and use—even for novice computer users and those just starting to research their family tree.

The online resources of The Church of Jesus Christ of Latter-Day Saints can be accessed by pointing your browser to <www.familysearch.org>.

**Free PAF
Family History Software**

Personal Ancestral File (PAF) is a free genealogy and family history program. PAF allows you to quickly and easily collect, organize and share your family history and genealogy information.

Download PAF

FAMILYSEARCH

Username Password Sign In
Register Forgot Password?

Home Search Records Index Records Share Research Helps Library Help

SEARCH FOR ANCESTORS - ALL RESOURCES

▶ All Resources
▶ Ancestral File
▶ Census
▶ International Genealogical Index
▶ Pedigree Resource File
▶ US Social Security Death Index
▶ Vital Records Index
▶ Search Family History Web Sites

▶ About The Church of Jesus Christ of Latter-day Saints

Enter at least your deceased ancestor's last name and then click *Search*.
Tips on How to Search for Your Ancestor

Father   Last Name

*First Name   *Last Name

Mother   Last Name

Spouse   Last Name

Event   Year   Year Range
All

Country   State
All Countries

☐ * Use exact spelling   Search   Clear

An official Web site of The Church of Jesus Christ of Latter-day Saints
© 2008 Intellectual Reserve, Inc. All rights reserved. Conditions of Use Privacy Policy

About Us | Contact Us | Press Room | Site Map
Records Custodians | Developers | LDS Church Sites | LDS Country Sites

Immigrant Ships Transcribers Guild

Established in 1998, the Immigrant Ships Transcribers Guild website represents the collective efforts of hundreds of volunteer researchers who have transcribed over 8,000 passenger manifests as of this writing. While many passenger records have been made available through other sources in the decade since this site was launched, its offerings continue to be freely available to all researchers. In addition, the technique used to publish these transcribed records makes them fully searchable by Google, so you can quickly and easily research these records for one or more of your ancestors.

In addition to passenger records, the site also has maritime newspaper articles, ethnic information, and resources for adoption research.

You can access the Immigrant Ships Transcribers Guild website by pointing your browser to <www.immigrantships.net>. Most recently, an index to this collection has appeared on <www.worldvitalrecords.com> as a free, searchable resource.

One-Step Search Tools by Stephen Morse

Necessity is the mother of invention and genealogists worldwide should be thankful that Dr. Stephen Morse of San Francisco is not only an extremely capable software engineer, but was also a frustrated genealogist at one point. That point was 17 April 2001 and, like many, Morse was up late into the evening trying to access the new Ellis Island website. After too many attempts submitting queries to a system offering few options to refine his search, Morse decided to build a better mouse trap. He studied the underlying query structure, wrote some code, and, well, the rest is now part of genealogy history.

The One-Step Search tools for finding passengers in the Ellis Island database were his first effort, but Stephen Morse and a group of like-minded and equally skilled volunteers have since created dozens of tools for researching passenger records, census records, vital records, and many other subjects of interest to genealogists.

The One-Step Search Tools by Dr. Stephen Morse can be accessed by pointing your browser to <www.stevemorse.org>. As Steve likes to point out during his presentations, don't make the mistake of typing .com or you'll end up on the imposter site of a guitar-playing rock star. This is truly one of my favorite sites.

Random Acts of Genealogical Kindness

The concept is simple and just as the name implies, this website focuses on volunteers performing not-so-random acts of kindness for other members of the genealogical community. Say, for instance, that you live in Florida and doubt you'll ever get to the small town north of Boston where your ancestors lived for several generations after coming to America. Or, you might need a copy of a vital record, photograph of a headstone, or an obituary from a small local paper not published online. You can visit the Random Acts website, navigate to the geographic area of interest, and view a list of volunteers willing to perform various acts of genealogical kindness for you.

The hope, of course, is that some day you, too, will be willing to perform a similar act of kindness for a stranger far away, but with research interests that may be just minutes from your home. This cycle of kindness touches every U.S. state and many other countries around the world.

You can access the Random Acts of Genealogical Kindness website by pointing your browser to <www.raogk.org>.

Wayback Machine (Archive.org)

The Wayback Machine, now called Archive.org, is an attempt to archive the pages published on the Internet over time. Old newspapers can be saved or microfilmed, other records can be digitized, but who is thinking about the research that will be conducted ten or twenty years from now? You may not see this site listed on other genealogy top-ten lists, but understanding what it has to offer will convince you to add it to your list of favorites.

In Chapter Two, you learned how Google maintains a snapshot or cache of a Web page from its most recent visit. But what if you want to revisit a page or site after a year or two, hoping to find the content that you knew you found once but forgot to print or save? This site may be your only chance of retracing your steps to an earlier time in cyberspace.

You can access the Wayback Machine website at <www.archive.org>.

Wikipedia—The Free Encyclopedia

Wikipedia is a clever adaptation of online technology that enables millions of contributors worldwide to share their expertise on a given topic. This very open exchange of information to create a free worldwide encyclopedia is also what draws harsh criticism from some educators. Genealogists should use Wikipedia with the same healthy skepticism they apply to any record—online or otherwise. You can learn a lot about surnames, place names, and other topics here, but you are encouraged to check the validity of facts against other sources before you assume they are 100 percent accurate.

The Wikipedia encyclopedia is also integrated as a feature of the Clusty search engine described in Appendix C (see page 308).

Wikipedia can be found by pointing your browser to <www.wikipedia.org>.

The WorldGenWeb Project

The statement on its website says it best: "The WorldGenWeb Project is a non-profit, volunteer-based organization dedicated to providing genealogical and historical records and resources for world-wide access!" When conducting research for almost any part of the world, I routinely visit the WorldGenWeb or USGenWeb sites to connect with the people and resources closest to where the individual or families lived. Many carefully crafted Google queries involving place names for genealogy will likely include a GenWeb page as one of the result listings. If you have been researching your family tree for years, but have never visited the local GenWeb page for the home of your ancestors, be sure to take a peek. You may make some interesting discoveries.

The WorldGenWeb Project can be accessed online at <www.worldgenweb.org>.

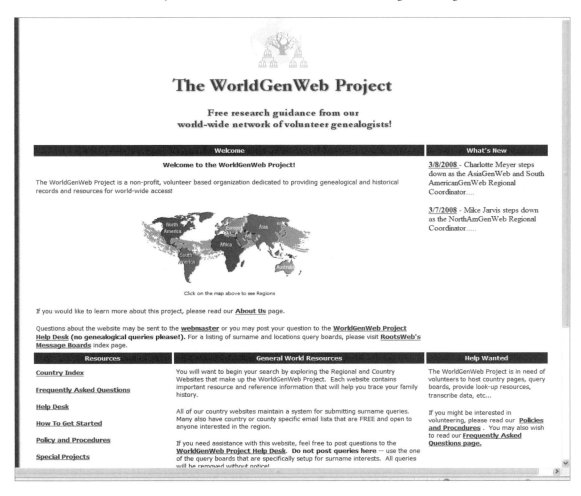

Your Favorite

No, you're not seeing things and we didn't make a mistake during the edit process. This page was put here in the Number Ten spot on the list to emphasize a point. When learning about genealogy—online or offline—there are many different sources of information. Most magazines, many books, and even many popular genealogy blogs publish an annual list of Top Ten. But your list certainly shouldn't stop at ten.

By using the search techniques described in this book, you may find a very small website published by an individual, club, or society active in recording the history for a particular geographic area. If that town happens to be the place your ancestors called home for several generations, that small website can hold more value for you than any of the so-called "Top Ten" sites listed in this book or on any other list. There are many aspects of our research that we as genealogists share in common, but the pursuit is also a very personal one. This is not a "one size fits all" activity. Enjoy the search—and when you find a great site, share it with others!

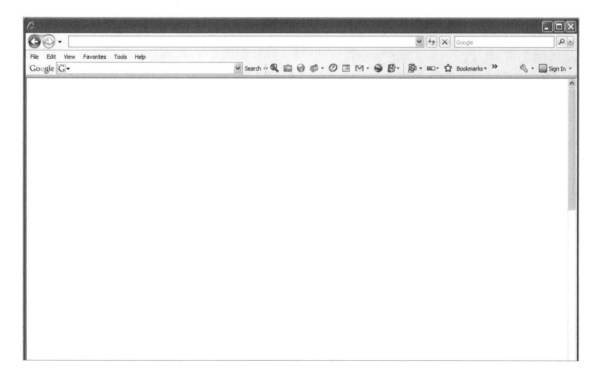

Following is a list of other useful websites that will help you in your family history search.

General

Association of Professional Genealogists

A U.S.-based nonprofit organization with more than 1,700 members worldwide, the group seeks to support, guide, and protect all aspects of genealogy as a profession and promotes the highest standard of ethics and professionalism among members. If you need professional assistance for any aspect of your family research, this is your place!
<www.apgen.org>

Cyndi's List of Genealogy Sites on the Internet

A category structured listing of genealogy and related sites that has served the online genealogy community since 1996. This site is a long-time favorite among online genealogists worldwide.
<www.cyndislist.com>

Federation of Family History Societies (UK)

The FFHS is an international nonprofit organization established in the UK. It represents, advises, and supports over 210 family history societies and other genealogical organizations worldwide, with a combined membership of over 300,000. The FFHS website includes a search of more than 67 million records including parish registers, memorial inscriptions, census, and more.
<www.familyhistoryonline.net>

Federation of Genealogical Societies (USA)

FGS is a U.S.-based nonprofit organization representing the interests of all genealogical societies. It hosts an annual conference in August/September and also publishes the FGS *FORUM* magazine with articles pertaining to society management, genealogical news and various other topics of genealogical interest—both at the professional and beginner level.

National Genealogical Society

NGS is a U.S.-based nonprofit organization founded in 1903 that serves everyone from the beginning researcher to the most advanced family historian. The society hosts a national conference every May.

<www.ngsgenealogy.org>

Genealogy / Family History Magazines

Ancestry

Long before the Ancestry.com website, *Ancestry* magazine was a premier publication featuring articles about all aspects of family heritage and genealogy research. The magazine is now published six times a year by The Generations Network and is celebrating its twenty-fifth year.

<www.ancestrymagazine.com>

Australian Family Tree Connections

An independent monthly magazine for Australian and New Zealand family historians that publishes a great collection of product and book reviews, surname features, computers and genealogy tips, and more.

<www.aftc.com.au>

Discovering Family History

Published by Moorshead Magazines (Canada), this bi-monthly magazine is for those just starting their genealogy, in need a refresher course, or tackling a new aspect of genealogy.

<www.discoveringfamilyhistory.com>

Family Chronicle

Published by Moorshead Magazines (Canada), this bi-monthly magazine is a how-to journal for individuals tracing their family roots. Each issue explores a different aspect of genealogy, providing readers with a variety of solutions to their research challenges.

Family Tree Magazine USA (**F+W Publications**)

This beginner-friendly genealogy magazine covers a range of topics of potential interest including ethnic heritage, family reunions, oral history, scrapbooking, historical travel, and more.

<www.familytreemagazine.com>

Your Family Tree (UK)

One of the leading family history publications in the U.K., this monthly magazine includes great articles, case studies and expert advice on various aspects of family history research.

<www.yourfamilytreemag.co.uk>

Internet Genealogy

Published by Moorshead Magazines (Canada), this specialty publication addresses the growing market need to highlight all that the Internet has to offer to the modern-day genealogist.

<www.internet-genealogy.com>

Canadian Records

Canadian Genealogy Centre

The Centre includes all physical and online genealogical services of Library and Archives Canada. It offers genealogical content, services, advice, research tools, and opportunities to work on joint projects, all in both of the country's official languages—French and English.

Census Records

1930Census.com

A site dedicated to census research for genealogy that helps you understand techniques to research and interpret census records and related facts. The website also links to popular fee-based sites with searchable census records for the United States, the UK, and Canada.

Heritage Quest Online

Heritage Quest offers a popular online service sold exclusively through the library market. The collection includes the United States Federal Census, 1790 to 1930, but you will need to contact libraries in your area to determine if they can provide you with free access.
<www.proquest.com>

Passenger Lists (Emigration & Immigration)

Castle Garden Records

Before the opening of Ellis Island on January 1, 1892, passengers were already arriving through the Port of New York. This website has a searchable index from 1820 to 1913, but no digitized images of passenger manifests. If you find your ancestor mentioned in these records, you'll need to find the image elsewhere.
<www.castlegarden.org>

Genealogy Community

RootsWeb

The oldest and largest free online community for genealogy. The site was established in 1993 and was acquired by Ancestry (now The Generations Network) in 2000. The message boards and mailing lists connect family historians who share similar research interests, and a great historical archive of messages are available here for searching. (You can use the Google **site:rootsweb.ancestry.com** command for more precise results.)
<www.rootsweb.ancestry.com>

Other Favorites

Your Google search skills will certainly be the best way to find the lesser-known specialty sites focused on your niche interests. The following is a collection of sites that I have relied upon for one or more aspects of my family research. For a more complete listing, visit this book's companion website <www.GoogleYourFamilyTree.com>.

Legacy

Working in collaboration with more than 500 newspapers in the United States, this site is a leading online destination for obituaries, death notices, and memorial pages. <www.legacy.com>

Library of Congress

This is an outstanding site for anyone conducting genealogy or history research for any aspect of United States history. The American Memory project provides free online access to a wide range of historic maps, photographs, documents, audio, and video. <www.loc.gov>

National Archives and Records Administration (NARA)

While many records are available online, the National Archives of the United States has far more in its collection than you might imagine. Find the location of the nearest regional archives and correspond by phone, mail, or email about the specific nature of your family research. NARA's holdings include original military files, naturalization papers, and much more. <www.archives.gov>

Newseum

This site features a digital collection of nearly 600 front pages from newspapers in fifty-nine countries. It also has an archive collection of front-page coverage for major historical events, but only dating to 2001. A very fun and educational site! <www.newseum.org/todaysfrontpages/>

We Relate

A free service sponsored by the Foundation for On-Line Genealogy and the Allen County Public Library in Fort Wayne, Indiana. Launched in 2007, its goal is to become the leading community website for genealogy with tools for research and collaboration. <www.werelate.org>

Leading Fee-Based Commercial Sites

The following are the leading commercial genealogy sites. Call or visit the libraries or genealogical societies in your area as many offer on-site access to subscription-based content, which can be a great way to conduct your own personal trial of each site.

Ancestors on Board

A partnership between The National Archives of the UK and FindMyPast.com, this site offers a complete collection of UK outbound passenger lists from 1890 to 1960. Classified as the BT27 collection, these 24 million records represent all long-distance voyages made from any British port bound for international destinations including North America, South America, Australia, and elsewhere. Searching is free, but you'll need to purchase vouchers or credits to view the full record transcription or full-color digitized passenger manifest. <www.ancestorsonboard.com>

Ancestry

One of the best-known online collections for genealogy research, Ancestry.com has been offering online content for more than ten years. Through its U.S. and World collections, members can access more than 6 billion records. The company also publishes *Family Tree Maker* software for use on your personal computer. In addition to its U.S. site, the company offers content through international versions including Australia, Canada, and the United Kingdom. Subscription options include monthly, quarterly, and annual memberships. <www.ancestry.com>

FamilyLink (World Vital Records)

Officially launched in 2006, the company has partnered with many leading content owners worldwide and has quickly created a valuable offering comprised of more than 2 billion searchable names. The company has also partnered with FamilySearch and will place the Family History Library Catalog of the LDS Church online—one of the most significant genealogical indexes ever created. The company offers U.S. and World collections. Subscription options include monthly and annual memberships. <www.worldvitalrecords.com>
<www.familylink.com>

Find My Past

A leading UK-based website offering civil registrations (birth, marriage, and death from 1837), census records (1841 to 1901), military records, passports, and more. The site also offers a free *Family Tree Explorer* application for building your tree. Searching is free, but you'll need to purchase vouchers or credits to view complete transcriptions and digitized images of original records.

<www.findmypast.com>

<www.1837online.com>

Footnote

Working in partnership with the National Archives and Records Administration of the United States (NARA), the collection features documents, most never before available on the Internet, relating to the Revolutionary War, Civil War, World War I, World War II, U.S. presidents, historical newspapers, and naturalization documents. The collection currently includes more than 30 million digitized images. Subscription options to premium content include monthly and annual memberships.

<www.footnote.com>

GenealogyBank

This consumer offering is from NewsBank Inc., a provider of content to libraries and educational institutions for more than sixty years. The collection includes obituaries and other historical newspaper content, historical books and documents, and more. Subscription options include monthly and annual memberships.

<www.genealogybank.com>

Newspaper Archive (Heritage Microfilm)

A collection of digitized newspapers currently offering over 80 million pages covering 240 years and over 725 cities. The company notes that it is adding over 80,000 images per days (about 2.5 million per month). Subscription options include ten-day passes and monthly, quarterly, or annual memberships.

Other Internet Search Engines

As great as Google is, it is not reasonable to assume that any one Internet search engine can index the entire World Wide Web. While there is certainly overlap, it is likely that others have indexed pages that Google hasn't yet included in their index of the Web. For a relative comparison of the penetration of any search engine, conduct a query for common words—I use *then OR than OR from* as a quick means of comparison. Google has more than 12 billion results, Yahoo registers 23.2 billion, MSN has 2.6 billion, and AOL just 2.1 billion. Since each search engine also uses its own weighting factors and proprietary algorithm to determine the relevancy and priority of results, you should routinely check important family lines on one or more search engines—in addition to Google.

The search engines listed in this section are a combination of market leaders as well as those with one or more unique features that may be of interest to family history enthusiasts. According to Nielsen Online (August 2008), Google represents a 60 percent share of the search market, with Yahoo and MSN a distant second and third, with 18 percent and 11 percent respectively. The only other offerings to represent more than 1 percent of the market share are AOL (at 5.2 percent) and Ask.com (at 2.0 percent).

Market Leaders

- Google ....<www.google.com>
- Yahoo! Search .... <www.yahoo.com>
- MSN Search (Windows Live Search) .... <www.live.com>
- Ask.com ....<www.ask.com>
- AOL Search .... <www.aol.com>

Other Interesting Search Engines

- Clusty (Vivisimo, Inc.) .... <www.clusty.com>
- Mamma (Copernic Inc.) .... <www.mamma.com>
- Cuil .... <www.cuil.com>
- ChaCha (ChaCha Search, Inc.) .... <www.chacha.com>
- Dogpile (InfoSpace, Inc.) .... <www.dogpile.com>
- Lycos (Lycos Inc.) .... <www.lycos.com>
- AltaVista (Overture Services, Inc.) .... <www.altavista.com>
- AllTheWeb (Yahoo!) .... <www.alltheweb.com>
- Euroseek .... <www.euroseek.com>
- Kartoo ....<www.kartoo.com>

Yahoo! Search

Currently ranked as the No. 2 Internet search engine in North America, Yahoo! was founded in 1994 and established a strong leading position through the late 1990s and into the new millennium. One of the primary differences was that Yahoo! was based on a categorized directory structure. Users seeking information would click their way through category and sub-category levels or search the directory.

Yahoo!'s customer loyalty came in part because of its strategy of offering free email accounts to users. With millions of visitors to the Yahoo! homepage each day, online advertisers have long been attracted to this Web portal. For some—including me—the attraction to using Google during its beta period was an escape from the cluttered Yahoo! homepage. The empty white utilitarian design of Google was a breath of fresh air.

The majority of commands and syntax discussed during Chapters One, Two, and Three will also work for searches conducted on Yahoo! An advanced Web search form is available by visiting <http://search.yahoo.com/web/advanced> or by searching for *yahoo advanced search*.

Yahoo Keyword Suggestions

A useful feature available directly from the Yahoo! homepage at <www.yahoo.com> is the keyword suggestion box. Google offers this feature through its toolbar and through Google

Labs as Google Suggest, but Yahoo! has enabled it as a permanent feature on its site. As you begin to formulate your query, the drop-down box comes into view and suggests other queries based on intelligence gathered from millions of previous searches.

Yahoo! is typically more aggressive with its display of advertising messages, including sponsored listings at the top and right side of the page, as well as other so-called "rich media" ads that can annoy some users. In the example below, a search for *1930 census* displays ten results similar to Google, but includes suggested alternate links above the natural listings. Because Google and Yahoo! use different factors and calculations to determine relevancy of results, the first result on Google (the site at <www.1930census.com> in this example) may not necessarily appear first—or even in the top ten—for Yahoo! or other search engines.

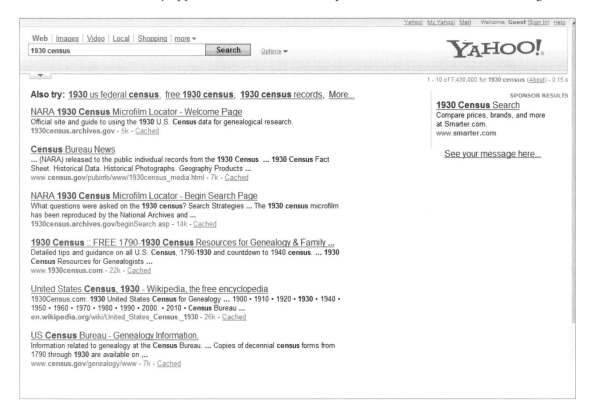

MSN (Windows Live Search)

Officially launched in September 2006 after six months in beta, this is Microsoft's latest volley in the battle to capture search engine market share. One look at the main homepage located at <www.live.com> and you can see the influence Google has had on search engines. Microsoft's previous search engine (and still a very popular site located at www.msn.com) has much more in common with the look and feel of Yahoo!.

Notable differences between Live Search and Google are the number of search terms allowed (just ten for Live Search versus thirty-two for Google) and support by Live Search for the **NOT** operator. Although Google does support exclusions through use of the minus sign, it can be more intuitive for some users to see the **NOT** command as part of their query definition.

An advanced search capability is available by clicking on the *Options* text link appearing on the homepage (see the arrow in the graphic above). As of this writing, the so-called advanced search capabilities are limited and users will be required to use command-line syntax to filter results of complex queries.

Live Search Maps—Birds Eye View

Aerial and satellite map views are certainly not new online (see Chapters Ten and Eleven), but you will appreciate the Bird's Eye View feature found on Microsoft's revamped search engine. With functions very similar to *Google Maps*, you can quickly navigate to a specific address by typing it into the search box and selecting the *Maps* text link. There are as many as seven different views for each map including 2D, 3D, Road, Aerial, Hybrid, Bird's Eye, and Traffic. Once you select the *Bird's Eye* link, you can rotate clockwise or counterclockwise to view four individual bird's eye images. This can be especially handy when shadows obscure your view from a particular angle. This is one of my favorite features!

To access this feature, point your browser to <http://maps.live.com>.

The image below is a bird's eye view of Ellis Island in New York Harbor. The circle in the lower right is the American Immigrant Wall of Honor, which includes the names of more than 700,000 American immigrants. See details at <www.wallofhonor.org>.

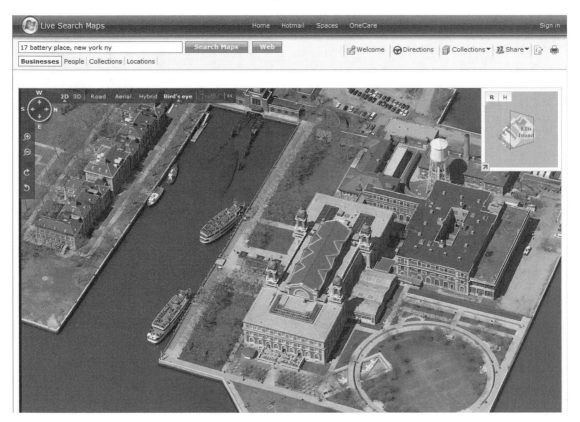

Ask.com

As the current No. 4 provider of Internet search, Ask.com has a loyal following, many of whom have used the service since it was branded Ask Jeeves and encouraged users to enter natural-language queries (e.g., Where can I find information about the 1930 census?). The homepage has adopted the look of Google, but has retained a distinctive feel all its own.

Founded in 1996 as Ask Jeeves, the company has similar functionality to Google, Yahoo!, and Microsoft. The Jeeves character was retired in February 2006 and the company's site can now be accessed by pointing your browser to <www.ask.com>. In addition to the U.S. version, the company operates international versions in more than a dozen countries and supports Dutch, French, German, Italian, and Spanish languages in its advanced queries.

Ask.com Search Results

The ask.com search results page offers a variety of clever features not found on other search engines. In a left-hand column, related links are suggested in categories to *Narrow Your Search* and also to *Expand Your Search*. The quick links can sometimes suggest a query you may not have thought to type on your own but that lead to unexpected, relevant results.

Another useful feature is a binocular icon that appears to the left of many text links. Without leaving the results page, you can slide your mouse over the binocular icon and a preview box will automatically appear with a miniature view of the Web page associated with that result. A second tab labeled Statistics shows a twelve-month trailing view of the traffic for this particular website (based on statistics provided from Compete, Inc.).

AOL Search

America Online, owned by Time Warner, is certainly one of the best-known brands on the Internet, but it lacks the innovation offered by others competing for market share in Internet search. AOL currently receives feeds from Google to respond to user queries, both natural results and sponsored results. While the natural results obtained through an AOL query will be nearly identical to those obtained through Google, you may find more sponsored listings appearing on the AOL site. From a genealogical point of view, there is no distinct benefit to using AOL as a tool to research your family tree.

The search function of AOL can be accessed at <http://search.aol.com/aol/webhome> or by searching for AOL advanced search from the homepage at <www.aol.com> or the small *Advanced Search* text link appearing to the right of the input text box. The Advanced Search is similar to the old version of Google Advanced Search, but substitutes other links in place of certain Google services (e.g., MapQuest in place of *Google Maps*).

Clusty

This search engine can be found at <www.clusty.com> and is one of my long-time favorites among the lesser-known search engines. The name Clusty is derived from its most distinctive feature—clustering results into logical groups to help you more quickly identify relevant results. This offering is well worth a visit and offers a clean Google-like interface, both in query and results. In addition to recognizing many of the same commands and operators supported by Google, Clusty also supports use of the word **NOT** as an exclusion operator. You will have to look elsewhere for maps, however, as Clusty does not offer this as part of its service. Google and Microsoft have this nicely covered, so not to worry!

Wikipedia Integration

Another nice feature of Clusty is the integration of Wikipedia—an online open-source encyclopedia. Without leaving the clusty.com environment, you can click on the Wikipedia link to automatically view the results summary before making your selection.

The Clusty technology was launched in 2004 after several years in development.

Clusty Search Results Page

In the example below, a query for ***connecticut vital records*** finds over 300,000 results, but clusters them into a much smaller number of logical groups or clusters—in this case, just twenty.

Actual search results are obtained from a combination of sources including Ask.com, Live.com, the open source directory project (see <www.dmoz.org>), and others. Clusty also incorporates sponsored listings similar to those found on Google.

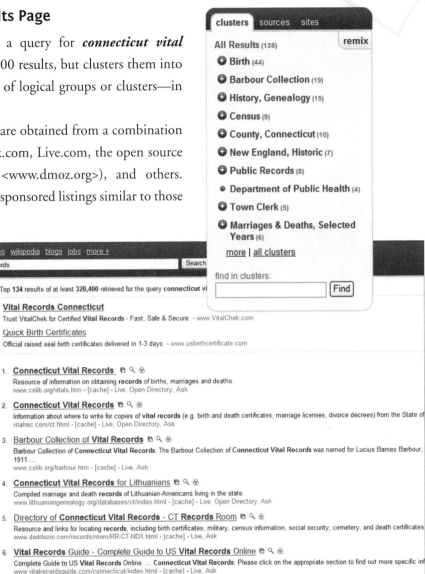

ChaCha

A fairly young entrant to the search engine space (launched in 2006), this site's search results are based on input and ratings from human guides. Offering search results online and on your mobile phone, this small upstart has an innovative approach that may help it carve out a niche among some tech-savvy researchers on the go. I included this in my list more because of the novelty of their approach and not because I thought you'd have a research breakthrough with their results. Given that the service does not provide actual result statistics along with search results, I suspect that the number of pages in its index is very small. But they all have to start somewhere.

The emphasis of this company appears to be the mobile consumer sending and receiving queries and responses via their cell phones—both voice and text messaging. The website offers results for Web pages, news, images, video, and audio.

Cuil

In July 2008, a new search engine joined an already crowded market. Although I wouldn't typically get excited about such an announcement—this one had a few things that made it worthy of my recommendation as "one to watch." You see, Cuil (pronounced "cool") is based in Menlo Park, California. That's not far from Google territory. And the founders include some very bright people, some with a Google pedigree and others with an equally impressive background in search architecture and relevance. With both the talent and access to funding, I do expect that we will see some very interesting things from this company over time.

Their current site at <www.cuil.com> claims to have the largest online index of Web pages at 121.6 billion pages. Indeed they report 121 billion results for the sample query of '***then OR than OR from***'. Results are displayed in a column layout (either 2 or 3 columns, your choice). A place name query for ***campobasso italy*** yielded 212 million results, but included a clever box in the upper corner of the screen which allowed one-click access to many links that will be appreciated by family historians. So, it's a relative newcomer, but give it a try! And be sure to report any special findings at <www.GoogleYourFamilyTree.com>, our companion website.

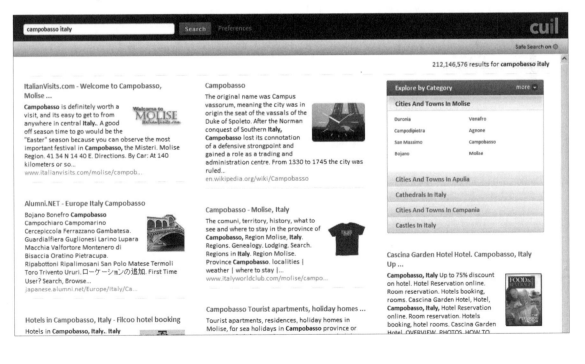

Dogpile

This search engine is fairly well-known among genealogists and is most recognized for aggregating results from Google, Yahoo, MSN/Live Search, Ask, and others. This type of search engine is known as a metasearch engine. The default search results page displays up to twenty numbered results—a combination of sponsored and natural listings. It can often be difficult to determine the difference between the sponsored results and those that show up as a result of natural relevancy for your query.

Owned and operated by InfoSpace, Dogpile adds two distinct search categories not often broken out by other search engines—White Pages and Yellow Pages search. While this can be helpful in certain instances, you will also appreciate the advanced reverse search features found at <www.infospace.com>. For example, using the Search by Phone option, there are several good reverse search features. Be forewarned, however, that many of the results screens are confusing and will steer you toward fee-based results from Intelius. Try Dogpile as a secondary option, especially for ancestors that have eluded your attempts to date. You will find that many of the same commands and syntax described for Google will work on Dogpile as well.

Mamma

Billing itself as "the Mother of All Search Engines," this search site, found at <www.mamma.com>, is recognized as a pioneer in the metasearch category. A metasearch engine is one that aggregates results from many other search engines and then presents relevant results based on its aggregate formula. The official company name is Copernic, Inc., but you continue to access the service through their clever domain and branding.

Results are a heavy mix of sponsored results and aggregate natural results from other leading search engines including Ask.com, Entireweb, About.com, and others.

This site also includes U.S. phone book results—White Pages and Yellow Pages—provided through partnership with Switchboard and data by Acxiom.

Five More for Good Measure

The second page of this appendix listed a total of fifteen search engines—certainly more than you need, but there were a few that I just couldn't ignore for this book. Lycos and AltaVista were pioneers in Internet search and still produce relevant results. AllTheWeb is a variation on Yahoo! with a cleaner interface. Euroseek.com provides strong results for European queries and Kartoo.com offers a radical approach to displaying results—although I sometimes find their graphical results confusing. As you have read many times in this book, don't be afraid to experiment. Try one, try them all—the great news is that once you've mastered the techniques of searching on Google, much of that learning can be applied to other search engines as well.

Web Search Engines Defined

For a more complete understanding of Google, some readers may find it helpful to understand more precisely the definition and evolution of Web search engines in general. Think of this as the lineage or family tree of Internet search.

The text that follows is from Wikipedia®—The Free Encyclopedia and is used with permission under the terms of the GNU Free Documentation License. As is required, the text is included in its entirety, without modification or edits of any kind.

A copy of the license is included in the section entitled "GNU Free Documentation License."

Content on Wikipedia is covered by disclaimers.

Additional information is available online at:

<http://en.wikipedia.org/wiki/Wikipedia:Copyrights>

For information on the **GNU Free Documentation License**, visit:

<http://en.wikipedia.org/wiki/GNU_Free_Documentation_License>

Web Search Engine

A Web search engine is a search engine designed to search for information on the World Wide Web. Information may consist of web pages, images and other types of files.

Some search engines also mine data available in newsgroups, databases, or open directories. Unlike Web directories, which are maintained by human editors, search engines operate algorithmically or are a mixture of algorithmic and human input.

History of Popular Web Search Engines

The very first tool used for searching on the Internet was Archie.[1] The name stands for "archive" without the "vee". It was created in 1990 by Alan Emtage, a student at McGill University in Montreal. The program downloaded the directory listings of all the files located on public anonymous FTP (File Transfer Protocol) sites, creating a searchable database of file names; however, Archie did not index the contents of these files.

The rise of Gopher (created in 1991 by Mark McCahill at the University of Minnesota) led to two new search programs, Veronica and Jughead. Like Archie, they searched the file names and titles stored in Gopher index systems. Veronica (Very Easy Rodent-Oriented Net-wide Index to Computerized Archives) provided a keyword search of most Gopher menu titles in the entire Gopher listings. Jughead (Jonzy's Universal Gopher Hierarchy Excavation And Display) was a tool for obtaining menu information from specific Gopher servers. While the name of the search engine "Archie" was not a reference to the Archie comic book series, "Veronica" and "Jughead" are characters in the series, thus referencing their predecessor.

The first Web search engine was Wandex, a now-defunct index collected by the World Wide Web Wanderer, a web crawler developed by Matthew Gray at MIT in 1993. Another very early search engine, Aliweb, also appeared in 1993, and still runs today. JumpStation (released in early 1994) used a crawler to find web pages for searching, but search was limited to the title of web pages only. One of the first "full text" crawler-based search engines was WebCrawler, which came out in 1994. Unlike its predecessors, it let users search for any word in any webpage, which became the standard for all major search engines since. It was also the first one to be widely known by the public. Also in 1994 Lycos (which started at Carnegie Mellon University) was launched, and became a major commercial endeavor.

Soon after, many search engines appeared and vied for popularity. These included Excite, Infoseek, Inktomi, Northern Light, and AltaVista. Yahoo! was among the most popular ways for people to find web pages of interest, but its search function operated on its web directory, rather than full-text copies of web pages. Information seekers could also browse the directory instead of doing a keyword-based search.

Search engines were also known as some of the brightest stars in the Internet investing frenzy that occurred in the late 1990s. Several companies entered the market spectacularly, receiving record gains during their initial public offerings. Some have taken down their public search engine, and are marketing enterprise-only editions, such as Northern Light. Many search engine companies were caught up in the dot-com bubble, a speculation-driven market boom that peaked in 1999 and ended in 2001.

Around 2001, the Google search engine rose to prominence. The company achieved better results for many searches with an innovation called PageRank. This iterative algorithm ranks web pages based on the number and PageRank of other web sites and pages that link there, on the premise that good or desirable pages are linked to more than others. Google also maintained a minimalist interface to its search engine. In contrast, many of its competitors embedded a search engine in a web portal.

By 2001, Yahoo was providing search services based on Inktomi's search engine. Yahoo! acquired Inktomi in 2002, and Overture (which owned AlltheWeb and AltaVista) in 2003. Yahoo! switched to using Google's search engine until 2004, when it launched its own search engine based on the combined technologies of its acquisitions.

Microsoft first launched MSN Search (since re-branded Live Search) in the fall of 1998 using search results from Inktomi. In early 1999 the site began to display listings from Looksmart blended with results from Inktomi except for a short time in 1999 when results from AltaVista were used instead. In 2004, Microsoft began a transition to its own search technology, powered by its own web crawler (called msnbot).

Timeline		
Note: "Launch" refers only to web availability of original crawl-based web search engine results.		
Year	**Engine**	**Event**
1993	Aliweb	Launch
1994	WebCrawler	Launch
	JumpStation	Launch
	Infoseek	Launch
	Lycos	Launch
1995	AltaVista	Launch (part of DEC)
	Excite	Launch
1996	Dogpile	Launch
	Inktomi	Founded
	HotBot	Founded
	Ask Jeeves	Founded
1997	Northern Light	Launch
1998	Google	Launch
1999	AlltheWeb	Launch
	Naver	Launch
	Teoma	Founded
	Vivisimo	Founded
2000	Baidu	Founded
2003	Info.com	Launch
2004	Yahoo! Search	Final launch
	A9.com	Launch
2005	MSN Search	Final launch
	Ask.com	Launch
	AskMeNow	Launch
	Lexxe.com	Founded
2006	wikiseek	Founded
	Quaero	Founded
	Ask.com	Launch
	Live Search	Launch
	ChaCha	Beta Launch
	Quintura	Beta Launch
	Guruji.com	Beta Launch
2007	wikiseek	Launched
	AskWiki	Launched

As of 2007, Google is the most popular Web search engine worldwide.[2] [3] A number of country-specific search engine companies have become prominent; for example Baidu is the most popular search engine in the People's Republic of China.[4]

How Web search engines work

A search engine operates in the following order:

1. Web crawling
2. Indexing
3. Searching

Web search engines work by storing information about a large number of web pages, which they retrieve from the WWW itself. These pages are retrieved by a Web crawler (sometimes also known as a spider)—an automated Web browser which follows every link it sees. Exclusions can be made by the use of robots.txt. The contents of each page are then analyzed to determine how it should be indexed (for example, words are extracted from the titles, headings, or special fields called meta tags). Data about web pages are stored in an index database for use in later queries. Some search engines, such as Google, store all or part of the source page (referred to as a cache) as well as information about the web pages, whereas others, such as AltaVista, store every word of every page they find. This cached page always holds the actual search text since it is the one that was actually indexed, so it can be very useful when the content of the current page has been updated and the search terms are no longer in it. This problem might be considered to be a mild form of linkrot, and Google's handling of it increases usability by satisfying user expectations that the search terms will be on the returned webpage. This satisfies the principle of least astonishment since the user normally expects the search terms to be on the returned pages. Increased search relevance makes these cached pages very useful, even beyond the fact that they may contain data that may no longer be available elsewhere.

When a user enters a query into a search engine (typically by using key words), the engine examines its index and provides a listing of best-matching web pages according to its criteria, usually with a short summary containing the document's title and sometimes parts of the text. Most search engines support the use of the boolean operators AND, OR and NOT to further specify the search query. Some search engines provide an advanced feature called proximity search which allows users to define the distance between keywords.

The usefulness of a search engine depends on the relevance of the result set it gives back. While there may be millions of webpages that include a particular word or phrase, some pages may be more relevant, popular, or authoritative than others. Most search engines employ methods to rank the results to provide the "best" results first. How a search engine decides which pages are the best matches, and what order the results should be shown in, varies widely from one engine to another. The methods also change over time as Internet usage changes and new techniques evolve.

Most Web search engines are commercial ventures supported by advertising revenue and, as a result, some employ the controversial practice of allowing advertisers to pay money to have their listings ranked higher in search results. Those search engines which do not accept money for their search engine results make money by running search related ads alongside the regular search engine results. The search engines make money every time someone clicks on one of these ads.

The vast majority of search engines are run by private companies using proprietary algorithms and closed databases, though some are open source.

Syntax Summary & Quick Reference

The most basic search ingredient used by Google and other Web search engines is called a keyword, a word representing the topic you're trying to research. While single-keyword queries will generate many results, you will typically find a more manageable number of highly relevant results by using a carefully crafted query comprised of multiple keywords (called a keyword phrase) and perhaps one or more special commands or operators. Most can be used in combination with one another to more precisely define your query.

For genealogists, the most useful elements when structuring a query are names, places, dates, events, and data types. Consider how the following basic commands can be used alone or in combination with one another to filter billions of results and deliver just a few meaningful pages.

In the example below, I conduct a Google Web Search for pages that may contain information about my great-grandfather Eugene Lynch (aka, Eugene Patrick Lynch).

Google Web Search Query	Results
lynch	42,800,000
lynch family	363,000
lynch family connecticut	141,000
eugene lynch family connecticut	45,500
"eugene lynch" family connecticut	51
"eugene * lynch" family connecticut	815
"eugene * lynch" family Connecticut ~genealogy	117
"eugene * lynch" family Connecticut ~genealogy waterbury OR bridgeport	8

A single keyword query based on surname only yields 42.8 million results and is generally a poor query for genealogists. There are possible exceptions to this rule for very rare surnames or those with a frequently occurring alternate spelling—especially an Americanized version of a European name, which virtually ensures a family relation. You can see that as the query builds in complexity, the number of results drops to a very manageable number for closer inspection. This table and the commands that follow in this appendix should serve as your guide for searching.

Keyword Basics	
single word	*Find results containing this word* ▶ census
multiple words	*Find results containing all the following words, in any order or proximity (results appearing anywhere on the page)* ▶ eugene lynch ▶ eugene lynch waterbury ▶ eugene lynch waterbury connecticut
common words (stop words)	*Certain commonly occurring words or single characters may be ignored because they slow search without enhancing the quality of search results* ▶ the statue of liberty *(the and of may be ignored as common words)*

Basic Operators	
" " (quotations)	*Find results containing the exact phrase specified* ▶ "eugene lynch" ▶ "the statue of liberty" (<u>the</u> and <u>of</u> are included in this instance)
AND (optional)	*Find results containing all of the following words* ▶ eugene **AND** lynch ▶ eugene **AND** lynch **AND** waterbury
+ (plus sign)	*Find results containing this keyword, but not the plural* *variant or any synonyms for the keyword* ▶ "eugene lynch" +brother
OR | (pipe symbol)	*Find results containing either keyword* ▶ eugene **OR** patrick lynch ▶ "eugene lynch" waterbury | bridgeport
– (minus sign)	Find results containing one keyword or phrase, but exclude those results containing another ▶ "eugene lynch" waterbury –vermont
~ (tilde symbol)	*Find results containing this word or similar words* *(synonyms)* ▶ lynch ~genealogy ▶ "eugene lynch" ~genealogy ▶ "eugene lynch" ~birth
.. (numrange)	*Find results containing one keyword or phrase, but* *exclude those results containing another* ▶ "eugene lynch" waterbury 1880..1900

Combining Basic Operators

You will notice in many of the examples above (also discussed in greater detail in Chapters One, Two, and Three) that all operators can be used in combination with one another. It may take a little practice at first to ensure the proper meaning, but you can surely master this after just a few sessions of careful searching.

One of the most useful examples for genealogists appears below. In this instance, the query is looking for any one of three common occurrences for the name Eugene Lynch, but also requesting that the resulting pages references the term Waterbury (his known place of residence). Since there is a city named Waterbury in both Connecticut and Vermont, the query further removes the unwanted results for Vermont using a minus sign.

*"eugene lynch" OR "lynch, eugene" OR "eugene * lynch" waterbury -vermont*

Advanced Operators and Queries	
site:	*Finds results for your query as defined, but limits those results to a specific website* ▶ ohio **site**:www.1930census.com ▶ "trumbull county" **site**:www.1930census.com ▶ ohio OR connecticut **site**:www.1930census.com
link:	*Finds Web pages that include a link to the specified site or page being specified in the query* ▶ **link**:1930census.com ▶ **link**:1930census.com/ohio_census_records.php
info:	*Obtains summary information about the Web page specified, along with quick links to additional detail* ▶ **info**:1930census.com ▶ **info**:1930census.com/ohio_census_records.php
related:	*Finds other Web pages related to the same topic as that covered by the specified page* ▶ **related**:1930census.com ▶ **related**:1930census.com/ohio_census_records.php

cache:	*Displays a snapshot of the specified Web page as recently indexed by Google; if followed by one or more keywords, they will appear highlighted and bold* ▶ **cache:**www.1930census.com ▶ **cache:**www.1930census.com Soundex
allintitle:	*Finds Web pages that include the specified keyword(s) in the actual title of the Web page (as it appears in the top title bar of your browser)* ▶ **allintitle:**lynch ▶ **allintitle:**lynch family
intitle:	*Finds Web pages that include the specified keyword(s) in the actual title of the Web page, but also meet other search criteria as specified* ▶ "eugene lynch" **intitle:**genealogy ▶ "eugene lynch" **intitle:**"family history"
allinurl:	*Finds Web pages that include the specified keyword(s) in the actual URL of the Web page (URL being the full address of a given Web page)* ▶ **allinurl:**lynch ▶ **allinurl:**lynch family
inurl:	*Finds Web pages that include the specified keyword(s) in the actual URL of the Web page, but also meet other search criteria as specified* ▶ "eugene lynch" **inurl:**genealogy ▶ "eugene lynch" **inurl:**"family history"

More Advanced Operators & Queries	
inanchor:	*Finds Web pages that include a link using the word or phrase as the target of that link (called anchor text)* ▸ **inanchor:**orsatti ▸ **inanchor:**"pietro orsatti" ▸ **inanchor:**"pietro * orsatti"
allinanchor:	*Finds Web pages that include a link using all the words as the target of that link (called anchor text)* ▸ **allinanchor:**lynch family genealogy ▸ **allinanchor:**connecticut census records
filetype: or **ext:**	*Finds results for your query as defined, but limits those results to documents with a specific filetype extension* ▸ ohio genealogy **filetype:**pdf ▸ "trumbull county" ohio **filetype:**jpg ▸ ~genealogy (ohio OR connecticut) **ext:**pdf
site: *(image search)*	*Using the Google Image search, this command will display images found on the designated website* ▸ **site:**www.ditota.com ▸ **site:**www.statueofliberty.org
Fun & Convenience	
phonebook:	*Returns a list of names, addresses, and phone numbers based on the surname and place name specified (U.S. city or Zip); results also include link to Google Maps* ▸ **phonebook:**lynch new york ▸ **phonebook:**lynch 10017 ▸ **phonebook:**lynch patrick, boston ▸ **phonebook:**patrick lynch, boston

bphonebook:	*Returns a listing from the U.S. business phone directory of names, phone numbers, Web addresses, and links, along with a Google Map link to organizations matching your specified query* ▶ **bphonebook:**church bridgeport ▶ **bphonebook:**church 06708 ▶ **bphonebook:**church oswego ny
movie:	*Finds the time and location for a given movie playing in the geographic location specified (U.S. city or Zip); results also include movie length, rating, genre, and links to trailers and reviews* ▶ **movie:**"vantage point" 02048 ▶ **movie:**"vantage point" canton ohio
define:	*Finds various meanings for the word specified, useful for surnames* ▶ **define:**cooper ▶ **define:**schneider

Keyword Queries for Genealogy

In addition to the special syntax and commands that can be adapted for genealogical use, there are also some simple keyword queries likely to produce good results. As most seasoned family historians know, even the smallest clue can lead to an important find. While many facts about the lives of our ancestors are found in official sources, there are many others that can be equally as important originating from one-of-a-kind sources shared online by another researcher.

With more than 20 billion pages already indexed by Google and new pages being published daily, chances are good that someone somewhere is working on a similar aspect of your family history—albeit from a different point of view. The queries below are designed to help you quickly locate pages dealing with the key genealogical events in your ancestors' lives. Note that commands can be combined with one another to narrow results as needed.

Genealogy Keyword Queries	
was born **was born in**	*Designed to find pages detailing birth information for an individual, by adding "was born" or "was born in," you are further refining results* ▶ eugene lynch was born ▶ "eugene lynch was born" ▶ "eugene lynch was born" waterbury OR bridgeport ▶ "eugene * lynch was born"
married	*Designed to find pages detailing marriage information for an individual* ▶ eugene lynch married ▶ "eugene lynch married" ▶ "eugene lynch married" waterbury OR bridgeport ▶ "eugene * lynch married"
died **died on**	*Designed to find pages detailing death information for an individual* ▶ eugene lynch died ▶ "eugene lynch died on" ▶ "eugene lynch died" waterbury OR bridgeport ▶ "eugene * lynch died"
was buried	*Designed to find pages detailing burial information for an individual* ▶ eugene lynch was buried ▶ "eugene lynch was buried" ▶ "eugene lynch was buried" waterbury OR bridgeport ▶ "eugene * lynch was buried"

Calculator Functions

The following numeric calculations can be quite helpful for genealogists, especially when you are working with results from another website and need to quickly compare data between multiple sources. By using these numeric calculations, you can quickly calculate age at death, approximate year of birth or marriage, approximate year of arrival for immigrants, and much more.

Numeric Calculations & Conversions	
+ *(addition)*	*Adds two or more numbers* ▶ 1892 + 78 ▶ 1910 + 24 + 73
− *(subtraction)*	*Subtracts two or more numbers* ▶ 2008−1911 ▶ 1991−1911−17
* *(multiplication)*	*Multiplies two or more numbers* ▶ 13 * 17 ▶ 13 * 17 * 9
/ *(division)*	*Divides two or more numbers* ▶ 1908 / 9 ▶ 1908 / 9 / 8
( ) *(parenthesis)*	*Used to direct the Google Calculator as to which calculations should be performed first* ▶ (2008−1911) * 3 + (4 * 36)
in *(unit conversion)*	*Used to specify a unit type for conversion* ▶ 27 kilometers **in** miles ▶ 27 miles **in** kilometers ▶ 27000 days **in** years ▶ 789 months **in** years ▶ 78 years **in** months ▶ 50 years **in** minutes

Google does not (yet?) provide a function for the conversion of an exact date of death and precise age at death to result in a date of birth. I have written to Google suggesting this as a future enhancement, so we shall see if it makes the cut.

Note: In addition to the features shown above, Google supports more advanced calculations and conversions, but this text includes only those likely to be of use in conducting family history research. For more complete details on the other calculation functions performed by Google, visit <www.google.com/help/calculator.html>.

Synonyms for Genealogy

Google has a Similar Words feature that allows you to specify a search for a given keyword where your results will also include pages that have synonyms or other similar words commonly used in place of the original keyword. The words are not necessarily synonyms as might be found in a dictionary or thesaurus, but are rather an intelligent list of words known only to Google.

The word *genealogy* currently appears to have the following words tagged as similar words within the Google index:

- Ancestry
- Family
- Family History
- Family Tree
- Genealogical
- Genealogical Records
- Genealogists
- Geneological
- Geneologists
- Geneology
- Records
- Roots
- Surname
- Tree
- Vital Records

I was able to determine the previous list of similar words by submitting a series of Google queries, then increasing the complexity until no results were found. The initial query was:

~genealogy -genealogy

By removing the primary keyword (genealogy) immediately after searching for synonyms of that same word, you are left with results including only similar words, but not the word itself. By carefully inspecting the results and removing keywords one by one, you are eventually left with a query that returns no results, therefore giving you a list of similar words. Using this technique, you can determine similar words that result for the term **birthplace**.

~birthplace –birthplace –born –birthdate –birth place –biography

I have tried this technique with given names and surnames, but with varying degrees of success. Google will recognize William as a similar word for Bill, but not the reverse. It will not recognize common similar words for Patrick, Daniel. It will not recognize Edward as a similar word for Ed, but it will include Edmund and a variety of educational terms. A search for words similar to Pete will find Peter and Petersburg, but will not find Pietro. Since there are thousands of names I would never have time to try, I recommend testing several of the names important to your research—you just might be among a lucky few.

Symbols

3-dimensional views in Google Earth, 206–207

* (asterisk) as search operator, 23–24, 329

- (minus sign) as search operator, 26–28, 323, 329

( ) (parentheses) as search operator, 329

.. (periods) as search operator, 64–66

| (pipe) as search operator, 24–25, 323

+ (plus sign) as search operator, 28, 323, 329

" " (quotation marks) as search operator, 21–23, 323

/ (slash) as search operator, 329

~ (tilde) as search operator, 29, 323

A

accounts, setting up, 215

accuracy of family stories, investigating, 273

addresses
  locating on maps, 187–188
  viewing in Google Earth, 203–204

Adobe Acrobat Reader, downloading, 113

advanced search
  accessing, 54–55
  building queries, 56–57
  college and university websites, 62
  compared to search operators, 62–63
  filtering options, 58–59
  by topics, 60–61
  by URL, 60
  U.S. government websites, 60

advertisements in search results, 39–40

airline flight status, checking, 240

airport conditions, checking, 240

alerts
  example, 171
  managing, 172
  overview, 168
  setting up, 169–170

alerts (*continued*)
  and spam, 168
  tips for creating, 172–173
  worksheets for recording, 174–175

Ancestors on Board website, 296

Ancestry.com website, 296

Ancestry magazine, 292

anchor text, searching, 326

AND as search operator, 19–20

AOL search engine, 307

Archive.org website, 287

Ask.com search engine, 305–306

Association of Professional Genealogists website, 291

associations and societies, websites of, 291–292

asterisk (*) as search operator, 23–24, 329

Australian Family Tree Connections magazine, 292

automated searching, 167–173

B

birth records
  search example 84, 328
  as sources, 276

blogs
  alerts for, 169–170
  creating, 135
  overview, 133–134
  posting to, 136–137
  searching
    advanced, 135–136
    basic, 134–137
    specific, 137
  search results for, 138–139
  spam on, 140–141

blogs (genealogy)
  Eastman's, 281
  search tips, 141

(photo by Eliza Catherine Lynch)

Daniel M. Lynch is a marketing and technology consultant and professional genealogist based in Connecticut. A fourth generation American of Irish and Italian descent, Dan has enjoyed the challenges of researching his family history since the late 1970s—the era of the American Bicentennial and Alex Haley's *Roots*. His hometown of Waterbury, Connecticut is rich in history and was one of four cities featured in the 2007 Ken Burns documentary, *The War*.

After 15 years in the computer industry, Dan turned his focus to the emerging online market for genealogy and in 1998 joined Ancestry as vice president of business development. In 2002, he founded Mattatuck Consulting, a private consulting firm specializing in Internet and search engine marketing solutions. His clients include The Statue of Liberty-Ellis Island Foundation (New York), FindMyPast (London), FamilyLink and WorldVitalRecords.com (Utah), as well as other organizations outside the genealogy sector.

Dan is a member of the Association of Professional Genealogists, a Life Member of the Connecticut Society of Genealogists where he has also served as a board member and vice president, and is a frequent lecturer at local and national genealogy conferences. He has appeared on ABCs *Good Morning America*, has published and maintains several popular genealogy websites, and his articles have been published in leading genealogy publications including *Internet Genealogy*, *Family Chronicle*, and *Family Tree Magazine*.

A list of articles and presentation topics can be found online at <www.danlynch.net>.